Who and What Govern in the World of the States?

A Comparative Study of Constitutions, Citizenry, Power, and Ideology in Contemporary Politics

Tukumbi Lumumba-Kasongo

University Press of America,® Inc.
Lanham · Boulder · New York · Toronto · Oxford

Copyright © 2005 by
University Press of America,® Inc.
4501 Forbes Boulevard
Suite 200
Lanham, Maryland 20706
UPA Acquisitions Department (301) 459-3366

PO Box 317
Oxford
OX2 9RU, UK

Library of Congress Control Number: 2004117544
ISBN 0-7618-3077-4 (paperback : alk. ppr.)

Table of Contents

DEDICATION

To all the citizens of the world of the states who have been betrayed, for different reasons, by the policies, the political activities, and the claimed legal sovereignty of their states, but who have also been fighting against the broken promises of the states on behalf of the principle of distributive social justice for all.

Preface

As a scholar whose main discipline of teaching and research deals with power in its multidimensional forms, I do not know exactly when I started to develop a specific interest in the topic of this book because the process is generally cumulative, gradual, and complex. Nonetheless, I do know when the general interest started to manifest itself in a concrete, specific research agenda that was cultivated and gradually led to the writing of this book.

The question of "who and what govern in the world of the states" is, first, a political leadership question. Second, it implies the origins of the dominant thoughts and institutions that manage societal affairs and govern the world. And third, it is about examining and understanding the nature of state-society relations, their policy and social implications, and how they impact human lives. It is difficult to imagine how complex contemporary societies and communities could effectively function without any visibly identified, accepted, and committed leadership. However, in light of contemporary political history, especially with various forms of power struggle that have occurred in the pre- and post-Cold War era and the adoption of the justifiable militaristic approach to deal with terrorism led, after the tragic events of September 11, 2001, by the United States, as nation-states, ethnic and social groups attempt to redefine themselves and also affirm their cultural and political identities and particularities in relationship to the imperatives of globalization, many scholars and people have become sceptical vis-à-vis the main claim of this book, which implies the existence of systems of governance with some basic rules and institutions.

This author has articulated the position that despite the fact that there is no single authoritative personality, state, or institution that is capable of totally ruling the world or influencing the course of history from a single dominated and accepted perspective, the world of the states has institutions and rules that have made the world and people behave the way they do. Thus, it is possible not only from an ethical perspective, but also from a political and economic approach, to assess comparatively how those institutions have been functioning and also to discuss their origins. The author recognizes very much the fragility and fluidity in the institutions, ideas, and the rules of governance, and lack of moral values within the contemporary systems of governance. However, the world of the states is not absolutely anarchic without any intention, purpose, or *raison d'être*.

In the twenty-first century, regardless of people's political and social locations, their level of economic and social progress, the strength of their cultures, ethnicities, and history, and their human intelligence, world politics is in an unprecedented global and structural crisis. Many states, societies, and people are daily losing confidence in their existing social institutions, in their political leaders, and in themselves to understand why world politics is almost upside down and what can be done or agreed upon to change its status for the better of the majority of people on the planet.

Does the nature of the political leadership, both at individual and institutional levels, matter in the complexity of the structures and hierarchies of contemporary world of the states? Who really has power among the states, the people, multinational companies, and transnational institutions in the world politics? How much do we know about the quality and values of those who govern us? Do we know or are we interested in knowing the origins of the ideas and thoughts that govern us and how they govern us? These questions, although not separately examined here, were used to guide the analysis through which I framed the issues raised and propositions articulated in this book. I firmly believe that in any society or any social institution the quality of the leadership makes a difference: it matters. However, the important questions are: What is the kind of leadership that matters? How can it be created? How does it function? How can it relate to the society and community at large? Thus, understanding the origins of the institutions that govern the world of the states is an analytical imperative toward changing the world.

It was in the fall of 2000, while I was planning to take a sabbatical leave from my teaching responsibility at Wells College, that I produced the first draft of the book proposal, which finally was developed in this book. I presented the project as a public lecture in the Faculty Club at Wells College, where some colleagues found it interesting although ambitious. I am grateful for the comments and the questions I received from my colleagues on that occasion. Many parts of the chapter on democracy were presented in my paper entitled: "Principles and Values of Liberal Democracy and the Politics of International Debt: Can their Dynamics Engender New Developmental Paradigms Towards the Reconstruction of the African States and Societies? This paper was presented in the 14th Biennial Congress of the African Association of Political Science (AAPS) held in Durban, South Africa, in June 2003.

The book project was enriched and developed when I taught as a visiting professor in the Department of Political Science during the 2001 spring semester at the University of Massachusetts, Boston. Several topics of the course I taught related to my research project. Thus, I was able to project some issues of my research into class discussions, which were beneficial to my work and my students as well. Some of these issues include the relationships among constitutions, the social validity of citizenry in the city-state in ancient Greece, and in nation-state in the contemporary world.

As already indicated, several chapters of the book were developed out of papers that were presented in several congresses, annual conferences, and seminars in many parts of the world long before 2000. Furthermore, the origin of my specific curiosity in power relations was consolidated as a student of political science since my graduate student days at the University of Chicago. Two specific courses I took with Professor Zdzislawa J. Coleman on "Comparative Approaches to Problems of Power" and Professor Edward O. Laumann on "Seminar: Elites and Networks" respectively were complex, historically and sociologically challenging, and intellectually fascinating. Since then, as a student of politics and international relations, I have been interested in studying the minds and thoughts of world leaders in academic, political, and social institutions.

Who are those people who have been governing the contemporary world? Where do they gain their ideas and strength from? Why do they behave the way they do? Do they have anything in common despite the obvious differences in the political regimes, societies, political cultures, and the levels of economic and industrial progress in their respective countries? As indicated earlier, this book does not specifically deal with all these questions in any systematic manner. But they have been constantly in the back of my mind while developing my philosophical assumptions, hypotheses, and my arguments in this book. Thus, earlier, I developed an interest in conducting research and writing a book strictly on the theme "Who governs in the world of the states?" using a comparative political thought inquiry in which I wanted to explore the views of government, governance, and governing, and the relationships among them from the perspectives of political and intellectual figures such as Ake, Aristotle, Althusser, De Gaulle, Houphouët-Boigny, Ibn Khaldun, Fanon, Ghandi, Lenin, Lumumba, Madison, Mosca, Pareto, Mandela, Marx, Mao, Nyerere, Nkrumah, Nzinga, Senghor, Ricoeur, Plato, to cite only few. After teaching and studying political economy, development theories, social and political movements, and their implications in the processes of the state and societal building, and world politics in many universities and colleges in Africa and the United States, however, I felt that it was imperative to contextualize the analysis of my theme within the dynamics of the international political economy and historical perspectives.

A component of the title of the book, specifically the part of "what governs" was suggested to me by a good friend and colleague, one of the best-known political scientists, Theodore Lowi of Cornell University. I benefited a lot from several discussions we had on this project. I am grateful for his encouragement as well. I also thank Pierre Clavel, a colleague and the Chair of the Department of City and Regional at Cornell University, for his encouragement every time we had an opportunity to discuss some aspect of this project.

Furthermore, many aspects of this book project were significantly enriched and enlightened when I participated in the Germany Today program on June 15–28, 2002. This was an exchange program where twenty selected scholars and policymakers from North America (the United States and Canada) visited many parts of Germany and Brussels (Belgium) to participate in workshops on biological and chemical sciences, cloning and environmental policy issues; citizenship in Europe, copyrights, and the European Union's institutions. I projected some of the issues of the book such as citizenship, welfare states in Europe, and state and regional sovereignty in various discussions that took place in this program.

Many of my thoughts for this book, especially those related to democracy, leadership, and political instability in Africa, were also "tested" and explored further when I participated in August–September 2002 in the CODESRIA Institute of Governance to train young African scholars (laureates) in social science in conducting specific research on "Intra-and Inter-state movements in Africa," Dakar, Senegal. I benefited enormously from the intellectual interactions I had from this Institute.

The corrections of the last chapter of the book were completed in July 2003 in Hiroshima, Japan, where I started to serve as a Visiting Research Fellow in the Center for International Cooperation in the Study of Education at the University of Hiroshima. My appointment is for two years renewable. My visit to Japan in July 2003 was beneficial as I had an opportunity to discuss the question of how Japan rose up as a highly industrialized country and at the same time, the Japanese society at large is still very much "Japanese," culturally less Americanized and Europeanized. Partially, I learned that historically the Japanese political leadership and social institutions matter for the Japanese society.

I thank Kristen Williams Powlick, my former teaching assistant, who is presently a Ph.D. student in economics at the University of Massachusetts, Amherst, for the quality of the sources and references she identified for me, which allowed me to complete the work as planned. I also would like to thank greatly my research assistant, Judit Temesvary, who is now a Ph.D. student in economics at Cornell University, for tirelessly assisting me in identifying relevant and rare major sources through her effective usage of the Internet medium. My sincere thanks go also to Janet Mapstone of the Department of Public Relations at Wells College who, despite an extremely busy schedule, carefully proofread each chapter of this book more than once and who also helped in fixing technical problems related to camera-ready exigencies. I also thank Jan Schwartzberg who edited the first version of the whole manuscript and the second version of a few other chapters.

I, with much love, thank members of my family, the Lumumba-Kasongo family (both the nuclear and extent African family systems), for the unconditional, tangible and untangle, and unwavering support I always enjoyed from their patience to my long hours of work and the sacrifice they make to allow me to miss some of the family's obligations. Without their unique love and interest in my work, this book would not have been completed despite my professional commitment and external expectations and support.

My greatest gratitude goes to Mô N'Dri, who despite her extremely busy professional schedule and many international commitments, responsibilities, and duties as a well-recognized world scholar, read the entire manuscript, made the most constructive and relevant comments and suggestions, and paid attention to every single detail of the manuscript. Her commitment and encouragement are the most motivating forces that gave me energy to complete the book on schedule.

Finally, I must insist that I, alone, am fully responsible for any misinterpretations or any errors that slipped past my eyes, creativity, or of the computer screen while writing the book.

Tukumbi Lumumba-Kasongo
Aurora, New York
October 2004

Chapter 1

INTRODUCTION

The study of politics is beset by paradox. Though there are many who choose to overlook this source of perplexity, the exploration of paradox remains one of the conditions of our understanding social and political life, signifying recognition of the readiness of human beings to pursue different and contrary courses at the same time, to struggle forward without entirely destroying their past, and to pursue ideals of which the consequences are incalculable.

Nevil Johnson, 1977, p. 80.

Issues and Problematics

This book deals with the elements that form the contemporary state and its corporate foundation, covering forces such as institutional power, constitution, citizenship, ideology, and the nature of the dynamic relationship among them. This first chapter identifies general themes and subtopics elaborated later in this book and raises the interrelated and specific issues that are important and relevant when dealing with them. It describes specific and general objectives pursued in this work. The chapter also examines the importance and the relevance of the intellectual perspectives and various political science approaches used in this comparative study.

The identification of major issues helps to contextualize the subject matter. The question of who and what govern in the world of the states entails several layers of political and social configurations that need to be addressed in both historical and philosophical terms. It touches on the ethos, the functions, and the claims of the states and their political realities as well as the people and their desires, interests, and social projects. Economic imperatives at the national and international levels that shape the behaviors of political realist and idealist thoughts and practices, and people's ideologies, are directly part of this discourse. That is to say, the above question implies the existence of dynamic relationships among the state, especially its executive power embodied in the government and its institutions; the people, who are citizens and consumers; and the economic forces at a given society and at a given time. Each of these actors, which is also considered an agent of social and physical change, has its own social and power base. Each also has its constituency, its zone of influence, its operational rules, and its internal and external environmental constraints. However, the power base of each actor in itself is not a sufficient factor to deal effectively with the question of who and what govern in the world of the states. This question must be examined within the perspective of a dynamic relationship (Chazan, Lewis, Mortimer, Rothchild, and Stedman, 1999). It is essentially a question of a power relationship.

Some of the important manifestations of political changes that have been taking place since the 1990s include people's various struggles to redefine the power of the state, its limits, and its social base; the state's resistance to these redefinitions; the state's effort to redefine itself within the new conditionalities articulated by the liberal, transnational economic dogmas and policies; and people's struggles to redefine their rights. Power and rights, though they dialectically relate to one another, also work together in a kind of "uneasy cohabitation" situation. Comparative dimensions of the study of constitutions have helped clarify the nature of the relationship between the above phenomena and identify the basis of their conflict.

A holistic analysis of the question of who and what govern in the world of the states and the complexity of social implications of this analysis require that we go beyond the simple established functionalist logic of who decides or formulates the major policies in a given society at a given time. Within this analytical perspective, the question not only implies the classical study of institutions such as parliaments, political parties, presidencies, and public administrations and their outcomes (Sartori, 1994), apparatuses which are centrally and internationally expected to make decisions and policies and implement them in a given country. Rather, it also concerns the issues of the nature of society-state relations in a broader context. Further, it implies the existence of systems of rules and their ideological bases that shape the behaviors of the state, society and its actions, and social relations.

It is significant that historically and sociologically, the three groups of actors which are central to this book—the state, its citizens, and private corporations—have had almost permanently conflicting relationships on the basis of which each of them defines its own being, rationality, and objectives. That is to say, these relationships are in most cases characterized by the struggles for interests, self-preservation, and some forms of consensus, depending on the nature of the nation-state and its geopolitical location. The state, through its legitimized use of force and the control of its resources, tries not only to define its own actions and justify them, but also to provide the legal and political parameters for the behaviors of its citizens, corporations, and social institutions. This is partially the foundation of the permanent conflicting relationship among the state, its citizens, and private corporations.

Within the context of the arguments and assumptions developed in this book, the question of who and what govern is not conceived or discussed as an intellectual or philosophical abstraction. Whether the question is examined from a socially and historically defined holistic approach or from a solely social class perspective, it implies the functional existence of an authoritative body, person, or institution that has legitimate and appropriate political skills or abilities to rule or to govern. These skills and abilities include some relevant level of training (or formal education), associated political rights, supporting traditions, individual or "personal" intelligence, and professional experience in government and decision making.

Other related sets of qualifications include mental and social dispositions, interests, and the desires of empowered social groups (political consciousness) to effectively and efficiently manage their political systems, to control their resources, and to distribute values and material resources. Abilities, within a functionalist approach, for instance, also concern the availability of effective human resources and the role of institutions and their values within a given social political system or regime which allow the system to make decisions and to create and maintain social "equilibrium." Are those general qualifications most relevant, or most needed, or strong enough for any one person or institution to have in order to be part of the dynamics of a governing body? Can these qualifications be generalized?

Despite the importance of the questions posed above and of the social values related to them, which are taken into account in the overall discussion, this book does not deal with all these issues as isolated, atomistic, individual subtopics separate from the central question of power or power relations. It is articulated furthermore that, in addition to the above sociological and political issues related to the dynamics of nation-states, the question of who and what govern has to be examined within the framework of the power of ideology because, as advanced in this book, nation-states are essentially ideological constructs.

The nineteenth and twentieth centuries were essentially the centuries of ideology, where major "isms"—such as capitalism, liberalism, socialism, Marxism, nationalism—and their associated paradigms dominated the ways in which societies and states were organized and managed, and also in the ways states and citizens generally were supposed to behave. These "isms" also determined the criteria of what was perceived as "good" and "bad" (or normative behaviors) or "relevant" and "irrelevant" at individual, societal, and international relations' levels. As Terence Ball and Richard Dagger stated, "An ideology provides its adherents with criteria and standards of evaluation—of deciding what is right and wrong, good and bad" (2002, p.1). In short, the contributions of ideologies to the processes of resource and value allocation, social production, and management cannot be denied or underestimated. Will the twenty-first century, embodying the elements of the past, continue to have similar imperatives in the rapidly changing world of the states? For instance, demographics, the level and the nature of communication technologies, the rapidity of financial transactions, and the redefinition of the contemporary states have become some of the important factors in this globally changing world.

At the level of world politics, state-society relationships are often characterized by power struggles, strong ideologies, and the constant processes of redefinition of people's cultural and political identities. These various processes, despite the fact that they are generally resisted or even rejected by the nation-states, are part of the dynamics of world politics.

Power takes the form of either a state interest, known also as "an iron law of politics" (Morgenthau, 1948), a protest movement, a social revolution, a factor of influence, a moving force, or an instrument of social control and domination. Thus, Foucault, for instance, perceives it as a multiform production of relations of domination, which should be analyzed as "something which circulates in the form of a chain" (1980, p. 98). It embodies a transformative feature. This feature does not necessarily imply social progression in a community. A phenomenon can be transformed negatively or regressively, as it can also transform other phenomena negatively or positively. When it is stipulated that citizens, the states, or private corporations have power in a given social context, what does it mean in political, social, and economic terms at the social class, national, and international levels? What kinds of power and rights do the states, citizens, and private and public corporations have in democratic and nondemocratic societies? Does political participation imply that the participants have real power? What does real power mean for the ordinary citizens who partially or fully participate in the electoral process in their countries? How does power manifest itself in the world of states, citizens, and private corporations? What are the power bases of these actors?

Intellectual and political interests, which are elaborated in this book, go beyond the technical or legalistic definition of the expression of power. Such interests lie in the philosophical meanings of power in the social and policy spheres, and in the implications of these meanings in the context of the dynamic relationship between the states and citizens. The nature of the societal and political effects of power in a given context depends on how such power was produced, its intended objectives, and the nature of its support from its institutions and agencies.

As alluded to above, the world of the states has been undergoing both substantial and symbolic changes since World War II in the geopolitical arena; in the domains of the management, distribution, and productivity policy of the mega-companies; in the sphere of labor policy; and in the redefinition of capitalist orbits of power as regional organizing and accumulating forces. At the same time, in all parts of the world, people and societies, and citizens and states, are also undergoing the process of redefining themselves, either by adapting to the new imperatives of liberal globalization or by challenging them based on local realities. These new definitions or new processes of political and economic remapping are manifested in different forms depending on the nature of the state and societal relationships, the history of state formation, and the dynamic interactions of civil and "indigenous" societies within the global context.

The state continues to lose or to compromise, in many forms, its past "tendencies of having almost total hegemonic power" or "sovereignty" in domestic and international political and economic affairs as a result of the ramifications of the power of global liberalization. Paradoxically, in many countries, many people through social movements and many citizens through civil societies have also been demanding their civil or legal citizenship—more today than thirty years ago, especially in the developing world. That is to say, they are reclaiming greater visibility for the state in the societal managerial affairs and in the delivery systems of that state than previously. This is partially due to the effects of judicial activism and the internationalization of human rights debates. The idea that no one is above the law has generally become a reality. It should be emphasized that crimes committed even by a head of state or government can be pursued more easily at many levels of the courts despite the pragmatic tendency of the sole remaining world power, the United States, and its allies, to resist this idea and its international implications. The principle of sovereign immunity is now being challenged in many parts of the world. The popular principle of "one can run but one cannot hide" has advanced many dimensions of this activism.

In fact, the question, in this author's view, of who and what govern the world of states has become pragmatically more relevant today than thirty years ago, when the world was ideologically divided between only two military and ideological powers, the United States and the Soviet Union. This results also from the changes in the world of the states that have further weakened many dimensions of people's and citizens' political and cultural identities to such a degree that one can characterize the status of some existing states as "confused." These are the states that can be perceived as totally or partially lacking in political direction and vision; they are irresponsible, unreliable, and disengaged. Similarly, confused citizenship in a global system may be characterized as lost, uncivil, uncivic, and disengaged. The situation described above explains partially why apathy has become a vehicle of withdrawal from the electoral process for many people, especially in the industrial countries. Yet, at an international level, as underlined earlier, judicial activism has increased.

Robert A. Dahl's book, *Who Governs? Democracy and Power in an American City*, published in 1967 by Yale University Press, which was based on an empirical policy study dealing with the interaction between the state and federal governments in New Haven, Connecticut on specific projects, has been without any doubt a well-read reference text among undergraduate political science students. It would be interesting to recontextualize it, or to revive and broaden the debates on similar questions and issues at the international relations level, where, according to the author's categorization, "the U.S. domination and the only superpower minus hegemony formula" has become an established dogma in the post–Cold War era. One of the shortcomings of the text mentioned above, however, is a tendency to project the United States, as compared to Western European nations, through the exceptionalist lens articulated by some American historians and foreign policymakers, a position that Dahl himself clearly does not advocate. The elite pluralism and its consensus base are not uniquely American. Nonetheless, for historical and geopolitical reasons, the U.S. political cul ture has been firmly consolidated in the belief of "the extreme market liberalism" which stipulates, in the point of view of the author, that "everyone who can work harder can make it based on the protection of individual freedom and constitutional rights." This belief is uniquely American. It is also an essential part of the American dream. This experience has not been successfully replicated or emulated elsewhere. Yet, so far as it is noteworthy that by and large millionaires, or aspiring millionaires, or the offspring of millionaires, or people of bourgeois origins in general are most likely to be elected or selected as United States presidents. In many ways even Ronald Reagan and Bill Clinton, who do not come from bourgeois family backgrounds, qualified to be associated with the aspiring millionaires. The same is true with John Edwards, John Kerry's running mate for the Presidency of the United States in the November 2004's elections.

It should be noted, as indicated by David Vogel (1987, p. 385), that many noted political scientists, before and after Dahl's work, have questioned the description of American political pluralism (Kariel, 1961; McConnell, 1967; Lowi, 1969). Given the centrality of the United States at the end of Cold War era as the only superpower (a "hyperpower") in the world, the issues these scholars have raised are still relevant in a comparative study of power in the twenty-first century.

Another interrelated issue that is analyzed in this book is the role of democracy in the systems of governance in a global, corporate world as the most important force in the twenty-first century. S. Deetz, for instance, in his book *Democracy in the Age of Corporate Colonization* (1992), added another important dimension, which Dahl did not directly and systematically raise, namely the issue of the control and exploitative characteristics as being an essential part of the logic and structures of governance. Jane Collier and John Roberts paraphrasing Deetz stated:

> This balance of rights and duties has been upset by globalization of product and capital markets, and asymmetries of power have been introduced by what many see as the weakening of the power of the nation-state associated with the growth of transnational corporations (2001, p. 67).

This discourse projects essential contradictions between democracy ("liberal democracy") and the corporate world, and not consensus. In fact, Dahl in the book mentioned earlier did not critically examine the corporate foundation of the contemporary state, as he, like many other political scientists, tends to regard the corporation as undemocratic because its managers are not accountable to its employees. Yet, in real world politics private corporation is hardly unique in this regard. In many countries, "democracy" ends at the elections.

Given the power of the corporations, Korten's publication, *When Corporations Rule the World* (1995), also alludes to the difficulty of dealing effectively with the question of who and what govern without linking it to the concept of a corporate world. One of the central issues raised in the analysis of corporate power is the fact that, since the domination of transnational financial institutions in world politics in the 1970s, the national institutions have been, in many ways, replaced by multinational corporations (O'Sullivan, 2000). And the ceremonial or genuine nationalist resistance to centralized financial supervision has been manifested through various forms of democratic pluralism as a contested political arena.

In studying the topic of who and what govern, it should be underscored that this work deals theoretically with three interrelated phenomena, namely, the concepts of power, ideology, and citizenry, and their political and policy implications in the contemporary world. How are they defined in constitutions, political culture, political parties, social movements, global corporations, and social or popular revolutions? These concepts were among the most important themes in the social sciences, especially in political science, international relations, and political sociology during the Cold War era. But, despite many changes that are taking place in the world of the states, it is no longer clear within the framework of the current trend of liberal global transition toward "unknown" or "unspecific" systems and the extreme weakening of the states in the developing world, for instance, what their real significance and implications are in the search for new paradigms of progressive social change, in the nation-state–building discourse, or in international relations.

In more than two decades of teaching, research, and publishing in various subfields of political science, this author has been also interested in studying the nature of the relationships among political elites, the systems of governance, and ordinary citizens, or those individuals who are called "the people," and how these relationships, using historical structural approaches, can produce policies to solve real societal problems. Political elites, in most contemporary societies, tend to hold the conviction that they are legally or traditionally entitled to rule based on the purported superiority of their ideas or because they technically know what is good (in a Platonic sense), they can philosophically articulate the best system in an Aristotelian sense, they know what is needed by the society at large (in a Marxian sense), or they have sufficient control over resources (in capitalist property-based discourse). Similar reasoning can be used for the charismatic leaders (in the Weberian sense) who claim to have superior talents for accomplishing prescribed missions.

Aristotle perceived the best in virtuous moral terms. For utilitarians, the best system, in its combined ideal and practical forms, should produce the highest good for the greatest number. Karl Marx evaluated the outcome of the best in the distributive power of a social system. It implies the abilities of a given social system to produce and promote social equality.

In most cases, with the end of Cold War politics, the above claims and social characteristics have been challenged by either the contradictions advanced by the elites themselves or the contradictions related to their relationships to society at large. It can be debated whether it is in the nationalist and socialist regimes, the representative democracies, or in the peripheral or the semi-democracies that political elites have always had the people's interests in mind or that they rule on behalf of their constituents. Some theorists have emphasized the view that historically constituents tend to count or rely on the accumulated credentials of the political elites, their claimed professional experience, their birthplace (origin), the quality of their family relations (or inheritance), and their social class. These theoretical assumptions should be reexamined in light of major social, economic, and political cleavages across countries and regions, which are associated with the increasing recent policies of global economic and political liberalism.

Within the above characteristics, other questions that may enlighten the issues in this book necessarily arise. What are the major or dominant ideas and institutions that effectively govern the world of the states? What are their origins, and which ideas are more powerful? How are those ideas appropriated? How are they used to govern and who actually uses them? Why is it that in some countries contemporary social and political institutions fail more frequently or are slower to adapt to changing exigencies of their societies and states than in other countries? Furthermore, the questions of what ideas, thoughts, and institutions and who rules as a social-class phenomenon are the central issues in this book. They contribute toward the understanding of how world politics is run or managed (or unmanaged).

One could argue that the stability of a given political regime and its ability to perform, deliver, innovate, and adjust to internal and external constraints, extreme pressures, and the people's needs, depend very much on the quality of the people who are involved in it (abilities of people as articulated in human capital theory and their traditions), the nature of the belief systems that sustain such involvement, the receptiveness of the national political culture, the "intelligence" (used not simply in its cognitive knowledge form) of the elite, the structures of the regime, and the history of the state formation. But international relations based on realist arguments and paradigms, and the comparative politics focusing mainly on the performance and stability or instability of the nation-states, have not produced a linear political theory that can show how the elements of political discourse can be universalized. Other scholars tend to put greater emphasis on the dynamics of a hegemonic class as the most important determining factor that deals with the quality of governance in a normative sense.

At the beginning of the twenty-first century, global liberalization in economic and market terms has become the pervasive policy and political dogma regardless of where the political actors are located, what they can offer, and who they are. Additionally, liberal democracy and multipartyism have been aggressively and authoritatively promoted as the agents of social progress and development. Indeed, many scholars and policymakers published books, articles, and monographs on the above themes between the 1970s, the time of the implementation of the policy of liberalism, and their recognized failures in the year 2000 as evidenced by some strategic shifts in the World Bank, the International Monetary Fund (IMF), and the so-called donors' policy guidelines on foreign loans (Stiglitz, 2002).

Thus, one cannot fully understand how liberal globalization works or how one can identify and examine its policy implications within the above transnational financial institutions without directly linking it to the concept of corporate governance or corporate power, which are the engine of liberal globalization. It is argued in the chapter that the concentration of economic power and the expansion of profit-making, which the transnational financial institutions promote, cannot be appreciated outside of a given social and political context. This is why several specific historical illustrations are examined.

It should, however, be noted that there remain many unanswered questions concerning the nature of the relationships among political culture, liberal democracy, and political stability as supported and promoted by the IMF, the World Bank, and other economic and financial institutions. Why is it that liberal democracy, or the multiparty system, and the liberal market economy have not yet produced a universal political culture that can transcend the constraints related to specific political and social capital as claimed by the global financial institutions? Why is it that the values, the convictions, and the beliefs associated with such a democracy encounter serious difficulties in being accepted, being effectively and productively operationalized, and being consolidated, especially in the countries of the Global South?

As mentioned earlier, within the dominant paradigms of the nation-states, it has been frequently argued by political scientists and political philosophers from various intellectual and ideological traditions that the best ideas, the best institutions, and the best people should or ought to govern. Nonetheless, in light of various forms of violence (civil wars, rebellions, invasions, etc.) related to the current dynamics of the states, the poverty associated with the contradictions of the world economy, the enduring and seemingly permanent racial/ethnic segregation, and the persistence of gender tension and inequality in the world of the states, the correlation between what and who should govern has been empirically problematic.

Other relevant questions in this book that complement those of who and what govern include discussion of whose ideas and institutions are considered the best and why, and by whom. For instance, which ideas and institutions would be historically considered within the Manicheism of contemporary society, the best between slaves and masters, the colonized and the colonizers, property owners and landless people, consumers and capitalists, peasants or rural people and urban dwellers?

One of the issues that should be pointed out in this discourse is the association of "best ideas" with "powerful ideas" within the state centric paradigm. In this case, the best states should be reflected in the nature of the strength of their institutions, in how they perform their duties and obligations, and also in the "rational" behavior of both these institutions and their citizens. How do the best ideas in a given social and historical context produce the finest (or the greatest) and most appropriate principles or doctrines to create the foundation of institutional formation? What are the criteria for defining the best ideas or institutions? How can they relate to a given people and in a given social context?

Despite intellectual and political controversies in defining the notion of the best idea—because this idea is an essentially relative philosophical concept—there is a belief or proposition, articulated by international institutions, that contemporary states and societies should be governed by the best institutions. Furthermore, these institutions are expected to produce stable policies that should rationally guide and manage the behaviors of their citizens and institutions according to mutually accepted or agreed upon international norms and rules.

It should, however, be noted that equating the best ideas or the best institutions with powerful ideas in the world of the states has, in the past, also implied domination and control in a militaristic manner. Powerful ideas tend to dominate and control other types of ideas. These ideas are fabricated and based on social-class. From this point of view, the best ideas, even within the premises of liberal democracy, are the ideas associated with the interests of those who govern. This logic of the world of the states in its classical and functional form has very little to do with the fulfillment of rights as expected by citizens, except in the national security (or sovereignty) arena and in some aspects of electoral process. Thus, one of the elements of justification in writing this book is that further critical studies are still needed, taking into account many factors, to redefine what the best ideas, the best institutions, and the best people are, ought to be, or should be. It was much easier to identify and describe them in the "limited and natural democracy" of the fifth century B.C.E. in Greece (within the city-state model of governance) or in Kingdom of Kongo before the 19th century than in the twenty-first century in Abidjan, New York City, or Seoul.

Why is it that countries with similar or common constitutional, historical, or cultural characteristics at the regional level, for instance, in Western Europe and Africa, have engendered different approaches, political performances, and outcomes? As the historical record shows, the stability of the world of the states was difficult to predict, maintain, and guarantee between the major European wars (World War I and World War II), even after the establishment of institutions such as the League of Nations and the United Nations. After the end of the Cold War era, consumed by the disintegration of the Soviet Union, a phenomenon that many social scientists were not able to effectively and accurately predict, the collapse of some nation-states as in the Balkans and Africa, the unconventional war between the Israelite state and the Palestinians, and the increasing number of people who live under conditions of extreme poverty have made the notion of "the best" intensively debatable and controversial.

All the chapters in this book are written in the form of analytical essays or critical reflections based on historical facts. Their main objective is to produce critical knowledge necessary to policy articulation and the understanding of various dimensions of the study of politics in a comprehensive fashion.

Objectives

General Objectives

An important general objective of this book, within this period of unpredictable behavior of the state and the citizens in world politics, is to make a theoretical contribution toward further understanding of the concepts of power, ideology, the ideas of governance, the dynamics of political culture, and the roles and rights of citizens. To achieve this objective and as part of the analysis, concrete illustrations are used from several regions of the world including developing countries, countries in transition toward liberal democracy, and industrial countries with liberal democratic traditions. In this book, the general study deals with power relationships and political culture: These relationships can build the foundation of political stability and shape the nature of the role of the political elite and its ideas, and determine how political institutions can become "immortal" or "mortal," since the beginning of the Cold War era. In short, this work is intended to deepen the understanding of how states, governments, citizens, and private corporations interact and how they produce social and political actions that can result in societal changes.

The imperatives of the dynamics of global economy on the movement of labor and the organization of the market, the role of multinationals in the promotion of resource distribution and allocation, and the development of the Internet and information technology have become increasingly prominent. The impression that stems from the characteristics of these imperatives is that constitutions, despite their centrality in defining the stability of the nation-states, do not seem to matter much and that citizenship has become a somewhat illusory concept as compared to labor. Is this era then witnessing the beginning of the end of the European model of the nation-state that, since the seventeenth century, has been consolidated through wars, agreements, peace accords, and political alliances in Europe and exported through colonial and neocolonial structures of domination and liberal economic liberalism?

Generally, my aim in this book is to explore the foundation of the major ideas and political configurations that have made the nation-state an effective functioning political entity. The book deals with the relationships among the projects of the political elites and their political ideas, ideologies, and institutions; the role of the citizens; and the foundation of both the people's rights and the elite's claims. One will not be able to understand the nature of these relationships without touching on some ideas of the origins of political phenomena, a subject that, in my view, has not been treated adequately and sufficiently in political science inquiry since the end of World War II.

As compared to classical political science as articulated by Aristotle and Plato in the evolution of the city-state (*polis*) and the development of Republicanism in the West, and to a certain extent in the subfields of political thought and political philosophy in Medieval Europe, contemporary political science deals insufficiently with the ideas or thoughts concerning the origins of political phenomena. This is partially due to the fact that since the nineteenth century, political science as a research and teaching discipline has gradually moved away, in its methodologies, its epistemologies, and on its policy base, from being part of the moral sciences, which essentially included ethics, legal studies, political economy, and moral approaches to empiricism.

In this era of extreme exploration of pragmatism, the ideas concerning the origins of phenomena in social sciences are not perceived as central to social analysis at large because these ideas tend to embody elements of "anti-rationalism" and "anti-utilitarianism" as they, epistemologically, focus on historical values and ethical imperatives. The interests developed here are not necessarily localized in ethnographical, linguistic, and anthropological studies of state formation and the behaviors of political communities, although in dealing with the questions of what and who govern, however, some issues related to the origins of political ideas in pragmatic, ethnographical, and historical terms have been touched on. There are several ways that one can approach the above questions: (1) One can explore the dominant ideas as articulated by major political thinkers such as Aristotle, Cabral, Castro, Jefferson, Houphouët-Boigny, Gandhi, Luxemburg, Madison, Marx, Mandela, Mao, Mitterand, Napoleon, Nyerere, Nkrumah, and Washington. What would be the nature of the impact of their ideas on the institutions of power in their geopolitical location? (2) One can explore these ideas from the points of view of the evolution of political culture, political parties, and political history. And (3) One can examine those dominant or governing ideas by studying the nature of the constitutions of given political situations. None of these approaches is theoretically self-sufficient to explain comprehensively the origins of the dominant ideas.

At the end of the Cold War era, within the framework of the globalization of political liberalism and multipartyism, the values associated with constitutions have literally exploded in many parts of the world. They have been elevated to the level that could even be characterized as "political mysticism." An important part of this work focuses on an analysis of constitutions in their concrete contemporary political forms, that is, constitutions in principle as unifying, reconciling, and transforming instruments of the states and citizens.

It should be stated that constitutions can be formal or informal, written or unwritten, general or specific, short or long, conservative or revolutionary. Nevertheless, despite their various origins, they all embody general rules or guidelines for governing a given society. Whether these rules are to be interpreted by a superior entity such as the U.S. Supreme Court or the Constitutional Council in France or Côte d'Ivoire, or any court for that matter, constitutions must embody the grand ideas or rules of what should constitute an organic political community. Just as the body is a dynamic organ which comprises many functioning parts, constitutions consist of major rules, general political definitions, clear definitions of citizens' powers, their rights, prerogatives, and duties, and well-articulated divisions of power, without which there is no functioning contemporary political community. In most cases, as elaborated further in Chapter 2, a constitution describes and dictates the present, while at the same time it embodies elements of the past and the future.

Specific Objectives

Keeping in mind the major questions of who and what govern in the world of the states posed in the above sections, and given the popularity and centrality of constitutions in the formation of states, and the citizens' expectations of what they should provide, the specific objectives of this book are:

(1) To define power and ideology in a historical context;
(2) To define constitutions and to identify and discuss the historical contexts that have produced them;
(3) To examine and contrast how various ideas of governance, governing, and the governed are articulated in contemporary constitutions;
(4) To identify the sociological, cultural, and intellectual characteristics of those who do or ought to govern;
(5) To contrast those characteristics across countries and regions; and
(6) To discuss the concept of citizenry.

The relationships between the objectives described in the section of general objectives and those described in the section of specific objectives were conceived and developed as complementary in an organizational basis.

In short, this author presents a comparative examination of how states define citizenship through constitutions, the political meaning of citizenship, and how the corporate world theoretically and historically influences the power base of the states and their citizens. The study is about examining within a historical perspective the nature of the relationship between the concepts of power, right, and profit-making, and their social and policy implications.

Approaches

In this book, a comparative approach is used to classify and examine the ideas of existing constitutions, citizenry, elements of political culture, and power. A historical approach also guides this comparative analysis.

One of the dominant propositions articulated in this book is that there is a world of states that has its particularities and that is different from other institutions or social entities. Thus to understand and appreciate its exigencies, its abilities, its goals, and how it operates, one must use a structuralist perspective. This perspective allows the use of causal, albeit nonlinear, relationship paradigms to determine why and how actors or institutions behave as they do.

A comparative approach combined with historical-structuralism provides the context as it improves classification. This is not a structural determinism approach that is generally and dogmatically associated with Immanuel Wallerstein's original scheme (Agnew, 2001, pp. 468-469). Further, comparative generalizations have potential for predictions. Despite their shortcomings and historical limitations, comparative social indexes, complemented by a solid historical perspective, may provide the grounds for measuring or evaluating some levels of social progress in a given society at a given time. If viewed solely through a descriptive historical lens, however, they may not tell us much about the quality of life associated with the institutions and people involved. In this context, the number of constitutions that has been produced in Central Africa alone, for instance, is not a sufficient or significant indicator of stability, democracy, anarchy, or dictatorship. The combination of dominant factors with a social and political classification is used to identify the origins or causes of certain political behaviors and the hierarchy of their relationship. What comparative analysis can do is to provide information that may make it possible to ask why this change has happened here and not there and what can be learned from each case individually and comparatively in relation to others. Globalization, in its diverse forms, is forcing scholars and policy makers to systematically, constructively, and critically examine, compare, and appreciate political phenomena on a broad basis.

It is anticipated that, in the current unstable and unpredictable global transition from the political culture dominated by the international power struggle of the Cold War era to some forms of multipolar politics, a comparative approach will continue to provide and create opportunities for students of politics and for policy makers to learn about other nations and states; and in learning about others, they may be able to better understand their own political systems. It is also believed that many developing countries, which have suffered from political instability, exclusive politics, excessive poverty, and wars, would be able to capture these new opportunities to learn about the relative constitutional stability of the industrial countries, especially the United States and France, and project how this learning can help them in their efforts to improve their own systems of governance. Regardless of their levels of economic progress and the citizens' political participation, however, what makes a comparative perspective more interesting and appealing, in my view, is the possibility that all the actors might have an opportunity to learn from one another.

Finally, it should also be mentioned that in this book the empirical and historical information and data that are examined or cited are used only to give an illustrative perspective. They are not examined as a fieldwork inquiry. My main interest in·this particular book is to try to make a contribution to the debates on theories of power, state, citizenship, and corporation, and the nature of the relationships among them in the twenty-first century, with the high expectation that the theoretical elements produced in this context can be used as tools for further investigation.

In short, I hope that theoretical elements or ideas that are discussed and sharpened in this book can be developed into a workable methodology and policy framework capable not only of being tested empirically, but also of being used as means of helping to address contradictions related to power relations among the state, private interests, and the community at large.

The relevance of this book stems in part from the fact that it draws its specific illustrations from both developing countries and the industrial world. The analysis and arguments advanced, and most of their illustrative supports transcend a "monologue" kind of approach, which is generally and mostly used by some political theorists in their examination of the principles and hypotheses of their individualized target political figures or a single political system or regime. It is also significant in that studying political regimes and power in motion has a pedagogical lesson, as it gives serious thought to comparative, historical, socio-logical, and policy arguments and assumptions. The interest in presenting the world as it is based on an assumption related to a critical theory, which supports the analysis of the world as it is, should embody elements of its future.

Finally, this book sheds light on the current burning debates in many developing countries related to the issues of citizenship and eligibility for elected office, especially the supreme executive office, the presidency and the prime minister's office. Selected illustrations from Africa, Asia, Europe, the Middle East, and North America are used in this text to clarify, support, or refute the arguments and assumptions.

The criteria for the selection of the countries used as illustrations in this work are somewhat arbitrary and personal. My own familiarity, intellectual interests, and curiosity led me to include some among equally informative cases. I also wanted to present a balanced regional representation, which provides an opportunity to build some diversity. In addition to regional considerations, I also took ideological factors into account. I also felt that it was a good idea to include the experiences of nation-states that have strongly influenced other nation-states regarding the ideas and practices of constitution-making. The element of anglophone and francophone colonial experiences in former colonies was also considered. But, the final selection was based on my own intellectual curiosity and professional trajectory.

Chapter 2

CONSTITUTION AS THOUGHT
AND PRAXIS

Introduction: Objectives and General Issues

Contemporary nation-states are generally supposed to be governed by the spirit of law and by the actual laws of the land, supported by political institutions. These laws, whether written codes of law or a general legal framework, are the instruments that in principle should protect individual rights, collective rights, and societies at large and promote social values such as justice, equality, liberty, and progress. These values are claimed as vital in any democratic struggle or regime and its various processes.

Since the end of the Cold War, with its extreme dualistic and antagonistic politics, the process which for many people "unexpectedly" started with the deconstruction of the Berlin Wall in 1989 and was formally finalized with the collapse of the Union of Soviet Socialist Republics (USSR) in 1991, the legal and social values associated with, and the significance of, political borders in many countries as the determining forces of the nation-states are being questioned in many parts of the world. Some borders are shifting rapidly, while others are either partially or totally disappearing. With the emergence of new nation-states, new borders are being created. Given the importance that political territoriality still occupies in the definition and construction of the nation-state paradigm, it is interesting to examine how these physical and political changes are reflected in constitutions or in constitutional thought, and also how constitutions reconfigure the debates on boundaries. Although these dimensions do not necessarily constitute the focus of defining and conceptualizing constitutions, in this section they are part of the contextually defined analytical framework that depicts important differences and similarities in the 'ways constitutions function and actually perform their tasks (praxis). Debates on constitutions and their values have intensified theoretically and practically as both states and citizens try to promote their "claimed immortality" through their redefinition of power, right, and interest.

What is possible or probable in terms of achievements and capabilities of a given state can be understood and appreciated by examining the nature of the structure of its political system or regime. Thus, the holistic analysis (an attempt to adopt a multidimensional perspective of looking at a phenomenon, or what is called a view of "totality") of constitutional arrangement in a given country may enable us to understand the important dimensions associated with a regime, its political behavior, and its policy basis.

There are, for instance, some people, and institutions that tend to perceive or define the nature of the failures of some regimes and their instability as a result of the lack of good or relevant constitutions. The nature of the procedures and rules of the political game may also inform us how and why some nation-states behave the way they do. Although the assertion prescribed above is valued in most cases, this author's general perspective is that the world of the states does not have any significant deficit concerning the availability of constitutions. In some countries, especially those in developing regions, nearly every new political regime invents or produces its own constitution. Even industrial countries like France, Italy, or Spain, for instance, in the past produced several constitutions before they reached a certain level of political maturity, which is characterized by an ensured degree of stability of political institutions. Institutional stability implies that the behaviors of the actors are generally predictable. Predictability is an important factor for policy planning, formulation, and implementation. Through amendments, the Federal Republic of Germany, for instance, has revised its basic laws (constitution) more than forty times since 1947 in order to participate in both North Atlantic Treaty Organization (NATO) military operations and United Nations Peace Keeping Operations (UNPKO) (Itoy, 2001, p. 311). However, instead of talking about a constitutional deficit, which seems to refer more to number, one might raise issues concerning the nature and quality of the conditions under which functionality of the constitutions can be defined. These conditions make a difference in the ways in which constitutions relate to political history, political culture, people's minds and hearts, and social conditions (general social environment) at a given time and in a given country. The question of the origins of constitutions is as important as the issues related to their functionality. This functionality is directly related to the dynamics of the social environment.

The most important questions are: Why is it that constitutions are functional in terms of their social and physical meanings in some countries while at the same time, despite similarities and differences among them, they are not so in others? Why is it that some constitutions can functionally last longer than others? What motivates people (citizens) and states (political classes and their institutions) to respect or violate constitutions? In taking into account the pertinence and the logic of these questions, the issue of constitutional deficit can only be addressed adequately in relationship to the questions of the origins of constitutions in a given social context and their applicability or functionality. In this context, a deficit is more of a philosophical concept than a quantitative one.

The question of who and what govern in the world of the states in all its complexity is directly related to the ideals and ideas of governance and the nature of the practical institutions that are established in a given society at a given time. The question also concerns how these ideals and ideas are used in collective decision making in order to deal with human and social conditions and factors. These institutions, whether private, corporate, or public in character, determine the nature of individual and collective behavior and their roles in the larger or broader community. They also shape people's expectations, produce laws and policies, and protect some specific social interests. Functionally, institutions should be the external manifestations or reflections of the internally defined individual factors such as visions, dreams, hopes, desires, and psychological dispositions, of organic life. However, it should be noted that if governance is reduced to merely the processes and mechanisms of decision making and institution building, we would fail to understand other important forces or factors that may influence decisions but which may not be directly related to the decision making or institutions. However, in this book, the focus is on the dynamics of the nation-state, institutions of governance, their dominant ideas, and the principles that govern political communities.

Furthermore, it should be emphasized that although citizens and people in all contemporary nation-states do not have the same kind of reverence for and expectations from constitutions as in the United States, it can be generalized that since the end of the Cold War era and especially toward the end of the 1990s, the claims for constitutions have become the essential fabric of world political culture and discourse. These claims and discourses, regardless of their origins, cannot be dismissed as being the fabrications of the technical minds of the states, bureaucracies, and political elites.

As previously stated, one of the main objectives in this chapter is to capture the dynamics of the most important moment in the history of the formation of constitutions in some specific nation-states and to identify the grand ideas that emerged behind them in such a moment. One cannot examine society–state relationships by either reducing them to a hermeneutic or to a descriptive study of the constitutions. That is to say, this chapter is not necessarily about comparing the legal codes or the texts called constitutions. It is not a historiographical study of or about the constitutions, an approach that in many instances tends to deal with descriptive forms and arguments rather than to raise philosophical issues. This section is not written from a technically defined legalistic perspective. Rather, it is an analytical effort to identify major ideas embodied in the constitutions in a historical-structuralist framework in order to discuss their political meanings and their praxis. The political meanings in this context refer to the behaviors or activities of the citizens in defining their rights, such as their participation in the electoral process, the quality of their input into policy formulation and implementation, and the formation of political parties. The discussion approaches what I can refer to as a phenomenology of constitutional study. The essence of a constitution does not lie in its rigorous legalism but in the strength of the ideas that constitute its foundation, the quality of political culture that supports such ideas, and the human vision it embodies.

As already indicated, this book is not a legalistic work, intended to provide some prescribed perspectives and purposes, with which one can use to make a case in a court of law. Its main purpose is to examine the ideas of constitutions and elaborate on how these ideas have become central to political discourse and state formation the world over. This section identifies the structural relationships between elements of political culture and the dominant political ideas concerning governance, the governed, and the governing. It is an attempt to explore and examine how various ideas of constitutions define who should or ought to govern, what major ideas are embodied in these constitutions, and how citizens are defined in them.

Various types of changes that are taking place in contemporary economies or trade relations, in technological communications, and in various aspects of state-societal relations, as well as in the ways governments govern or rule, have contributed to the sharpening of the debates on constitutions and constitutionality of the decision-making, policies, and rules. These debates are likely to be intensified in the twenty-first century. Will these debates lead to a better understanding of the role of constitutions? Who is most likely to benefit from the outcome of these discourses in the long run?

First, constructing or reconstructing a contemporary state or nation requires above all the thinking, selecting, and setting up of a set of general, central rules that embody the vital elements of the vision and the dominant ideology of what kind of society is to be established. Second, the question of who should be involved in this process of reconstruction or invention should be dealt with. Third, the issues of what major ideas should guide its formation and what resources should be available to do the job must be addressed. In general terms, a constitution refers to the existence of some philosophical ideas and assumptions about what kind of political society is to be constructed in a given context.

After 1991, following the end of international ideological and military struggles between the East and the West, the adoption or the pursuit of constitutional rule (*état de droit*"), or some of its aspects, has become popularized as a key slogan for political development, the process of building a political community or the means through which states and political movements promote their international accountability and acceptability. It should also be noted that even in the middle of the Cold War, when many authoritarian regimes were supported by either the United States or the Soviet Union, most of these regimes in countries in the Global South, for instance, the Democratic Republic of the Congo under Mobutu, Uganda under Idi Amin, Togo under Etienne Eyadema, South Africa under the apartheid regime, Iran under the Shah, the Philippines under Marcos, Haiti under the Duvalliers, and Nicaragua under the Samosas, claimed in different periods of their survival to have used and/or advanced some aspects of constitutionalism. Thus, constitutionalism is defined as the idea of constitutional rule (Hague, et. al, 1998, p. 151). The degree of the application of constitutional rule within given political regimes depends on whether those regimes are liberal democracies, or mixed, transitional, military, or totalitarian regimes.

The point being made is that the claims for constitutional rule have been made across nation-states, social classes, and ideological spectrums. One needs to understand first the nature of these claims within a given social and political context. The call for constitutionalism has became another means through which governments or political regimes attempt to build legitimacy while consolidating their power base and establishing international recognition of their actions and a degree of respectability.

The creation of the United Nations Commission on Human Rights (UNCHR) in 1993 has also played an important role in the advancement of constitutional human rights arguments and related issues. The creation of a specialized United Nations unit has given momentum to world recognition of what should constitute human rights. Since the 1990s, the majority of political contests and protests have taken place in the courts. Political opposition is also building its struggles toward obtaining power on constitutional claims. In many countries where opposition parties did not or could not win presidential or parliamentary elections, for various reasons, courts have been more or less used effectively.

Claims of voting irregularities, the malfunctioning of voting machines and punch cards, intimidation by the police, the conflict between popular vote versus the electoral college, and so forth—the factors which led to the disenfranchisement of a relatively large proportion of the population of the racial/ethnic minorities in Florida in the United States' presidential elections of 2000, in which George Bush, the Republican candidate, and Al Gore, the Democratic candidate, ran a very close election—were finalized with the intervention of the local courts, including the Florida State Supreme Court, and the United States Supreme Court. In the former Republic of Yugoslavia, particularly in Serbia, in the presidential election of 2000, the opposition party used the court in Belgrade to declare its victory against incumbent President Slobodan Milosevic. In Côte d'Ivoire, the unplanned and unfinished presidential electoral process of October 2000, in which coalitions of popular protests led by Laurent Gbagbo of the Ivorian Popular Front (*Front Populaire Ivoirien*), which drove the late military leader Robert Guei from power, used the Constitutional Court in Abidjan to declare the winner. (Although not an established fact, there have been rumors that Robert Guei, members of his family, and his domestics were assassinated by the Ivorian soldiers loyal to the government of Laurent Gbagbo as a result of a violent military coup d'état which he was accused of organizing on Thursday, September 19, 2002. Concerning the story of this assassination, there are alternative hypotheses that have not yet been ruled out.)

The result of the Ugandan presidential elections in March 2001, in which Museveni claimed to have won by 69.3 percent of the votes against his opponent, Colonel Besigye, who polled 27.8 percent, was also contested in court in Kampala. For several years of the Rawlings presidency in Ghana in the 1990s, the court was effectively used often by opposition parties to challenge or protest Rawlings' policies. In Madagascar, the leader of the major opposition party who challenged the incumbent president declared himself the winner in the presidential election of February 2002. Until July 2002, with two declared presidents in the country, at the last Organization of African Unity meeting in Addis Ababa, the decision was made by the heads of state to isolate Madagascar from the activities of the newly established African Union (AU) until its political situation become regularized.

Despite these few examples, it is in the non-state apparatuses that the ideas and the spirit of constitutionalism have become better articulated, especially in the activism of human rights organizations, nongovernmental social organizations, and popular movements. Many of these organizations tend to promote a greater sense of territorial belonging of the involved groups, such as rural women, environmental groups, or neighborhood clubs, into the civil citizenship but also into the world of humanity.

Although Western Europe invented "individualism" in political terms (Amin, 1989), the United States invented the concept of "individual rights" in its pragmatic sense. Thus, it should be emphasized that despite internal social and political contradictions in the domestic life and the political culture in the United States, the symbolic as well as real, pragmatic role it has been playing in world affairs as the incarnation of individual freedoms and rights until the tragedy of September 11 2001 and the invasion of Iraq in March 2003, has been an important factor in the expansion of constitutional rights the world over. This political, economic, and military role has promoted a political culture that embodies the myths, realities, and utopianism of liberalism. The insistence on, and belief in, constitutional rights have been much stronger in the United States than in any other liberal democracy in Western Europe. Even before the projection of the international ideological and behavioral phenomenon of Cold War politics, the articulation of the principle of self-determination by the United States inspired many colonized people and colonial subjects between World War I and World War II to start fighting for their political independence. Active members of international organizations also used the same principles as the United States itself did in the eighteenth century. Thus, a special ideological space was carved out for the United States as a world power. In addition, the states' efforts and demands toward the remapping of the colonial European powers after World War I and World War II also placed the United States in a special, superior ideological space, a united nation-state with a strong collective political culture. In the United States, the highest law is the Constitution. As Lucius Barker et al. indicated, "All other types of law—rules, regulation practices, statutes, administrative orders, customs—must be in conformity with the Constitution (1999, p. 2)."

Claims of producing, maintaining, implementing, and respecting constitutions have exploded since the end of the Cold War era. These claims, regardless of their social and political origins and what they can or should do to positively or negatively change the world, have become global or transnational in their forms. They have become part of global liberalization paradigms. Nation-states, or people who have decided to construct or deconstruct new political communities, have all engaged in the promotion of constitutional rights as an urgent requisite.

The ideas and ideals of a constitution became popularly associated with liberal democracies toward the end of the Cold War era. It should be emphasized, however, that even in Western European countries, which were economically and militarily rebuilt by, and with, the financial support and economic resources of the United States (the Marshall Plan and private capital) and protected by NATO, the thought and politics of liberal democracy were not fully adopted as fixed universal or regional menus. In post–World War II Western Europe, liberal constitutions were implemented through various gradual mechanisms of power and domestic ideological struggles, and which even met some resistance in countries such as France under Charles de Gaulle.

The formal colonial states in the West, as well as the formal colonies in the South at large have directly or indirectly dealt, at various stages of their state formation, with the issues of constitutions or constitution-making. What did the constitution mean to a colonial state in Europe and what did it mean to a colonial state in the South? Could or did these two situations produce common cultural or similar constitutional interpretative ideas?

It should be restated that "constitution" in its general, contemporary usage consists essentially of elitist ideas or ideals. These grand ideas or ideals are promoted by either self-selected social groups, by an elected political elite, or by the perceived leaders of revolutionary or nationalistic movements. These ideas embody the major mechanisms of how a given society should or ought to be governed. The ideas of "constitution," in general terms, also embody some ideals of futurism, or evolutionary and revolutionary progressive ideas. In this sense, "constitution" is also idealistic or utopian.

It should be emphasized that in most parts of the postcolonial regions of the world, even in countries such as Ethiopia, Liberia, and Thailand which were not formally colonized by the Western powers, constitution making in general has been shaped by the rules and values consolidated during the global colonial era. They include: the elements of the visions and interests of the local Western political elites; the imperatives related to the nationalistic debates about the postcolonial societies; and the conventions and agreements made in international organizations. The ideas and institutions of governance that expanded from the dynamics of the colonial powers were the grounds upon which most constitutions were constructed. This situation occurred in most cases regardless of whether any radical revolution or conscious decision of changing the old system was considered central in the transitional period.

Furthermore, it should be noted that political education of the political elites, their desires, and personal ambitions and the struggles to exclude or include some social groups based on claims related to ethnicity, ideology, gender, or class (intrastate groups) have influenced the ways in which constitutions have been designed and produced. As pointed out in other sections of this book, international agreements, covenants, resolutions, and conventions have also been firmly adopted or integrated into most constitutions. Still, it is difficult to clearly identify and distinguish which specific thoughts and ideological and cultural elements have dominated the process of the actual production of the constitution. This is partially due to the overlapping or antinomy between the ideas/ideals of constitutions and various struggles for constitutions. The identification can be facilitated by the nature of the political regime at the time of the debates on constitution, the preparedness of the people to engage in constitutional debates, the location of the country in the existing orbits of power, and the international political climate.

Definitions, Categorizations, and Sources of Constitutions

The technical definitions of constitutions in this book are used if and when they can help explicate the broader political issues of power, class, and gender relations and their implications in policy and governance matters in the political community. It is important to note that not all constitutions have written preambles. Preambles are, however, important in defining the content of constitutions and also in classifying them, as they inform the nature of the state that has been established in a given country. They help not only to inform why a given state was established, but also to address the question of who created it and the identity of the spirit behind its creation. This is a fundamental issue in state formation. Preambles also present national perspectives on the question of citizenship, which is framed in a historical or ideological context. Thus, they project who should or ought to be citizens in constantly reminding us of the context.

The examination of various aspects of constitutions in the modern world of the states is about identifying the social project behind them. Philosophically, the issue of social project refers to the question of what kind of society people or political elites would like to build in their contexts, as well as who should build the society and for what purposes? The issue of social project also seeks to determine the means or resources people and political elites need to do the work of nation-state building. Building a social project implies having a certain level of consciousness or awareness of specific reasons for building such a social system. It means also having individual and collective confidence and the sociological identities that may be the necessary instruments upon which the grand ideas and thoughts will be cemented. Constitutions do not deal with all the abovementioned pragmatic questions. However, they provide intellectual and legal frameworks for addressing the pragmatic issues related to who and what govern in the world of the states.

There is an ongoing debate on whether any constitution should be considered a noble document in itself, or a class document with some noble ideas, or a general guideline for pursuing some noble ideas that should be embodied in constitution-making. It is argued in this book that questions related to the nobility of constitutions should be addressed in view of the political culture and the history of political struggles (the struggles for acquiring or sharing power) of a given country.

It should be reiterated that within modern and contemporary nation-states, constitutions are born as the result of a combination of factors such as domestic political conflicts or power struggles among political actors, social and political revolutions, foreign invasions, international or regional conspiracy, or agreements or treaties among various forces. In many countries, private corporations are also involved in defining constitutions, either by sponsoring the process or by supporting the agencies/agents which are involved in the process.

In any case, most constitutions are amended through complex processes of referenda, votes, or decrees in which citizens (people), and the executive, legislative, and the judiciary branches of a given government participate at different levels and in various capacities. In addition, many constitutions contain fictive and decorative passages or sections omitting many of the powers and processes that occur in real life (Finer, et al., 1995, p. 3). "The constitutional texts are highly incomplete, if not misleading, guides to actual practice, that is to what is often called the working documents or the governance of a country" (Finer, op. cit., p 3). In some cases, "the texts themselves say little of the extra-constitutional organizations which generate and conduct the political process: churches, the pressure groups, ethnic and other minorities, the media, the armed forces, and so on" (Finer, op. cit., p. 2).

However, despite definitional or perceptional shortcomings, Finer et al. conclude that constitutions, at least in three industrial countries, notably the United States, France, and Germany, provide exact knowledge of what happens and of who does what, where, and when, on highly important occasions (Finer, op. cit., p. 3). Even in those countries that have no codified constitutions such as the United Kingdom, New Zealand, and Israel, there is a remarkable consistency and continuity in their constitutional rules (Finer, op. cit., p. 2). In these countries, the spirit of constitutionalism was mainly influenced by nationalism or patriotism, democracy movements, a welfare economy associated with the industrial revolution, and liberal notions.

The optimism about the values associated with constitutionalism, which derives from the fact that despite different moments and sets of circumstances (political status quo, political culture, history of power struggles, and political economy) that have contributed to the production of specific ideas and movements that led to constitution-making in some countries, the nature of the world system, and the interactions among nation-states have convinced students of politics that constitutions convey some universal philosophical ideals and ideas that help define citizenship, power, and ideology in broad yet accurate terms.

In the West, for example, the origins of formal study of constitutions are as old as the discipline of political science itself, a practical or the master science, as articulated in the classical studies of the Republic of Plato and more so in Aristotle's Politics between the fourth and fifth centuries B.C.E. For Aristotle, the basis of the city-state (*polis*) is the constitution. It was defined as "a certain ordering of the inhabitants of the city-state" (Politics, Sections, 1274b32-41). It is an organizing principle, a way of life of citizens (Politics, Sections 12954b32-41). An important question in this context is, Who were the citizens?

As articulated in this chapter, constitutions manifest themselves differently as organizing principles. However, at the theoretical level, as Aristotle states, "Constitutions that aim at the common advantage are correct and just without qualification, whereas those which aim only at the advantage of the rulers are deviant and unjust," (Aristotle, Book 3, 1958, p. 114). In relationship to this definition, constitutions embody normative collective values and common advantage.

In the East, especially in classical India, constitutions can be referred to according to Kautilya (ca. 360-280 B.C.E.) as a sacred law and tradition in which the *Dharmik* code and order was prescribed (Kohli, 1995). Cheikh Anta Diop (1987, pp. 43-55) citing the works and the testimony of Al Bakri, Ibn Khaldun, and Ibn Battuta argued about the validity and solidity of the structures of the African constitutions of the empires of Ghana (tenth and eleventh centuries) and the empire of Mali (fourteenth century). In the Toranic and the Shari'a' traditions, Yahweh and Allah had established rules through their prophets, Moses and Muhammad respectively, of how the world of Jews and Muslims sought to be governed. The Old Testament and the Koran are legalistic-religious documents written as dictations that provide the foundation of both the states/institutions and human conducts within the Judeo-Islamic traditions.

A constitution in political science at large is defined as "a set of rights, powers, and procedures regulating the structures of, and relationships among, the public authorities, and between the public authorities and citizens. Constitutions are the laws that govern the governors" (Hague, op. cit., 1992, p. 460). They continue to define it in the following: "A constitution sets out the formal structure of government, specifying the powers and institutions of central government, and the balance between central and other levels of government. In addition, constitutions specify the rights of citizens and in so doing create limits on and duties for the government (Hague, et al., 1998, p. 154)."

From the above definition, a constitution is formal. Further, it defines rights and powers. It implies constitutional rule, which is defined as "government by law." "It places limits on the scope of government, sets out individual rights and creates opportunities for redress should the government exceed its authority. Constitutional rule is a defining feature of liberal thinking which predominates in the West and especially in the United States" (Hague, et al., 1998, p. 152). S. E. Finer, et al. also define constitutions: "Codes of norms which aspire to regulate the allocation of powers, functions, and duties among various agencies and officers of government, and to define the relationships between these and the Public" (1995, p.1). Jan-Erik Lane defines a constitution as a "compact document that comprises a number of articles about the State, laying down rules which State activities are supposed to follow, (1996, p. 5)."

As noted earlier, most people and states seem to be interested less in the question of the origins of constitutions. The questions related to the origins of political phenomena are not well examined and appreciated in the mainstream discipline of political science, except in relationship to the discussion of political culture, political anthropology, and some aspects of public policy debates. Myths and mythologies, which are part of the origins of things, are considered by some scholars as being intellectual distractions or weak political references.

More pertinent questions have been posed at the level of process, for instance, including how constitutions affect people's lives or their living standards; how they influence policies, or who manipulates them; or how they produce social values. This process should not be considered an end in itself behind which substantial issues may be hidden. However, there is a need to make a critical examination of the rise of various forms of ethno-nationalism as in Bosnia, Kosovo, and Macedonia; the increasing activism of "theocratic" regimes, as in the Sudan, Afghanistan under the Taliban, or the semitheocratic regime in Iran; the expansionism of the religious right, as in the United States; and the rise of both the state and ethnonationalism in some African countries such as Côte d'Ivoire and Nigeria.

"Ethnonationalism" is used in this context to define the sentiments and concrete actions of individuals with a given ethnic composition and their associates in organizing political opposition to, or rebellion against, the state in the name of ethnicity, claiming that they have been marginalized because of who they are. As stated elsewhere;

> Historically, the major premise of ethnonationalism and nationalism has been self-determination of various forms. Ethnic sentiments and nationalistic forces or organizations have been used to question some practices and policies of contemporary states and their dominant social associates....Ethnic groups which have been functionally or ideologically associated with the state powers have also benefited more than others which have not had any privileges or opportunities of being associated with the state apparatus (Lumumba-Kasongo, 2000, p. 113).

Although ethnicity as a clientilist phenomenon has often been manipulated, especially in Africa, because of the tendencies of the personification of state power by African politicians, the extreme weak social and economic conditions, and the weak delivery system, it cannot be denied that in many cases, people attempt to elevate ethnicity to the level of nationalist dogma. In short, the content and the claims of ethnonationalism are generally debatable and controversial, but their existence cannot be denied. Some scholars tend to argue that propositions and claims related to ethnonationalism should carefully be incorporated into the debates on the question of the origins of constitutions.

The question of the origins of constitutions is slowly reemerging in political science research. The extreme political and cultural tendencies in the contemporary world among marginalized social groups, whether real or imagined, are likely to provoke the rising question of the origins of rights and power. Origins should not be projected only in mythological, philosophical, and religious terms.

They can also be located in history, ideology, culture, or the grand ideas of a given period. They should also be analyzed from relational and sociological perspectives as historical processes.

Some constitutions have essentially had external or foreign origins. For instance, the U.S. Constitution and some European constitutions have inspired the constitutions of most countries that were colonized by the Western Europeans and Unites States, depending on how they gained independence. These former colonies decided in the postcolonial era to adopt these models in order to emulate their masters and also to maintain the status quo. In this regard, it should be noted that states that have been occupied by other states have had little or no chance to negotiate the establishment of their own, independent constitutions. In the process of constitution making, some local political elites have decided to maintain the status quo either because of lack of imagination and commitment to new national policies or because the old constitutions were literally imposed on them by force or by threat of force. Whether they were imposed or not, these constitutions serviced the interests of specific social groups. Furthermore, it should be mentioned that there are also pacifist, liberal, nationalist, socialist, or belligerent constitutions.

As a matter of illustration, the Japanese and German postwar constitutions are generally defined as pacifist, although amendments to the Japanese constitution, for instance, have led to the production of Self-Defense Armies (SDA) on land, at sea, and in the air (Itoh, 2001, p. 310). A brief comment on the nature of the Japanese constitution is necessary to explain its ambiguous pacifist characteristics, as this can also indicate how external, occupying forces can produce constitutions.

The principal feature of the occupation policy as outlined in the Potsdam Declaration and analyzed by Masland is that:

> Japan is to be completely disarmed, and militaristic, ultranationalistic and anti-democratic doctrines, practices, institutions, and organizations are eliminated. The economic basis for the Japanese military strength is to be destroyed. The desire for individual liberties and for the democratic processes is to be encouraged; likewise, encouragement is to be given to those forms of economic activity, organization and leadership deemed likely to strengthen democratic forces. Japan is to be permitted to resume peaceful economic activity at a level required to satisfy reasonable civilian needs and eventually to participate in world trade relations (1947, p. 567).

The Japanese Constitution was written by General Douglas MacArthur after Japan was defeated by the allied military forces led by the United States. As early as March 1946, MacArthur proposed the conclusion of a peace treaty with Japan (op. cit., p. 565). Thus, Japan's constitution was written in the United States' image according to a liberal democracy model (a representative democracy model). It was promulgated in 1946 and went into force in 1947. Japan has to be protected under the United States-Japan Security Treaty. However, since 1999, the second largest political party in Japan, the Democratic Party of Japan (DPJ), has been mobilizing debates about the possibility of revising Article 9 of the Japanese Constitution, which would give Japan the right to have an army (Itoh, p. 311). As Masland stated:

> The Constitution of 1946, together with accompanying legislation, fully satis-fies the specifications prescribed by General MacArthur in October 1945. It constitutes a complete revision of 1889, providing for a constitutional monar-chy in which the legislative branch is supreme over the executive and in which the independence of the judiciary and the rights of people are established and protected. Perhaps the outstanding innovations are renunciation of war and the clear-cut declaration of the sovereignty of the people (p. 572).

Thus, the origins of the ideas of Japanese constitution can be located in the project of the total military defeat of Japan, the final solution to war in Asia and Europe, the new role of the United States as the "champion of liberal democ-racy," and peace between Japan and the United States. It is a pacifist constitu-tion as perceived and defined by the victorious forces, the United States and its allies.

In short, recent claims about constitutions have focused more on principles of governance and the functionality or dysfunctionality of their systems. Their philosophical and historical origins have been perceived as peripheral to the core requests that people have demanded, that is, their rights and the basis of their power. As alluded to previously, however, in contemporary world politics, the origins of the constitutions cannot be disassociated from the following issues: history of state formation; internal and external power struggles among the el-ites; the history of conquests and imperialism; the expansionism of the Western powers; bourgeois and populist revolutions; decolonization and social move-ments; and the history of agreements and treaties among nations, political par-ties, and people. Constitutions have never been created from a *tabula rasa*. They are shaped by histories, ideologies, cultures, and particular dominant social in-terests at a given time.

Some scholars in social sciences tend to argue that no matter their origins in a given social milieu, ideals of constitutions in their essence embody some pro-gressive leftist or universalistic ideas. Furthermore, the liberal constitution of the United States, which was produced by its bourgeois revolution in the context of a slave society and its ramifications, the French constitutions based on, and de-rived from, the spirit of the French Revolution, and the constitutions inspired by the Marxist-Leninist regimes in Central and Eastern Europe, Africa, and Asia share some common forms of "ideals of democracy, equality, justice, freedom, and development." They embody some ideas of emancipatory politics. In princi-ple, they are concerned with the ideas of democratic transformation and political participation, or rights. It is not suggested in this context that despite similarities in their grand or noble ideas related to the constitutional ideas, the United States bourgeois revolution, the French bourgeois revolution of 1789, the 1949 Chinese revolution, and the Tanzanian African Socialist movement with the Ujamaa scheme of 1967, for instance, could possibly produce similar political and economic societies. We have to be able to classify constitutions by their dominant ideological and philosophical characteristics, their origins, and the political culture within the social context in which they are supposed to operate.

Thus, there are nationalist, conservative, revolutionary, left-wing, right-wing, and liberal constitutions. For instance, Germany under Hitler and Italy under Mussolini produced extremist nationalist ideas that were intended to produce fixed societies based on the so-called essence of the nationalistic ethnic ideologies. Within the framework of the dynamics of the nation-states, these regimes at large were not intended to be ideologically "futuristic" in their international relations, although they were firmly supported by the actions of multinational capital.

A constitution is a power map that deals not only with the location and definitions of rights but also with the division of power and the relationships between political institutions and citizens. The author agrees with William Simon as he stated, "A constitution is both reflective of what has been achieved and, at the same time, programmatic of what remains to be done, and is not limited to describing the state structure alone, but also concerns social policy and relationships" (1980, p. 347). Borrowing from Hague, et al.'s categorization, the following types of constitutions have been identified as the ones that dominate the political scene in the contemporary world:
- loose frame of government;
- a state code;
- revolutionary manifestos;
- sets of political ideals; and
- the embodiment of ancient sources.

Rod Hague, Martin Harrop, and Shaun Breslin's classification of different types of constitutions provides an explanation that is linked to Cold War politics. The discussion of the classification of constitutions is philosophically and historically linked to the question of origins of the ideas of constitution and the social context that supports these ideas.

A loose constitutional framework calls for interpretation, adjustment, and contextualization. It has been dominated by the United States' constitutional model. This model allows amendments to complement and, more important, to make the constitution functional. Thus, the complex process of the judicial review that takes place through the court systems is a pragmatic means of making the U.S. constitution more relevant throughout history, as Lucius Barker, et al. indicated:

> Justice John Marshall proclaimed that emphatically the province of the judiciary to determine whether particular laws, rules, regulations, etc., conform with the Constitution. Thus, according to Marshall, the Constitution had authorized

the courts, and no other institution of government, to make such a determination of the Constitution. This is the power of judiciary review that has long since become firmly entrenched in our constitutional and legal fabric (p. 3).

The value of this loose framework lies in its ability to contextualize the political behaviors of citizens and the government and also to submit power systems to the supreme legal institutions of the country. In the case of the United States, for instance, the loose framework creates new opportunities to adopt the spirit of the constitution in the imperatives of the United States' conditions. Here the statutory aspect of the U.S. Constitution and the idealism of U.S. society meet in a marriage of convenience. That is to say, the rights (in the form of the Bill of Rights) and laws in their ultimate interpretation must ensure, in principle, individual happiness and freedom.

The constitution as a state code in which power relations between the political institutions and citizens are defined in specific forms provides limited room for legal speculation. This code contains most of the detailed, specific laws that should govern society. This kind of constitution has been popular in Western Europe, particularly in France, Germany, Italy, and Spain. There is an assumption here that it is possible for the society at large to classify and codify human behaviors in the public domain. The constitutions here are veritable legal documents that stipulate concrete cases. Codified constitutions contain an internally consistent set of laws which control the conduct of government. These laws have a special or superior status vis-à-vis other laws (Finer, op. cit.,1995).

Although the U.S. model has inspired many countries and people the world over, which are also moving toward an interpretative legal sphere, in general terms, the role of the judges or the courts in many of these countries has not necessarily been to interpret the laws but to interpret the context and the behaviors of individuals or institutions. In short, judges or other legal functionaries are not expected to make laws by themselves but to manage and promote them.

Between 1917, with the Russian Revolution (also known as the Proletarian Revolution), and the formation of the Eastern bloc in the 1950s, constitutions as revolutionary manifestos spread from the Marxist-Leninist revolutionary dogmas to Maoist, Castroist/Guevarist, Cabralist, and other revolutionary leftist movements as Leon Trotsky, the Soviet Commissar of Foreign Affairs from November 1917 through March 1918, indicated:

We know not the day nor the hour; and every day, every hour, every minute which separates us from the decisive day, it is our duty to use. We must subject ourselves to self-criticism, prepare ourselves politically so that our part in the coming decisive events will be worthy of the great class to which we have linked our fate as revolutionaries: the proletarian class. ....Of course, when these decisive events come—even if they come tomorrow—we, as communists, as pioneers of the new socialist world, will know how to carry out our revolutionary duty towards the old bourgeois world....We have to look forward, not only beyond the criminal head of Tsarism, but further still, over the top of the revolutionary barricades, beyond the smoking ruins of the Peter and Paul fortress, towards our destiny; the irreconcilable fight of the proletariat against the whole bourgeois world (pp. 4-5).

Within the context of the question of who and what govern the world of the states, a brief discussion on the sources of constitutions and their major characteristics is vital. What can be learned about their sources in terms of commonalities and differences of constitutions based on the illustrations discussed in this book?

As defined earlier, constitutions are not static, fixed documents, or fixed grand ideas. In general, they embody a spirit of change. Thus, they may be transformative tools as well as transforming agencies. They can be defined as historical memories of a state, a nation, or a people. Additionally, it is important to insist that constitutions do have selective, cumulative or mixed sources. Thus, one may not be able to use linear logic alone to examine and understand the original elements that compose a given constitutional history at a given time. Social processes can change the grand ideas and political guidelines of any society.

What seems to be more important in this discussion concerning the sources of constitutions is to identify and to separate the primary influences from the secondary ones and to examine how these influences have shaped the history of constitution making in certain countries. Although this book deals primarily with power, ideology, and citizenry in the broad context of the contemporary world of the states, for the purpose of this section it is important and necessary to briefly identify and discuss some dimensions of the sources of constitutions in some selected countries as empirical illustrations.

Let's begin, once more, with the United States of America, because of the maturity of its constitution and the centrality of the country in world politics, being the only military superpower after the collapse of the Soviet Union. The U.S. Constitution provides a framework that produced a republic in which, in principle, neither kings, nobles, nor privileged church organizations had any permanent, inherited power.

It should be noted that the most important sources of the Constitution are the English colonial political and social institutions, grand philosophical ideas of colonization, and the existing political practices. During the colonial era, the institutions were governed by the royal system, property ownership (gentry), and self-governing bodies. The system of self-government, which seems to have been influential or popular in some colonial states included "codes of civil and criminal law, trial by jury, the right of habeas corpus, the system of representative government (as yet imperfect because of limited suffrage), the idea of a bicameral legislature; the tradition that the lower house, representing the people more directly, should control the purse" (Dorf, 1955, p. 24). The struggles between the royal governors, representing the central power of the crown, and colonists, most of whom did not trust the centralized powers, are also important sources not only of the ideas that contributed to generate constitutional ideas but also the social forces that sustained the debate. In short, the fundamental principles and the specific provisions of the U.S. Constitution are derived from the following general sources (Dorf, op. cit., p. 47):

- traditions of constitutional government development in England's representative government, personal liberty, and an independent judiciary;

- the experience in self-government acquired under the colonial charter and, after 1776, under states' constitutions (Declaration of Independence);

- the influence and the contributions of the eighteenth-century political philosophers, notably John Locke (1632-1704) and Montesquieu; and
- lessons learned from the Articles of Confederation (1781).

As evidenced by the above points, the sources of constitutions are diverse. But in terms of ideas and the procedures of managing constitutions, many nation-states, especially those that were colonized by the Western political powers and those that were born after the formation of the League of Nations in 1919 and the United Nations in 1945, have borrowed heavily from outside of their own history, culture, and power struggles. Thus, the constitutional influences of Great Britain, France, Germany, Portugal, and Spain in the constitution-making experiences of other nation-states can be considered as a historical and imperialistic fact. The nature and the quality of such influence however, is still an issue of intellectual debates, personal curiosity, and political contests, especially in situations where political independence was gained by some form of national or popular revolution.

How have the ideas of constitutions been appropriated by political elites? How much has Great Britain, with its so-called unwritten constitution, influenced the written constitutions of countries that are members of the Commonwealth such as Canada, India, Ghana, Jamaica, Nigeria, Pakistan, Sri Lanka, South Africa, and Zimbabwe? How much of the French constitution has been translated or transplanted into the Cameroonian, Ivorian, Senegalese, or Togolese constitution-making efforts? How much of the Belgian Basic Law became part of the Congolese constitutions? Before concluding this section, it is relevant to briefly clarify the popular notion of the "unwritten constitution" of Great Britain as used in this book.

Many scholars refer to the United Kingdom's Constitution as "unwritten." In my view, this definition is, in many ways, misleading in that the United Kingdom does not officially use oral traditions as a significant mechanism for conducting policies and dealing with social problems. As Nevil Johnson said:

> To a certain extent the description of our Constitution as "unwritten" is misleading: there are clearly some statutes which look like constitutional law, such as the Parliament Acts, the Ministers of the Crown Act 1937 or the Crown Pro-

ceedings Act of 1947. What is really being said about the Constitution when it is described in this way is that it is not formalised. There is uncertainty about what counts as a constitutional provision, there is a grey area between particular constitutional enactments and political convention and habit, and there is no special procedure by which constitutional provisions are made, amended or repealed. This, of course, means that constitutional law in Britain is quite a tenuous and elusive subject, and great deal of what passes for constitutional practice is no more than conventional political habit. Britain is quite exceptional in all this. Practically every other developed political society has a writen or formalised constitution which attempts to define the structure of political institutions, to guide the manner in which political life is to be conducted, and to define the rights and obligations of citizens in relation to the state (1977, p. 31).

The United Kingdom has a firm written culture of education, communications, industrialization, and militarization. Thus, it can only be said that it does not have a single codified document that can be reached by all at any time and that is comparable to the Constitution of the United States. I also agree with the features articulated by Finer, et al. who describe the British Constitution as "indeterminate," "indistinct," and "unentrenched." The indeterminate content of this constitution is described as follows:

> Her majesty's Stationary Office publishes the Official Revised edition of the Statutes in force. The two volumes devoted to 'Constitutional Law' give the text of 138 Acts of Parliament (from the Tallage Act 1297 to the Welsh Language Act 1993), while a quite separate volume on 'Rights of the Subject' gives another thirty-two (including what is left of Magna Carta). From these hundred of pages, what is or is not 'the Constitution' is a matter for scholars' individual judgments (p. 41).

The Magna Carta is the great charter of English political and civil liberties granted by King John at Runnymede on June 15, 1215. Later, it was used as any document or any piece of legislature that served as a guarantee of basic rights.

In addition to Magna Carta, one should also mention another element of the history of the constitution of England, which is the Petition of Rights of 1628. This Petition was "exhibited to His Majesty by the Lords Spiritual and Temporal, and Commons, in this present Parliament assembled, concerning diverse Rights and Liberties of the Subjects, with the Kings' Majesty's royal answer thereunto in full Parliament."

England is also one of the first countries among the European monarchies to have produced a clearly articulated Bill of Rights. As stated in the introduction to the 1689 English Bill of Rights (Lloyd Duhaimer's Law Museum on the Internet, 2003):

> The Bill was formally passed through Parliament after the coronation. On December 16, 1689, the King and Queen gave it Royal Assent, which represented the end of the concept of divine right of kings. The Bill of Rights was designed

to control the power of kings and queens and to make them subject to laws passed by Parliament. This concession by the royal family has been called the "bloodless revolution" or the "glorious revolution." It was certainly an era for a more tolerant royal prerogative. William, for example, did not seek to oppress the supporters of the deposed and Catholic King James II, even as James tried as best he could to rally the Catholic forces within England, Scotland and Ireland against King William III. The Bill of Rights was one of three very impor tant laws made at this time. The other two were the 1689 Toleration Act (which promoted religious toleration) and the 1694 Triennial Act, which prevented the King from dissolving Parliament at his will and held that general elections had to be held every three years.

The indistinct structure of the United Kingdom's constitution implies that "there is no special device to signal the repugnancy of 'ordinary' laws to those we choose to regard as laws forming part of the constitution. The constitution is a rag-bag of statutes and judicial interpretations thereof, of conventions, of Law and Custom of Parliament, of Common Law principle, and Jurisprudence, (op. cit., p. 43)."

Further, an unentrenched feature means that there are no special formal requirements for enacting or amending constitutional forms. Statutes relating to political practices, "that is constitutional law," are changed or repealed in exactly the same way as any other statute (ibid.,).

The brief discussion above supports the view that the United Kingdom has a different kind of written constitution, which constitution also has a different status compared to those of other nation-states around the world. This constitution has been as stable as that of the United States; it is a functionally legitimate constitution.

The following points summarize the sources from which ideas of constitutions have been drawn, as briefly touched on above:

- national or social revolutionary situations;
- grand philosophical ideas;
- national conferences or forums;
- militaristic ideas as results of military victories;
- international and regional treaties;
- colonial political ideas and institutions;
- Magna Carta;
- 1689 English Bill of Rights;
- existing laws; and
- traditions and cultures (political culture).

In short, this kind of constitution has been sustained by appropriate convention and understandings, which implies traditions, faith in them, and habits. As Nevil Johnson concludes: "The contemporary account of the Constitution of this country stills owes nearly everything in it to the writers of the last century, and notably A. V. Dicey. For it was he who gave a such a large place to convention and attempted to explain how it operated as an indispensable complement to constitutional law proper"(1977, p. 32).

Liberal Democracies

The Case of the United States

Between the Pilgrim Covenant of 1620 in Plymouth to the drafting of the Federal Constitution in 1787, individuals and states initiated and produced various plans of governments—some which were decreed by the crown while others organized by individuals and communities by their own free will. This section is concerned mainly with the ideas and principles of the Federal Constitution.

> WE THE PEOPLE of the United States, in order to form a more perfect Union, establish justice, insure domestic Tranquility, provide for the common defence, promote the general Welfare, and secure the Blessings of Liberty to ourselves and our Posterity, do ordain and establish this Constitution for the United States of America.

The issue of "we the people" will appropriately be raised and expanded on in the section on citizenship. The original United States Constitution is a short written document that contained seven articles. However, as of 1996, it also contained twenty-seven amendments. But still, it is a smaller document than the French or Spanish constitutions, for instance.

In the United States of America, government was conceived as a government of laws, not of "men" (or citizens). At the same time, it is also a society built on the grand ideas of freedom, acknowledging a level of systematic rebellious tendencies of the settlers to the English colonial administration and rule. The American society is a litigious society. However, this litigious society has an extreme and profound reverence for the individual human being, his/her talents, dreams, spirit of adventure, and the pursuit of his/her happiness. From the institutional stability point of view, the constitution has played a more visible and constructive role in the United States than perhaps in any other industrial society.

The territories that today comprise the continental United States were colonized for 150 years by England, France, and Spain after wars and negotiations. The Louisiana Purchase from France, for instance, is one of the best-known outcomes of one of these negotiations and wars. It should be quickly mentioned that in 1819, Spain sold Florida to the United States. In 1821, Spain lost the vast areas of Texas and California (Knight, 1990, p. 260) to the United States as well. Furthermore, Knight shows how American political influence, including its constitutional model, expanded after its civil war in the nineteenth century as he indicated,

At the Treaty of Paris in December 1898, Spain weakly ceded Puerto Rico, Cuba, and the Philippines to the United States—so that they could more effectively spread their dream of an American hemisphere—and agreed to pay $20,000,000 of war reparations. America emerged after the war as a major world power (1990, p. 266).

In these three cases, after the imposition of military governments during the period of occupation, quasi-republican forms of governments were established, based on the United States model, along with the free-market paradigm as an instrument of political economy and industrialization.

Within the United States and its so-called autonomous territories, the constitution was a struggle for liberty first, among the people of the middle class against the factions. Furthermore, as argued in this chapter, constitution making, even in the United States, is essentially a historical and sociological process in which struggles and compromises concerning certain ideas and principles among various social groups with conflicting purposes must be reached. Some historical moments can be regarded as more important than others in this process of constitution making. Several important phases in defining the development or evolution of the ideas that shaped and/or consolidated the U.S. Constitution, include: the production of the Articles of Confederation, the Constitutional Convention of 1787 that produced the federal constitution, the adoption of the Bills of Rights in 1791, and the implications and consequences of the Civil War. The rigorous interpretation of history and social activism have contributed to more accurately defining the United States' Constitution as a functional, pragmatic contemporary document.

Finally, what are the major characteristics of the U.S. Constitution? Before examining some of its major themes and aspects of the constitution, it is important to link it to the political significance of the Articles of Confederation.

It should be indicated that Thomas Jefferson's Declaration of Independence, which was unanimously adopted on July 4, 1776 by the thirteen British colonial states, namely Virginia, Massachusetts, New Hampshire, Maryland, Rhode Island, Connecticut, North Carolina, South Carolina, New York, New Jersey, Pennsylvania, Delaware, and Georgia, was made without any specific allusion or reference to promoting a concrete agenda of a united republic. The Declaration embodied the ideals of liberty and self-government, which were inspired and supported by political theories and beliefs of the writings of great philosophers such as John Locke. It took several years before Great Britain officially recognized (by the Treaty of Paris in 1783) the independence of these thirteen states under the Articles of Confederation. The nature of this loose, weak union was described by Dorf as he stated:

In theory, the States shared their sovereignty with a central Congress in which each State had one vote. Actually, the powers granted Congress were so inadequate that it was overshadowed by the State governments. Congress lacked the power to levy taxes or control the commerce. It could request money from the state government, but could not compel them to contribute. While it could make laws, it lacked the proper agencies to enforce them, since the Articles failed to provide for a separate executive or a system of national courts. It was difficult for the Congress to enact important laws because such measurements required the assent to nine States; it proved impossible to adopt amendments to remedy weaknesses because such changes required the consent of all the States (1955, p. 41).

In my view, the Articles of Confederation were concerned more with a commercially or trade-driven arrangement than a political resolution. The urgency for improving trade relationships at the time of mercantilism was one of the key objectives that produced the movement toward independence. At the beginning of the struggle for independence, the network of Committees of Correspondence set up by Samuel Adams condemned not only the acts of Parliament (the British measures such as the Writs of Assistance, the New Sugar Act of 1764, the Stamp Act of 1765, and the Townshend Acts of 1767, which infuriated and alienated many members of the middle class from the British policy), but more important, the nature of the British political economy at large.

What did the delegates from twelve states want to achieve in the Constitutional Convention of 1787 in Philadelphia? As Francis Biddle, Attorney General, and Ugo Carusi, Commissioner on Immigration and Naturalization, stated:

> The Constitutional Convention met in 1787. Its members wanted a nation strong enough to survive and enjoy the independence it had won. They hoped to make a plan that would improve the union of the States and enable the people to live more happily. They made a plan of government, the Constitution. They hoped to preserve free government by dividing government powers among three separate branches (1944, p. 4).

As indicated earlier, the United States' Constitution framed in 1787 was a conservative document which drew more heavily upon its experiences and the political institutions of England and the English-speaking peoples. However, its genius lies in its flexibility to accommodate new factors and views in the redefinition of the citizenry, power, rights, and the state. Later, the great ideas of freedom and liberty associated with the Civil War also contributed directly to the redefinition of the Constitution.

To be able to give a comprehensive answer to the question of what the delegates wanted, it is important to identify some of the delegates and describe their social origins and personal characteristics. The combined characteristics of delegates to the Philadelphia Convention of 1787, in which twelve of the thirteen states sent delegates to revise the Articles of Confederation, clearly reflected an elite model of societal organization. Among the fifty-five delegates were the leaders of the changing society. For instance, George Washington, the President of the Convention, served as Commander-in–Chief of the army during the revolution; Alexander Hamilton was one of the delegates from New York; Benjamin Franklin had been minister to France during the war years; and James Madison, who later became the fourth President of the United States, was one of the youngest delegates at the Convention.

According to a short report written by the United States Department of Justice (1942, pp. 17-18), the delegates had the following social characteristics:

1. Most of the delegates had been in public affairs either in their states or in the national government.
2. Eighteen were members of Congress.
3. All but twelve had served in Congress at one time or another.
4. Eight of them had signed the Declaration of Independence.
5. Many of the delegates were wealthy.
6. About half of them were college graduates.

Further, most of them were land owners, lawyers, and businessmen and they were all men of European descent.

In short, these fifty-five people belonged to the bourgeoisie (the upper middle-class structure). The constitution that they drafted was intended to first protect the interests of the settlers against England's interests. It was philosophically an economic document and can also be classified as a social class document. The government that was defined by this constitution was clearly a strong government with the intention of protecting property rights and imposing high taxes on farmers and small entrepreneurs. It should be remembered that the idea of taxation without representation was the engine of the Boston Tea Party and the instrument of the American Revolution at large. This was one of the most important reasons why there was a resistance to its ratification. Farmers in many parts of New England, especially in Massachusetts, revolted against it as a result of the high taxation imposed on them. There was a need to produce the Federalist Papers to explain what this document was about and persuade people to support it.

Still, compared to the Articles of Confederation, the United States Constitution is first of all, a political document that articulates the citizens' rights, functions and limits of government, its institutions, and mechanisms of the circulation of power.

In short, the origins of the United States' Constitution can be summarized in what Edward Conrad Smith wrote:

The Constitution of 1787 was the product of seven centuries of development in England and America. Magna Carta (1215) is as much the heritage of Americans as of Englishmen. So is the common law which limited the authority of the King's minister as well as governed the King's subjects. The rights and privileges of Parliament were claimed by colonial legislatures against royal governors. From experience in living under charters in some of the colonies, Americans learned the value of written documents, which explicitly stated the rights of the people and the government's powers. They were constantly trying to adopt

English institutions to the conditions of a new continent and a relatively classless society (1972, p. 1).

The Case of France

What are the historical and philosophical foundations of the principles of liberty, equality, and fraternity in the French constitutions? As compared to other liberal democracies, the French people at large seem to be more skeptical, suspicious, distrustful and critical of authority and of the state and its executive power. Does this result from their different interpretations of human nature and nation-states? This attitude may have arisen from the nature of the unbalanced centrality of the powers of their kings and emperors throughout French history and the attitudes and behaviors associated with the 1789 revolution. Despite controversies concerning specific functions that the French Revolution have played in France and Europe, and various struggles that took place to reverse history and re-recreate the empire, its principles have clearly been the foundation of the contemporary French state and French society. Efforts towards the creation of a unified political system among diverse social groups and the fear of diversity of ideologies or opposing values are the most central elements of the legacy of the French Revolution.

Based on the dogma of assimilation and a foundation of French universalism, the French constitutions (a total of sixteen since the first in 1793), have influenced, in various ways and forms, many other constitution-making experiences in the former French colonies. For instance, how much has the French Revolution influenced the power and class struggles among the *petits blancs, grands blancs*, the creole, people of color, etc., in Haiti, the struggles which finally led to the first "real democratic revolution" in the world (Knight, 1990). Furthermore, the ideas related to the French Revolution of 1789 were essentially centered on democracy as participation but not necessarily as representation, which historically has been described by many scholars as an English invention. Even Napoleon Bonaparte, who claimed to continue the revolution, was hostile to representative ideas in the National Assembly. Rule was sanctioned by the voices of the sovereign people, the practice of direct democracy (Ehrmann and Schain, 1992, p. 12).

In 1989, France celebrated the bicentennial of the French Revolution with special expositions, fanfare, parades, and commemorations (Ehrmann and Schain, 1992, p. 3). Although France is among the oldest nation-states in Europe, this celebration was not about political stability or national unity. Rather, it was mainly about French ideas and their influence the world over. Indeed, the French Revolution had an impact beyond Europe and the United States in the nineteenth and twentieth centuries. As Ehrmann and Schain indicated:

Wherever historical events have created deep divisions, mutual distrust has been frequent and agreement on fundamentals tenuous. It was natural enough that Revolution of the eighteenth century opened long, drawn-out controversies between the monarchists and republicans. However, it also shook and split, on the most sensitive level, the conscience of a broad range of elites and common people (p. 7).

Consolidated by the industrial revolution in England, the dogmas of the French Revolution, as articulated by workers and middle classes in many parts of Europe as part of their emancipatory politics, centered on democracy. Thus, the spirit of systematic questioning of authority or the state, a critical democratic discourse, is one of the most important elements of the French Revolution's contribution to world politics.

The French Constitution of 1958, which was promoted by a unique historical situation (occupation by Germany) and a high level of patriotism or nationalism, was a product of the dynamics of a combination of factors. France was engaged in a war against the National Liberation Front of Algeria. The crisis in Algeria was larger and deeper than any other crisis of the French colonial experience. In their psychology and power relations, the French perceived Algeria as part of France, a settler's colony where about one million French had lived for more than three generations, owning more than 40 percent of the fertile land. More than 150,000 Algerians were also working and living in France between 1954 and 1956. As Leslie Wolf-Phillips noted:

The Algerian insurrection of May 13, 1958, followed nine days later by revolts in Corsica, gave rise to fears of disorder in metropolitan France. On May 29, President Coty—who had refused to accept the resignation of the Prime Minister (M. Pflimlim) until it was possible to form a new government—warned the National Assembly that France was on the brink of civil war, and informed them that he had asked 'the most illustrious Frenchmen' to form a 'government of national safety (1968, p. 11).

Furthermore, France's memory of defeat in Indochina was still vivid. This memory psychologically and politically promoted a reconciliatory national agenda. France had also been occupied by Nazi Germany, which led the country to be divided between the collaborators (the Vichy government) and the nationalists. Thus, Charles de Gaulle, a nationalist, was recalled by various national political forces to join the government in order to unify France and to make sure that France did not lose its colonies in possible national revolutions that were taking place in most parts of the world, including Africa. Immediately after he was elected Prime Minister in the National Assembly on June 1, 1958, Charles de Gaulle asked the Assembly to approve three measures:

1. a bill for the renewal of special powers in Algeria, as required of all new governments;

2. a bill conferring special powers on the government for a period of six months; and
3. a bill empowering the government to make constitutional reforms by revising Article 90 of the constitution and thereafter to submit the revisions to a national referendum, the government being assisted in its work of revision by a consultative committee of whom two-thirds would be members of the French Parliament (Leslie Wolf-Phillips, 1968, p. 13).

Thus, thirty-nine members of the consultative committee carefully studied the document that was drafted by a small group of highly respected cabinet ministers, which included Mollet, Pflimlin, Jacquinot, and Houphouët-Boigny (Leslie, op. cit.). It should be noted that Félix Houphouët-Boigny was the founding father of the contemporary state in Côte d'Ivoire, an enterprise which he firmly undertook with strong collaboration of the French colonial administration. The text of these ministers was approved through the national referendum of September 28, 1958. Thus the Fifth Republic came into being on October 6, 1958 with a new constitution. In its constitutional governance, this republic departed from the tradition of absolute parliamentarian sovereignty, a tradition that is traced to Rousseau's influence (Rohr, 1995, p. 130). The framers put trust and confidence in the executive. However, in terms of the dominant ideas, the 1958 constitution was consistent with the previous constitution of 1946. The 1946 constitution was produced at a time marked by widespread political reform in former colonies, the impact of World War II, and the weakening of France as a world power. Both the nature of the political crisis in French society and the ideal of political and historical continuity shaped the 1958 French Constitution. Its preamble states:

> The French people solemnly proclaim their attachment to the Rights of Man and the principles of national sovereignty as defined by the Declaration of 1789, confirmed and complemented by the Preamble to the Constitution of 1946. By virtue of these principles and that of the self-determination of peoples, the Republic offers to the overseas territories that express the will to adhere to them new institutions founded on the common ideal of liberty, equality and fraternity and conceived with a view to their democratic development.

What should be emphasized is that the Constitution of the Second Empire as well as that of the Fifth Republic implicitly referred to the "great principles proclaimed in 1789" and boasted of having given the constituent power back to the people (Ehrmann and Schain, 1992, p. 12). Some scholars go so far as to characterize French constitutionalism as the embodiment of some elements of "egalitarian socialism." Liberty, equality, and fraternity have become a permanent, powerful moral and political tool in the struggles against the state, the state that is claimed to be national and which creates a rallying arena in French political society.

The Socialist Models

The Union of Soviet Socialist Republics (USSR)

The USSR was a powerful military "empire." It also articulated a grand and powerful ideology to build a society around the notion of *Pax Sovietica* (Magstadt, 1998, p. 165), with nations composed of different nationalities, such as Albanians, Hungarians, Germans, Moldavians, Finns, and Ukrainians, forming a unity of purpose. This society was projected on the concept of the Union of Soviet Socialist Republics (USSR) as a unitary, federal, multinational state, formed on the principle of socialist federalism and as a result of the self-determination of nations and the voluntary association of equal Soviet Socialist Republics. The USSR was composed of a complex of various geopolitical entities including, the Soviet Socialist Union Republic, Autonomous Soviet Socialist Republics, Autonomous Provinces, and Autonomous Areas. The Soviet of the Union and the Soviet of Nationalities had one common denominator, namely the adoption of socialism as the ideology of the state. It should be noted, however, that this union constantly redefined itself as the world around and in it also changed with the emergence of new states as a result of either war or new negotiations within the dominant elements of the axis of power (for instance, the Baltic states of Latvia, Lithuania, and Estonia, plus Moldavia and Karelo-Finland, which joined the union in 1940).

The Bolshevik Revolution, also known as the October Revolution, produced its constitutions to support the socialist revolution and the establishment of social and political institutions which lasted until the collapse of the USSR in 1991. Unlike the U.S. Constitution, which began with the preamble as "We the people of the United States...," the Soviet constitution started with an articulation of revolution as stated in the 1977 amended constitution (in the midst of the Cold War), known as the Brezhnev Constitution:

> The Great Socialist October Revolution, carried out by the workers and peasants of Russia under the leadership of the Communist Party, headed by V. I. Lenin, overturned the power of the capitalists and landowners, broke the chains of oppression, established the dictatorship of the proletariat, and created the Soviet state—a state of a new type, the basic instruments and to build socialism and communism. The world-wide historical turning-point of mankind from capitalism to socialism began.

During and after the October Revolution, the Bolsheviks and the left social-revolutionaries worked very hard to influence the dynamics of the Third Congress of Soviets, which was responsible for producing the constitution. Thus, after many meetings of the Constituent Assembly and the Central Executive Committee, the Constitution of 1918 was approved by the Fifth All-Russian Congress of Soviets on July 10, 1918 (Wolf-Phillips, 1968, p. 166). But this constitution was only for the Russian Soviet Federative Socialist Republic

(RSFSR). Like any constitution in the world of the states, this one went through amendments to take into account the positions of the leadership and the momentum of the revolution. It had six parts, which were:

1. Declaration of the Rights of Toiling and Exploited People;
2. General Statutes of the RSFSR;
3. Constitution of Soviet Authority;
4. Active and Passive Right of Suffrage;
5. Budget Law; and
6. Coat of Arms and Flag of RSFSR.

The RSFSR was an unfinished story. Debates for the formation of the Soviet Union continued until 1922, as Wolf-Phillips indicated:

> The decision to unite the Soviet Republics into a single Union was made formally at the First Congress of the Soviets of the Union of Soviet Socialist Republics after the Congresses of Soviets of the RSFSR, Ukraine and White Russia and the republics of the Transcaucasian Federation (Azerbaijan, Armenia, and Georgia) has decided on December 29,1922 to accept the 'Compact' concerning the formation of the USSR (1968, p. 167).

A new constitutional committee drafted a document which was ratified on January 31, 1924, ten days after the death of Lenin. Thus, the unification was established with a clear division of labor within this federalist revolutionary state. This vast multinational state, based on the dictum of the new constitution, had a mandate to strengthen its revolutionary legality and legitimacy. The document was flexible enough to accommodate differences and conflicts among social groups and various nationalities. The system of governance was highly centralized, with the supreme organ of power in the Congress of Soviets and, between its sessions, the Central Executive Committee, with the Soviet of the Union and the Soviet Nationalities, enjoying equal rights and status (ibid.,).

Stalin, like Charles de Gaulle in France, was interested in acquiring total state power. He was also interested in "strengthening and regularizing the state structure and at the same time, making it superficially more attractive to world democratic union" (ibid., p. 168). Another new constitution (not an amendment to the 1924 Constitution) was enthusiastically supported by the Soviet people and voted on by the All-Union Congress of the Soviets of the USSR between November 25 and December 5, 1936. It contained 146 articles.

According to William Simons, the 1977 Brezhnev Constitution with its 174 articles was more inclusive or, from a liberal point of view, more Western European. For instance, the principles of the 1975 Helsinki Agreement are enshrined in Article 29 of this constitution. Article 28 can be traced to international human rights' covenants, and new articles in this constitution speak of rights to health care, housing, the achievement of culture, participation in the administration and state affairs, and freedom of scientific, technical, and artistic creation. Judicial protection was raised to the level of a constitutional provision (1980, p. 348) rather than being articulated at the party level. Although these ideas were not alien to the dogmas of the proletarian revolution as they represented the core programs to be advanced in the new society, they became more publicly and internationally institutionalized during the détente period.

The Soviet approach to constitution making is summed up in a celebrated passage from Vyshinsky's *The State of the Soviet State*, as cited by Wolf-Phillips

> Soviet Constitutions represent the sum total of the historical path along which the Soviet State has traveled. At the same time, they are legislative basis of the subsequent development of state life. Thus, the development of Soviet Constitutions is indissolubly linked with the development of the Soviet State. Changes in the socio-political life of our country are reflected in the corresponding changes that Soviet Constitutions accepted by the highest organs of the state authority. In the Soviet Constitutions we have the formal record and legal confirmation of socialist conquests won in the formal separate stages of historical development of the Soviet state. Soviet Constitutions are not a program (1968, p. 169).

It is clear that the Soviet constitutions embodied elements of democracy (socialist democracy) and universal revolution. Finally, it is necessary to briefly discuss some elements of the current constitution of the Russian Federation, keeping in mind the historical development of the Soviet Union as reviewed above.

The new Russian Federation is not a socialist regional entity. However, its members were part of the Socialist Soviet empire. Russia is still the most powerful entity and the engine of political change in the region.

As compared to the 1924, 1936, and 1977 constitutions, which started with expressions of revolution, the constitution of the Russian Federation begins with the people, as does that of the United States:

> We, the multinational people of the Russian Federation,
> united by a common destiny upon our land, asserting human rights and freedoms and civil peace and concord,
> preserving the unity of the state as formed by history, preceding the unity of the states as formed by history,
> proceeding from the generally recognized principles of equality and self-determination of peoples,
> revering the memory of our forebears who bequeathed us love and respect for the Fatherland and a faith in good and in justice,
> restoring the sovereign statehood of Russia and asserting the immunity of its democratic foundation,
> striving to ensure the well-being and the prosperity of Russia,
> accepting responsibility for homeland before present and future generations,
> recognizing ourselves as part of the world community,

adopt this Constitution of the Russian Federation.

The Russian Federation emerged out of the ashes of the collapsed Soviet Union in 1991. It is divided into eighty-nine federal administrative units, including twenty-one independent republics. Its constitution was adopted on December 12, 1993. At that time, it contained nine chapters and 137 articles. What is the nature of the Russian Federation? I have identified only a few items from among those articles of the constitution that reflect the nature of this form of governance.

Article 1 states that the Russian Federation is a democratic federative law-governed state with a republican form of government.

Article 3 states:

- The holders of sovereignty and the sole sources of authority in the Russian Federation are its multinational people.
- The people shall exercise their authority directly and also through organs of state power and organs of local self-government.
- The supreme direct expression of the power of the people shall be the referendum and free elections.
- No one may appropriate to himself or herself power in the Russian Federation. The seizure of power or the appropriation of its competences shall be prosecuted in accordance with federal law.

Article 5 states:

- The Russian Federation consists of republics, areas, provinces, cities of federal significance, an autonomous province and autonomous districts which are equal components of Russian Federation.
- A Republic (state) has its own constitution and legislation. An area, province, city of federal significance, autonomous province or autonomous district has its own charter and legislation.

Article 7 states:

- The Russian Federation is a social state whose policy shall aim at creating conditions ensuring a worthy life and free development of the individual. In the Russian Federation people's labor and health shall be protected, a guaranteed minimum wage established, state support ensured for the family, motherhood, fatherhood, and childhood, invalids and elderly citizens, the system of social services developed, and state pensions, allowances and other guarantees of social protection established.

Chapter two, entitled "Human and Civil Rights and Freedoms," contains forty-seven articles. These rights, even their formulations, clearly and literally echo the 1789 French Declaration, as S. E. Finer et al. suggest (1995, p. 250), the United States Federal Constitution, and the United Nations Human Rights Covenant and Conventions.

Have all or most of the constitutions produced by revolutionary ideas, movements, or social movements in the contemporary period embodied the elements discussed in the constitutions of the United States, the USSR, and the Russian Federation? To elucidate this question, it would be interesting to examine some major characteristics of the case of the constitution-making experience in the People's Republic of China.

People's Republic of China (PRC)

The People's Republic of China like the United States, France, the Soviet Union, and the Russian Federation has redefined itself in contemporary world politics through its constitutions. The amended Chinese constitutions were produced through the complex process of debates within various committees of the Chinese Communist Party and voted on by the National People's Congress, which was proclaimed the highest organ of the state under the leadership of the Chinese Communist Party in the 1975 constitution (Chaube, 1986, p. 78). The first revolutionary constitution was produced in 1954, followed by ones in 1961, 1975, 1978, and 1982. Each of these constitutions addressed the following items: issues related to the nature of the Chinese revolution; the role of its leadership in the international socialist world; the relation between the state and the working class or people; and agrarian and modernization issues. In my views, the most important constitutions in the history of the PRC are the 1954 constitution, which had to set up the framework for a Marxist-Leninist type of revolution and provide political guidelines; the 1961 one, which was produced in the middle of the Cold War era; and the 1978 constitution, which was produced at beginning of economic reforms and after the passing away of Mao Zedong. What do these constitutions have in common in terms of their origins and sources?

Since the economic reforms of the early 1980s, Chinese society at large has been undergoing considerable changes which have led to unprecedented economic growth. Some of these reforms have led to some aspects of political openness and to the formation of political clubs and new political parties. Nonetheless, the question of how far and how much the People's Republic of China has reformed its constitutions is still relevant.

There are scholars who tend to link the cultural strength of the People's Republic of China and its leadership style to the empire-building heritage of the Han Empire of 200 B.C.E., the Xia (Hsia) dynasty of about 2200-1700 B.C.E., the Shang dynasty of 1766-1122 B.C.E. (Magstadt, 1998, p. 344), and some dimensions of the search for a "Greater China." Despite the richness of these periods in the history of the constitution-making experience in China, in this section, as indicated earlier, we will limit our discussion to the ideas of constitution making as they relate to the formation and proclamation of the People's Republic of China in 1949.

It is the proletarian revolution conceived as popular revolution, with its victory in 1949, that produced a constitution in 1954, which was aimed at guiding the revolution and making it "pragmatic." Although in a revolutionary context it is difficult to identify historical evidence and links that justify claims of the theory of revolution as a natural process, it is clear that similar ideological elements embodied in the Russian revolution can be identified and examined in other revolutionary contexts, including the Chinese case. Historically, most constitution-making forces have borrowed from other experiences. However, this section is not directly concerned with what China borrowed or did not borrow from the Soviet Union or other experiences, but rather it addresses the question of similarities and political meanings of the grand ideas that constitute the philosophical foundation of the vision or the future of a political community.

The preamble of the Constitution of People's Republic of China, adopted in March 1978, two years after the passing of Chairman Mao, in the midst of Cold War politics, after the Cultural Revolution of the 1960s, and at the beginning of economic reforms, begins differently than those of the United States, France, and the USSR. It states:

> After more than a century of heroic struggle the Chinese people, led by the Communist Party of China headed by our great leader and teacher Chairman Mao Tsetung, finally overthrew the reactionary rule of imperialism, feudalism, and bureaucrat-capitalism by means of people's revolutionary war, winning complete victory in new-democratic revolution, and in 1949 founded the People's Republic of China. The founding of the People's Republic of China marked the beginning of the historical period of socialism in our country. Since then, under the leadership of Chairman Mao and the Chinese Communist Party, the people of our nationalities have carried out Chairman Mao's proletarian revolutionary line in the political, economic, cultural, and military fields, and foreign affairs, and have won great victories in socialist construction through repeated struggles against enemies, both at home and abroad, and through the great proletarian revolution.

The roles of Chairman Mao, the Chinese Community Party (CCP) as an agent of change, and their revolutionary ideology for creating a new society and political culture are central to this constitution. The preamble recalls the history of contradictions of Chinese society and the dialectics of change that were produced.

As in the case of the Russian Revolution of 1917, the Chinese Revolution produced a constitution that was initially based on Marxism-Leninism, a movement of ideas and actions that led to the victory of the Chinese Communist Party over the partisans of the Kuomintang regime (the nationalist party). Thus, as Wolf-Phillips indicates (1968, p. 1), on September 29, 1949, the Chinese People's Political Consultative Conference (CPPCC) adopted three fundamental laws: (a) the Organic Law of Central People's Government, which was intended to establish the structure of the central government; (b) the Organic Law of the CPPCC aimed at outlining the organization, powers, and the functions of the CPPCC, which was going to exercise supreme state power; and (c) the Common Programme of the CPPCC. This program stated the guiding principles to be followed during the new "democratic stage." All three of these organs emphasized the need for promoting the notion of "democratic dictatorship" as the political foundation of the national reconstruction of China. According to Wolf-Phillips:

> The Common Programme outlined a wide range of personal freedoms (of thought, speech, public assembly, correspondence, person, domicile, religious beliefs, demonstration) for those who worked with the regime, but denied them to 'feudal landlords, capitalists, and reactionary elements in general;' It dealt with the military and with policies for economic organization, education and cultural matters, and it provided for the exercise of state power through people's congresses and people's executives, abolishing all laws and decrees of the former Kuomintang regime (1968, p. 1).

It is the principles contained in this Common Program, after public debates, that became the core of the first draft of the constitution, which had over a million amendment proposals before being voted and approved by the National People's Congress on September 20, 1954. Some of the characteristics of this new constitution are defined by Shibani Kinkar Chaube as follows:

> The 1954 constitution envisaged China as a multinational, multi-class and multi-party state in which, unlike the Soviet Union, no party was officially recognized. Liu Shaoqi while moving the constitution, said: 'a broad people's democratic united front still exists under our country's system of people's democracy.' The first article of the constitution provided that the leadership of the new state, based on the worker-peasant alliance, was with the working class. Indeed, the CPC was the acknowledged vanguard of the class. The people's democratic united front envisaged an alliance of the workers with those nonworking people with whom cooperation was possible. Having eliminated the compradors, the regime was ready to accommodate the national bourgeoisie in the transitional period while carrying on the step-by-step socialist transformation (op. cit., pp. 47-48).

The amended constitution in 1961 had 106 articles and five chapters. In its form, it is a shorter document than the United States, the French, and the Russian constitutions.

The first chapter sets out general principles; the second and longest chapter concerns state structure; the third chapter is concerned with fundamental rights and duties of citizens; and the fourth chapter, the shortest, is entitled "National Flag, National Emblem, Capital." What are some of the major characteristics of this constitution? What is its major policy significance within the Chinese revolution and society at large?

For the purpose of identifying the major characteristics that define what kind of constitution is discussed in this section, the content of a few articles should be cited and briefly discussed. In Chapter 1, Article 1, the constitution describes the PRC as "a People's democratic state led by the working class and based on the alliance of workers and peasants." In Article 2, it states "All power in the People's Republic of China belongs to the people." The organs through which the people exercise power are the National People's Congress and the local people's congresses at various levels. The National People's Congress, the local people's congresses, and other organs of state practice "democratic centralism." This democracy implies that the elections of officers at all levels of society take place though people's congresses.

Article 3, for instance, states that the People's Republic of China is a unitary multinational state. All the nationalities are equal. Discrimination against or oppression of any nationality, and acts which undermine the unity of nationalities, are prohibited. In the center of the question of governance is the place of the individuals and institutions which make decisions, or laws, and also implement or enforce them.

In Chapter 2, sixty-three articles define the state structure (Articles 21 through 84), namely the division of power, legislative mechanisms, the limits of power, and the nature of the interactions among various agencies. However, only few articles have been cited to provide some ideas, in theory, about the dynamics of the governance system. Article 21 states "The National People's Congress is the highest organ of state power." Article 22 also states "The National People's Congress is the sole organ exercising the legislative power of the state." Article 27 describes the power of the National People's Congress as vital and central to Chinese politics. It exercises some of the following selected powers:

- to amend the constitution;
- to make laws;
- to supervise the enforcement of the constitution;
- to elect the Chairman and the Vice-Chairman of the People's Republic of China;
- to decide on the choice of the Premier of the State Council upon recommendation by the Chairman of the People's Republic of China;
- to decide the Vice-Chairmen and members of the Council of the National Defence upon recommendation by the Chairman of the People's Republic of China;
- to elect the President of the Supreme Court;
- to decide on the national economic plan;
- to examine and approve the state budget and the final state accounts; and
- to ratify the following administrative divisions: provinces, autonomous regions and cities directly under the central authority.

In short, although the Chinese constitutions, as any others, were amended to respond to the demands of the internal forces, the exigencies of its leaders and those of the Chinese Communist Party, they share some common characteristics. For instance concerning the place of the military and its relationship to the CCP, Chaube writes:

The 1954 Constitution put it under the command of the Chairman of the State. The 1975 and 1978 Constitutions put the army under the command of the Communist Party of China. The 1978 Constitution put the army under the control of the a Central Military Commission comprising of the Chairman, the Vice-Chairman and members, the Chairman having the overall responsibility for the Commission to the NPC (p. 131).

Despite changes in the 1954, 1961, 1975, and 1982 constitutions, some of the main themes that were consistently elaborated or clarified in all constitutions include people's democracy, the centrality of the CCP, the visibility of the national, regional, and local congresses in the decision making, systematic opposition to imperialism, colonialism, and hegemonism, and socialist political platforms. However, it should be noted that one of the new features of the 1982 Constitution was "the admission of foreign enterprises, other foreign economic organizations and individual foreigners into the economy" (ibid, p. 103). As Chaube explains:

> The most significant change in the Commitment of the PRC is the revival of the concept of the People's Democratic Dictatorship. The 1975 and the 1978 constitutions declared the PRC as 'a socialist state of the dictatorship of the proletariat' (in the very first article). The 1982 constitution calls the PRC 'a socialist state under the People's Democratic Dictatorship, thus returning to the political form of 1954. While the Preambles to the 1975 and the 1978 constitutions spoke of a 'revolutionary united front,' the Preamble to the 1982 constitution speaks of 'a broad patriotic front that is composed of democratic parties and people's organizations and embraces all socialist working people, all patriots who support socialism and all patriots who stand for reunification of the mother land.' (ibid, p. 98).

Selected African Experiences in Constitution Making

Introduction: General Issues

In this section, I identify and raise general issues related to the importance of constitutions in Africa in the postcolonial era. As the constitution-making experiences are diverse and vary from one country to another, I contrast only few selected cases/countries that may help reflect the diversity, similarities, and complexity in projecting the notion of a constitution as a constructive force in state formation. As in the cases of other regions of the world, the main objective here is to examine the historical arguments and philosophical roots of the grand ideas behind constitution making in Africa. What forces have influenced constitution making in Africa? Have African political elites been capable of integrating the ideas of the political resistance organized and used to fight the colonial powers into their constitutions or have they projected their own personal dictatorships as alternative forms of governance on national institutions? Have the national, political, and social movements that led to political independence been able to enlighten or inform postcolonial constitutions? Have selective African traditions and cultures been used as instruments of re-defining the African societies, states, and citizens?

Despite the large scale of transatlantic enslavement, an economic instrument used since the seventeenth century by the Western powers to build their empires, to colonize others, and to enforce their domination, Africa was the last region of the world to be colonized. Further, Africa was able to protect in many forms some elements of its own historical and cultural heritage. The Western powers came to the continent when colonial rules, their values, and their strategies had become sharper, better-defined, and relatively mature. In South America, for example, new or independent nation-states emerged in the nineteenth century. But in Africa, this period was the beginning of the Western powers' movements toward the continent's interior. In many parts of Africa, these powers used and promoted the concept of what I characterize as "scientific" or "rational" colonization, the notion that it was possible to calculate and predict with a certain level of precision and confidence the outcomes of colonial actions and policies. That is to say, they could take actions or make policies, and people's reactions or behaviors would be clearly predictable and reasonably deductive based on accepted premises practiced elsewhere. The colonial experiments in Africa were planned to be quick and brutal. However, as evidenced by historical facts, the concept of scientific or rational colonization in its policy forms did not work for either the colonial Western powers or the Africans.

For the approximately one hundred years of colonization, the majority of the population was not ruled by its own internal or indigenous constitutions. All colonial regimes were essentially militaristic, until the postwar reforms. Mapped within the geo-linguistic, cultural, and political legacies of colonialism, the experiences of constitution making in most parts of Africa are not the results of internal evolutionary processes. African constitutions were born out of the conditions and the history of domination, subordination, protest, resistance, and negotiation.

Historically, the African constitution-making experiences are divided into the cultural and political traditions of the anglophone, francophone (with the two components of French and Belgian), lusophone, and "spanophone" colonial legacies. Compared to the anglophone, francophone, and lusophone legacies, the spanophone represents a small, almost "invisible" tradition. It should be mentioned that only Equatorial Guinea and Western Sahara have Spanish cultural and administrative traditions. However, these traditions, and the Spanish history of colonization, have been seriously challenged by the francophone tradition of pragmatic politics. The fragmented elements of the Italian legacy in Eritrea, Somalia, and Libya were also quickly challenged and combated by British cultural and economic imperialism and elements of the rise of African imperial power (the Ethiopian case) and nationalism.

Thus, constitution-making experiences in Africa must be studied within the context of comparative political paradigms and colonial rule. These historical configurations, combined with the imperatives and interests of global political economy, have some direct and profound impact on the ways constitutions have been conceived, drawn, maintained, and implemented in Africa. It should be pointed out, however, that internal political factors such as nationalism, power struggles, ethnicity, political alliances, "intelligence" of the political elites and their professional experiences, and the dynamics of the international political economy have directly or indirectly influenced the processes of constitution setting in many parts of Africa.

Despite national revolutions and local revolts in the pre- and-post-independence periods, constitution-making experiences were generally shaped by the nature of the European strategies or politics of colonization. That is to say, colonization and decolonization processes were antithetical yet interrelated phenomena in Africa. They were related to one another dialectically as opposing forces. Epistemologically, one cannot fully understand one without trying to understand the other and vice versa. Although colonization was an alienating force, which was rejected and combated forcefully by all at various levels and capacities, it should be noted that people's reactions to it depended very much on how colonial powers organized themselves and what kinds of strategies and mechanisms they used to pursue their intended objectives of domination.

The British in general used the well-known dogma of "indirect rule." The indigenous or local African institutions played a role in recruiting new agents and supporting the new administration. The system did not intend to produce an "African Shakespeare." It was only possible to reform the functions of local agencies and social practices and traditions to feed the new systems based on a new loyalty foundation. However, this rule was not written in stone. It was applied only in a historical and sociological context where the social, military, and environmental conditions forced the British to use it as a negotiating scheme for maintaining their rule. The conditions and the nature of resistance, along with the physical environment, determined where and how the British used indirect or direct rule. For instance, in the settlers' colonies in Eastern and Southern Africa, the British used essentially elitist and centralized policies like those of the French. The major difference in this case between the British and the French policies was one of the degree of the so-called melting pot, or assimilationism. The French believed that it was possible to totally assimilate the colonized (although this intention was not actualized) into the French linguistic culture and consequently into the French political culture, while British centralized policies were rather pragmatic, technical, and institutional. French direct rule, which was based on an assimilation policy and cultural guidelines, was essentially articulated on the arrogant belief that French culture and the French language were superior to other cultures (as the British thought theirs was).

Thus the so-called civilizing mission of all European powers was promoted by the principle of the melting pot. In general, the French colonial administration articulated two dominant tendencies toward the creation of constitutions in

Africa, as indicated in the conference that took place between January 30 and February 8, 1944 in Brazzaville, that was convened by Charles de Gaulle. "A controversy arose among the delegates relating to the postwar constitutional connections between France and the colonies. Governor-General Eboué and Governor Latrille of Ivory Coast stood for the establishment of federal institutions, which could harmonize the social, economic and cultural differences between the French and the Africans. On the other hand, the colonial commissioner, Rene Pleven preferred centralized institutions under French control"(Harshé, 1984, p. 10). On the same subject, according to Michel Cromdwer:

> French policy was then a constant search for a compromise between the two extremes, for a formula that would conserve the unity of Great France by retaining ultimate political control in Paris and yet allow a degree of local autonomy both compatible with the thesis of unity and yet sufficient to turn African politicians' attention away from the ideas of independence (1965, p. 19).

Did the ideas of liberty, fraternity, and equality in France influence the francophone Belgian experiences in the constitution making of the Democratic Republic of the Congo? The Congo is the largest francophone country in the global South and was colonized by Belgium, not France. The Belgian population is predominantly composed of two groups, the Walloons and the Flemish. In the Congolese administrative and educational experiences both the francophone and Flemish traditions produced an eclectic model of governance.

A Reflection on the Case of the Democratic Republic of the Congo (DRC)[1]

Introduction: Objectives and General Issues

What are the socio-economic and political factors that have influenced the efforts toward constitution making in post-colonial Congo? Who have been the major actors in this process? I intend to discuss the political context in which constitutions were produced in the DRC and what kind of constitutions they were.

The political situation in the DRC is such that it will be a long time before a stable constitution is accepted by the majority of the Congolese people. It is very much hoped that by June 2005, as projected by the institutions of the transitional regime, the Congolese will be able to produce a new, solid, and viable constitution as the symbol of the unity and progress for the Fourth Republic and also as an effective functioning document shaped by African philosophy and conditions to guide all the activities of political life in the country.

Nonetheless, we have to examine the history of constitutions in order to ask one of the major questions in this book which concerns the origin of constitutions. We hope that this history can teach us some lessons about the nature of

Congolese politics. What are the sources of these ideas? What are the core ideas that constitute the centrality of constitutions in the DRC?

In the postcolonial politics of the Congo in the early 1960s, one of the major characteristics of the Congolese crisis was the ambiguity of its basic laws and their inability to articulate clearly the division of power and the general rules that should govern society at large. As Crawford Young stated:

The *Loi Fondamentale* had the fatal flaw of providing no method to secure a definitive interpretation of constitutional ambiguities. Articles 226 to 236 provided for a Constitutional court, but its functions were restricted to the delivery of opinions on the compatibility of legislative measures with the *Loi Fondamendale*, conflicsts in the division of powers between central and provincial authorities, and the legality of administrative acts where no other recourse existed (1965, p. 327).

The first step of state formation in the Congo was the phase of the extreme form of privatization and personalization of the state. After the end of the so-called Congo Free State in 1908, the status of the Congo was personal property of the King, "Colonial Charter provided the supreme supremacy of law as enacted by the Belgian Parliament. Yet, in practice, it was the King, who under ministerial responsibility, legislated by decree" (Gittleman et al. 1991, p. 1). It was only in 1964 that the Congolese produced their "independent" constitution.

However, given the current level of political instability caused by the elements of international and national power struggles and a high level of social cleavage, it should be emphasized that the Congolese have yet to enjoy constitutionality and the rule of law. Another constitution that was relatively well debated was the 1992 one. The DRC is a case where most of the constitutional changes and revisions or amendments in the postcolonial era took place under one single regime (1965-1997) with the exceptions of: (a) the 1964 constitution; (b) the drafted constitution of November 1998, which the late President Kabila approved; and (c) the current debate organized by the transitional government to produce a new constitution before June 2005.

One of the responsibilities of the transitional government that has been established as a result of the Sun City, South Africa peace accord among the so-called rebels and the government in December 2002, is to produce a constitution in the DRC. Finally in July 2003, a transitional working administration composed of thirty-five ministerial and twenty-five vice-ministerial posts and a 630-member transitional parliament (the Senate and the House of Deputies) were produced representing the major "rebel" movements, the civil society, the non-military opposition, and the government. The constitution that was formulated in April/May, 2003 would be used to define other political institutions in the country, which should support the elections projected to take place about two years hence.

The Third Republic, under the late Mze Laurent-Désiré Kabila, who was killed on January 17, 2001, and then Joseph Kabila, has not yet promulgated any constitution. Thus, the analysis is more historically and philosophically oriented rather than based on policy and law.

The Search for Constitution Making: A Historical Context

The Belgian Congo gained its independence as a secular republic on June 30, 1960. But its Fundamental Law was strongly based on the Belgian constitutional monarchy. This Law was voted on by the Belgian parliament and sanctioned by the Belgian king on May 19, 1960. Its legal system was based both on the Belgian civil system and on what was called "tribal" law. The Congolese people did not debate the Fundamental Law. To a large extent, it was imposed on the masses with the consensus of the newly emerging political elite.

However, after the 1960s, the Congolese national political elites produced several constitutions and amended them often to fit their political agendas and political tastes. They wanted to make some political reforms mainly as a means of consolidating their power. Thus, the constitution was the first issue that was touched on in various periods of postcolonial Congolese politics.

As noted earlier, the Fundamental Law, the first Congolese constitution, was similar in many ways to the constitutional monarchy of Belgium. In this constitutional monarchy, the king had in principle very limited practical powers, although his role in a constitutional crisis could be substantial. It established a unitary state with some elements of a "federal parliamentary form of government," including a bicameral legislature that comprised a house of representatives, the Chamber, based on direct and proportional representation, and the Senate, with equal representation from each of the six provinces.

The president would be elected directly by the people through universal suffrage. He/she was considered the symbol of the unity of the Congo and the key figure of the constitutional structure. His/her functions resembled essentially those of a constitutional monarch, including the power to appoint and dismiss ministers, although such ministers had to be invested by the parliament (Gittleman et al. 1991, p. 1). The premier minister was elected from the representative members of the parliament. The powers were shared between the central government and the six provincial governments, and between the Chamber and the Senate, and between the premier minister and the president.

After independence, inspired by monarchic constitution, the president behaved as a weak monarch. But the relationships between the head of the government and the head of the state were dangerously ambiguous. For instance, the president could dismiss the premier minister and the premier minister could also dismiss the president with the vote of two-thirds of the members of parliament. This is exactly what happened with the power struggle between President Joseph Kasavubu and Prime Minister Patrice E. Lumumba in July and September 1960.

The 1964 constitution was well debated among the political elites. In addition, it was believed that this constitution should address the causes of the Congolese crisis, which was also partially located in the nature of the inherited Basic

Law. It retained the bicameral parliament and gave it both legislative responsibilities and the power to approve the president's appointment or the dismissal of the premier minister. Some scholars believe that this 1964 constitution reflected, to a large extent, the people's aspirations and desires. Despite political instability, politicians were then very close to their constituencies, which brought their inputs to the constitutional debates. The division of power in this constitution became clearly articulated, with significant implications for "good" governance. The constitution of Luluabourg (now known as Kananga), provided for an executive president who coexisted with a cabinet government, under a prime minister. Thus, despite political crisis, the Congo produced its first constitution, which was approved through a referendum that took place between June 25 and July 10, 1964. President Joseph Kasavubu promulgated this constitution in July 1964. It formalized the primacy of the presidency.

For more than thirty years, the Mobutu regime was defined and shaped by the principle of *"après moi, c'est le deluge"* (after me, there is a deluge). He produced the most sophisticated form of clientilist regime in Africa. He was a maximum ruler who effectively used Machiavellian strategies to rule. But his neo-patrimonial rulership is different than those described by René Lemarchamp, who distinguishes five models of polities in Africa, namely: (1) ethnoregional hegemonies; (2) totalizing polities; (3) neo-patrimonial rulerships; (4) factionalist state system; and (5) liberalized transitional polities (1994). How were this principle, the form of his regime, and his strategies reflected in constitution making in the DRC?

After the November 24, 1965 military coup d'état, Mobutu increasingly assumed legislative powers as well as executive power. He produced the 1967 constitution in which he replaced the bicameral parliament with a unicameral national assembly. This body had little formal or real power, because of the power taken by the president to rule by executive order, which carried the force of law. This was the beginning of the process of setting up institutions of political control in the country. Thus, elements of federalism disappeared, and the number of twenty-one provinces was reduced to eight administrative units. In appearance, this is the first time the Congo became a unitary system. Some scholars believe that the source of this new constitution was clearly a direct inspiration from General de Gaulle's French Constitution.

In 1974, Mobutu amended the 1967 Constitution, which was also revised in 1978. He produced another constitution in 1981. In June 1988, he revised the 1981 constitution in which it is stipulated that the president of the *Mouvement Populaire de la Révolution* was by right the president of the republic according to Article 36 (paragraph 1). This constitution was also amended in 1990. In April 1994, the so-called "transitional constitution" was promulgated. Although this constitution contains many definitional elements related to the division of power, citizenship, territoriality, and the like, that are similar to the Constitution of Luluabourg (1964), the transitional constitution was not a mere copy of the 1964 Constitution. The 1964 Constitution was essentially framed within the logic and criteria of a federalist state, while the transitional constitution defined the Congolese state as firmly unitary.

Despite Mobutu's strong political resistance to the idea of a national conference, with visible and relatively well-organized internal pressure from the national political opposition, social and popular movements, international organizations, and foreign powers, the conference, which started in 1991, finally produced in August 1992 a draft of the constitution to be used for the period of transition to multiparty democracy. For the first time, under Mobutu's presidency, the Transitional Act of August 1992 created a parliamentary system. The draft of the constitution was adopted by the "Sovereign" National Conference on November 18, 1992.

Although the draft of the transitional constitution that was produced by the national conference was neither approved by the people nor implemented, for the purposes of this research, it is important to identify some of its general characteristics. These characteristics reflect either the nature of the struggles for power in the country under the Mobutu regime, the history of the Congolese political elites, or the nature of the Congolese political culture and civil society. What are the elements of the vision embodied in this constitution, if any? The preamble of the Constitutional Act of 1992 begins thus:

> We, representatives of the Zairean people, gathered around the High Council of the Republic the Transitional Parliament; Observing the profound, multiform and persisting profound crisis that is confronted in the country; Confirming our determination to consolidate our unity, and national integrate in respect to our regional particularities in order to promote, through the path of justice, our material being, our moral and spiritual blossoming...; Proclaiming our adhesion to the Universal Declaration of Man (sic) and to the African Chart of Rights of Man (sic) and People.

Two important aspects that characterize the constitution in the above statement must be pointed out. First, it starts neither with "We the people" as in other constitutions, nor with a revolutionary concept, like the Russian constitutions, which were based on the 1917 revolution. It began with the most important characteristics of the concept of liberal democracy, which is representation. Second, toward the end of the preamble, it shows its important philosophical sources or references, which are the Universal Declaration of Man (sic), and the African Chart of Rights of Man (sic) and People. These rights are both the products of the cumulative political notions related to the dynamics of great ideas in Europe and to the struggles of people in the developing world.

This constitution officially recognized both utilization of the names "Zaïre" and "Congo" throughout the document. The constitution was perceived and defined as the law to be used as a working document in the transitional period. It has 113 articles that are divided among the following titles: Territory and Republican Sovereignty; Fundamental Rights of Individuals and Duties of Citizens; Organization and the Exercise of Power; Provincial and Local Institutions; Public Finances; International Treaties and Accords; and Final Dispositions.

It should be emphasized that with this constitution the question of the colonial geographico-political boundaries as stipulated by the Basic Law were recognized and maintained. The Organization of the African Unity (OAU) also recognized and maintained all the colonial boundaries to defeat the articulation of pan-African ideas of Kwame N'Krumah. In addition, Zaïre (Congo) was defined as a unitary, indivisible, democratic, and secular republic. In the transition, four institutions were defined as vital: (a) the presidency; (b) the High Council of the Republic; (c) the government; and (d) the courts and tribunals.

Despite the fact that Mobutu resisted the national conference and he had also lost the people's confidence and support for the presidency, the most important arena of power as articulated in this constitution showed that there was a continuity between a strong and personal presidency that Mobutu created as a "figurative" soldier, a dictatorial executive president, and the inspiration of the new political leadership. The president was not only to represent the nation, but he/she was also defined as the chief of the armies and the person who should preside over the Superior Defense Council and High Council of the Republic. Furthermore, the president would appoint and dismiss by ordinance and under the proposition(s) of the government and approval by the High Council of the Republic, the ambassadors, high officers of the armies, and the top functionaries and directors of the public administration. In principle, this constitution rehabilitated the centrality of the power of the presidency in the political history of Mobutu and his regime.

Laurent-Désiré Kabila captured political power in Kinshasa (DRC) on May 17, 1997. He banned all political parties in 1997, with the exception of the Alliance for Democratic Force for the Liberation of the Congo (ADFLC). He proclaimed himself president of the country on May 28, 1997, by a decree which contained fifteen articles. Between that date and the time he was assassinated on February 17, 2001, Kabila governed the country by decree, with unelected members of the government either in provinces, districts, or in Kinshasa. To a certain extent, the country was ruled in a *de facto* state of emergency.

State power was centered on the president. The presidency was also personalized. But this model does not fit the client-patron model of Mobutu. The following articles define the centrality of the president. In Article III, it is stipulated that "the institutions of the Republic are the president of the republic, the government, the courts, and tribunals." Article IV states that "the president exercises the legislative power by decree-laws deliberated by the council of ministers." Article V defines the power of the president as "the chief executive and the chief of the armed forces; he exercises his powers by decrees; and he has rights to mint money and to issue paper-money in accordance to law." This decree was going to cease to function upon the elaboration, production, and ratification of the new constitution. Laurent-Désiré Kabila's government was only struggling to survive. However, within the framework of the planned pluralist general elections that were intended to take place in April 1999, he announced on May 29, 1997 a program for undertaking constitutional reform.

In March 1998, the work of a newly established constitutional commission began, with the late Anicet Kashamura, a member of the old generation of the Congolese political elite, as its president. He passed away on August 18, 2004. In November 1998, Kabila approved a new draft constitution. It awaited ratification by national referendum.

Between August 2, 1998 and October 2002, when most of the Ugandan and Rwandan soldiers withdrew from Congolese territory as a result of the Peace Accord of Pretoria, South Africa of 2001, the DRC was involved in a war of invasion (a neo-imperialist war) by its neighbors, namely Rwanda, Uganda, and also Burundi. This war was firmly conducted with the intrigues of the Congolese cronies of Uganda and Rwanda. It was also supported by the masters of the global capitalist system, who had perceived and defined the Congo since the nineteenth century as an international colony. From this perspective, this colony had to be fully exploited because of its extraordinary mineral deposits. Most of the efforts of the government of Laurent-Désiré Kabila focused on how to liberate the country and the people from this violent foreign occupation and pillage. Nevertheless, there were some efforts to establish political institutions.

In February 2000, President Kabila set up an advisory committee of thirty-members to draw up plans for a legislative assembly despite complaints from opposition political parties. This committee's main responsibility was to define who would be eligible to sit in an assembly of three hundred representatives. There were about 15,000 candidates. People freely submitted their *dossiers* until February 21, 2000. Some of the criteria for the selection of candidates included how the candidates saw their role, their projects, and their capacity to demonstrate nationalism and patriotism (Reuters, June 7, 2000). The government thought that this process would lead to "democratization" despite the continuation of the war. The opposition parties also insisted that this move violated the Lusaka Peace Accord of July 10, 1999.

On July 1, 2000, President Kabila announced the names of 240 members of the transitional parliament. They included some names from the occupied territory. And on July 10, 2000, he named the remaining sixty members. These new members of the transitional parliament were responsible for organizing debates on the constitution before the referendum. The unarmed opposition parties declared that they did not intend to participate in this process because, although the ban on parties was, in principle, lifted in January 1999, political parties had not been allowed to function. Still, the three hundred people would conduct debates on the new document before the end of 2000. The draft document tended to emphasize people's independence, national development, and democracy. It is difficult to appreciate and understand Kabila's approach to constitution making and the mechanisms of building political institutions without understanding how he came to power and how his political life ended in a short period of time. He was a catalyst of new energies in the DRC. As such, he would probably imagine a new constitution reflecting some aspects of his own social agenda, which combined strong nationalism with populism, Maoism, and the African socialism of Julius Nyerere of Tanzania.

Despite the intention of the current government with its fragile transitional institutions, and the intention of the Congolese people to unite and rebuild their society as they resist occupation in many parts of the country, these efforts will not be actualized as long as the social, economic, and political conditions created by the occupation by Uganda, Rwanda, and Burundi, and their Congolese cronies continue. Furthermore, it is not likely that the so-called rebels and their victims — the Congolese people — will clearly and sincerely agree to produce a constitution that would safeguard the interests of the nation-state and of the majority of the Congolese people. Thus, I consider the constitution that will be produced as a working document, which should shape the efforts of building the state and society as their objectives become better defined through people's struggles against poverty, social injustice, and the interests of the lumpen-intellectual-politicians. The war in the DRC has devastating consequences in any state-building endeavors, especially in creating a new constitution, which poor people are likely to associate with the efforts of the lumpen-intellectuals and cronies of the invaders to acquire and share power.

A Reflection on Constitutional Experiences in Côte d'Ivoire

Introduction: General Questions and Issues

Côte d'Ivoire, a former French colony in West Africa, which was also an active member of the *Afrique Occidentale Française* [(AOF)/French West Africa], and which was ruled for more than 40 years by Félix Houphouët-Boigny and his vision of politics and Africa on a one party-state model, is going through a serious multidimensional crisis of national identity, power struggle, political legitimacy, and economic degradation. The root of this crisis can be identified in the nature of the Ivorian State. Thus, it can be characterized as the crisis of political redefinition and/or of constitutional redefinition of a nation-state. Some Ivorian groups and the majority of their political parties have firmly decided or even overly made commitment to redefine themselves, their Ivorian political identity (*Ivoirité*), as an imperative of a nation state. This movement has been very much reflected in the debates on the question of citizenship.

What kind of constitutions have been advocated for, and adopted in, Côte d'Ivoire since the period of formal decolonization? That is to say, within the parameters of colonization and decolonization, what kind of state did the French government on the one hand and the Ivorian elite and the Ivorian masses on the other hand, envision to creating?

Although this section is not an analysis of political personality of Félix Houphouët-Boigny or his political thought as such, because of his political longevity and due to the fact that he was the "incarnation" of the Ivorian state formation and politics from the 1930s to December 1993, the year he passed away, this section examines the elements of state formation, especially the dimensions of constitution-making experience in light of his political roles, his choices, and his personal considerations and tastes. He was known as, and called, the father of the Ivorian nation, a title that is economically and politically not inheritable in a non-monarchic state like that of Côte d'Ivoire. Thus, no political leader or president after him has come close to calling himself or being called the father of the nation, which connotes the creation of the nation. The expression also implies a kind of patrimonial and paternalistic state's relationship that he developed in the country. There cannot be literally a new father, except figuratively, as the nation-state was created once for all. He was indeed the major factor in the state formation of Côte d'Ivoire.

In this section, I discuss, in general terms, the major factors that have had an impact on the African political elite choices of the governance system and people's struggles for rights and sovereignty. These factors include the rise of Félix Houphouët-Boigny in the national political scene and his political activism, the domestic and the regional movements in either the search for national autonomy or the effort of political elites to integrate or at least associate themselves with the global French community, and the class and ideological struggles in party politics in France. I am interested in the question of the origins of the constitutional ideas. These constitutional ideas are summarized in the ideas of rights, liberty, autonomy, and sovereignty. It has been reiterated many times in this work that the study of the origins of constitutional rights cannot be well analyzed and understood outside of power struggle. People's political struggles to free them from their oppressive conditions and the actions of the colonial powers to either maintain the status quo or to produce reformist agenda, provide the context of the analysis.

This section is not about making the hermeneutics of the Ivorian constitutions or the diagnosis of their technical contents. Rather, it is an effort to understand the dynamics of the social and political conditions and the major political ideas that were promoted by the political elites, and which also influenced the making of constitutions in Côte d'Ivoire. What ideas have dominated the constitution-making experiences in Côte d'Ivoire? What kind of political society did the Ivorian political elites want to create?

As already stated, Côte d'Ivoire was not legally a settler's French colony like Algeria where its one million of European descendents owned forty percent of the land and who had lived in Algeria for 3 to 4 generations at the time of the war of liberation (Pickles, 1963, p. 64). However, economically and adminis-tratively, Côte d'Ivoire was de facto a semi-settler's colony. The French colonists invested more here in the cash economic enterprises and plantations, and the small enterprises and service economy than in other West (*Afrique Occidentale Française*/AOF with its capital in Dakar) and Central French African colonies [*Afrique Equatoriale Française* (AEF)/French Equatorial Africa with its capital in Brazzaville]. Côte d'Ivoire has always had, since the 1930s up to the 1980s, a relatively large and solid population of French colonialists and colonists, who were almost settlers, and the so-called technical assistants. The country was never isolated from the dialectics of regional French colonial policies at large.

But, there was no local space/political institution either with a special political status associated with the metropolitan political and social rights based on the French citizenship like the four communes of Senegal where Africans were born as French citizens. Côte d'Ivoire also contributed a significant financial amount to the AOF federation budget. To a certain extent Félix Houphouët-Boigny continued this practice even after the independence of the French colonies in West Africa in paying the salaries of the public servants in Upper Volta (Burkina Faso and Senegal). According to Immanuel Wallerstein, as quoted by Harshé, "it provided about one third of the portion of the total customs revenue for the eight territories, which until 1956 constituted the Federation of West Africa (1984, p. 38)." There are arguments of Ivorian exceptionalism.

Elements of this exceptionalism of Côte d'Ivoire can also be discussed in the nature of the Ivorian resistances to the French colonial policy and politics, the nature of its ethnic composition and the weak sociological relations among them before colonialism, and the peculiar role that Félix Houphouët-Boigny played in the state formation.

After serving as a representative of Côte d'Ivoire in the French National Assembly and disassociating himself later from the alliance with the French Communist party and then, an esteemed Minister of Health in Charles de Gaulle's government in Paris in 1956-1958, did Félix Houphouët-Boigny have a project of creating a different political identity for Côte d'Ivoire or did he prefer to copy the French Constitution? Did he promote the ideas of "constitutional accommodationism," "constitutional integrationism," "politics of association," or an eclectical type, that is, a combination of both accommodation and assimilation to fit the imperatives and purposes of his regional and national agenda and political base? Given the fact that politics of association was not only controversial but also impracticable, how did its failures affect Houphouët-Boigny's societal project? What are the ideas, which dominated in his model of constitutional building? These questions and more will help identify elements of the specificities of the Ivorian political experiences and their qualities in relation to the problematics of constitution building.

I have been articulating that in contemporary Africa the constitution-making experience is a process in which political elites (sometimes with the people's support or in other circumstances without people's support) attempt to project what they want or wish their political communities to be, presently or in the future. This process has never been finite. It is the mirror of the substance whether or not that substance is an imitation or an original. Why is it that in some cases, constitutions have been more consistent with the dynamics of their political cultures than in other cases?

What should be argued is that many aspects of the constitution-making in many countries that are examined in this book have not been autonomous from the domestic forces and political struggles. The issue of borrowing the constitutional ideas or the ideas of constitutions, or some general ideas from others in the political struggles, is not necessarily the major focus here. The Japanese Constitution, for instance, which is characterized as a pacifist Constitution, is literally a photocopy of the United States' Constitution as it was written by General McCarthy. But in many ways, Japanese political behavior is qualitatively different from that of the United States. However, despite changes of Prime Ministers in recent years as results of scandals and corruption, and growing nationalistic sentiments among some young social groupings and parties, including the current Prime Minister Koizumi (2002), the Japanese political regime is firmly stable. What matters more in my reflection is the nature of what is, was, or can be borrowed and how it is, was, or can be either appropriated or owned by the people and their political elite. What is the situation in Côte d'Ivoire?

Currently, precisely since the 1980s, although this is not new in the history of state formation in Côte d'Ivoire, the national discourse on constitution has become an ethnically sensitive issue with tendencies of being a socially explosive subject. This is due partially to the fact that Côte d'Ivoire is a country with a large proportion of immigrants, some of whom have had access to lands, scholarships, and other state resources for many years. These immigrants also have contributed with their labor to building the state and the economy. Specific groups among them have controlled some specific commercial areas and small-scale manufacturing. But as the state's resources have become more scarce world wide with demographic pressures from the Ivorian citizens with high social and political demands, the Ivorian government, since the adoption of the structural adjustment programs (SAPs) in the early 1980s, has been obligated to review and re-assess how resources are distributed legally in the country. It should be emphasized that when it comes to the issue of national loyalty and cultural identity, many of these immigrants who are mostly from Burkina Faso, Mali, and Guinea-Conakry in most cases, have also remained active citizens of their respective countries participating in the political process in those countries. In a situation of extreme economic weaknesses and political fragility, the double or triple political loyalty tends to accelerate and exacerbate the level of political antagonisms. Despite the recent involvement of the Economic Community of the West African States (ECOWAS) in the regional peace monitoring arrangements, those countries have not yet produced double-citizenship policy.

Furthermore, the political crisis has also been exacerbated by the fact that a single individual, who is a member of the opposition party, Alassane Dramane Ouattara, who has been historically established as a Burkina Faso citizen (from the Mossi ethnic group), the former Deputy Director of the International Monetary Fund (IMF), and the first hand-picked Prime Minister of Houphouët-Boigny in 1991, has decided with an extreme arrogance and weak local political base to break all the laws of the citizenry of a nation-state in order to force himself into the office of presidency of Côte d'Ivoire.

Thus, it should be emphasized that the politicization of the issue related to constitution by the political elite and its usage as an instrument of mobilization or an instrument of alienation has negatively contributed to making the issue sensitive and controversial. The last census (1998) approximates the population of 'foreigners' or immigrants to constitute about 26 percent of the total population. It should also be mentioned that the border between Côte d'Ivoire and Burkina Faso, for example, was defined and redefined several times during the colonial period to fit the imperial interests.

Despite the fact that demographically, the *Parti Démocratique de la Côte d'Ivoire* (PDCI)-*Rassemblement Démocratique Africain* (RDA), which was in power from its creation in 1946 until the military coup d'État of December 1999, could be considered as the majority party or the ruling party. Since then, this party has lost its dominant momentum and its strength in influencing the political directions of the country as articulated in the political institutions of the country and among many social groups. To understand how Félix Houphouët-Boigny emerged in the political scene, his style of governing, and his vision may help localize why his party has lost the central domination and the control over political affairs in the country.

The Rise of Félix Houphouët-Boigny

Félix Houphouët-Boigny once said to university students: *Je vous ai sorti du trou* ("I took you out of hopelessness" or literally "out of the hole"). This reflects a claim of historical legacy in the process of nation building. He is the embodiment of the concept of "paternalism."

Côte d'Ivoire under Félix Houphouët-Boigny had many peculiarities in the history of the formation of the state. He was once the first chair of *Syndicat Agriculture Africain* (SAA) in 1944; the co-founder of the *Parti Démocratique de la Côte d'Ivoire* and its chair until 1993, and also co-founder and chair of the *Rassemblement Démocratique Africain* (RDA) in 1946. He forged a semi-patrician and semi-traditional state with a strong national and sociological base and regional and international consolidation. His personality as a son of a Baoulé chief, his experiences as one of the favored French Minister of State by Charles de Gaulle in Paris in 1956, and as the Prime Minister in Côte d'Ivoire in 1959 before the independence of the country, his international diplomacy as well as his strategies to develop a certain type of regionalism without strong pan-Africanism contributed to the formation of a particular kind of state.

However, despite this patrimonial characteristic of the state and the father kind of figure, as noted earlier, the social context in which political history of Côte d'Ivoire produced elements of a contemporary state can be characterized by power struggles in the colonies and in Paris.

Furthermore, the first constitution building experience in Côte d'Ivoire was also influenced by several factors such as the implications of the regional political reforms—Loi Houphouët-Boigny in 1946 (abolition of the forced labor), *Loi cadre* reforms (1956)—the restlessness in West Africa (beginning of political decolonization movements), Ho Chi Minh's armed struggle against France in South-East Asia (Indo-China), the years of political crisis in France, and the war of liberation in Algeria.

It was in 1905 that all French Socialist organizations were unified as recommended by the Second International and formed *le Parti Socialiste, section
française de l'Internationale ouvrière* (SFIO), "the Socialist Party, the French
section of the International labor."

According to Jean-Noël Loucou (1992, p. 29), it was in July 1937 that an
official branch of the SFIO was created in Côte d'Ivoire. Several members of the
office of federation were planters (commercial agriculturalists) such as Paul
Pons, Bernard Anglade, and Georges Kassi. By 1939, there were five sections .
notably in Abidjan, Grand-Bassam, Aboisso, Agboville, and Abengourou
though only the two first branches had effectively functioned (Ibid). In 1939, the
federation had 413 French people as members. It published the magazine called
Notre Voix ("our voice").

The main purposes of this federation were to denounce the abuses of the colonial regime and make claims that the colonial regime should be more humane
in its treatment of the indigenous groups. To a certain extent, the future traditions of the opposition against the colonial politics were also related to the dynamics of this SFIO. It accelerated further the traditions of claim making in the
political history of power struggles in Côte d'Ivoire. Later in the 1950s, the
movement became strongly associated with ethnic politics. In this case, through
Adrien Dignan Bailly of Gagnoa (West of Côte d'Ivoire), who became its member after claiming the deception by the representative Houphouët-Boigny of
PDCI-RDA, the representative to the National Assembly in Paris, the federal
branch of the SFIO became localized in the *Bété* country (Loucou, 1992, pp. 30-
31). But Gagnoa is not the only region that promoted elements of progressive
ideological nationalism. Dimbokro also is known for its furious organized
movements against the French administration in the same period.

These struggles and various processes of political "decolonization" or neo-
colonization were also shaped by the interests, the views, and political activism
of Félix Houphouët-Boigny. His political positions, his alliances with the local
and metropolitan forces, and his vision of Côte d'Ivoire formed the foundation
of what Côte d'Ivoire was during the period of colonization, especially from the
1940s to the period of decolonization. But his ideological shifts and
contradictions, his patriotism, and accommodationist tendencies reflect what
Côte d'Ivoire has become. Toward the end of his life, Houphouët-Boigny was
shocked and deeply upset faced with the failure of the world system in Africa
and the contempt that this system continued to project with respect to Africa,
even to the point of bringing "to the knees" those who had faithfully represented
the interests of the West and the liberal system since the turn of the fifties
(Lumumba-Kasongo and Assié-Lumumba, 1999, p. 6.). However, he seemed to
have finally understood the nature of the sources of the contradictions of the
world system as reflected in the Ivorian economic situation. Thus, despite
philosophical contradictions that reflect his politics and policy, especially
between the 1980s and the 1990s, Félix Houphouët-Boigny remained relatively

consistent with himself in terms of what he wanted Côte d'Ivoire to be as a contemporary state in the world system.

Félix Houphouët-Boigny, from the time of the formation of the African Agricultural Trade Union in 1944 by seven growers to the time of his death in 1993, was an institution in himself, the founder of the Ivorian nation-state. He produced rules of the political games and he made them functional according to imperatives of the moment. That is to say that before political multipartyism of the early 1990s, he acted and made major public decisions in the name of the legislative, executive, and judiciary body politics.

It should be noted that this Union was co-formed in collaboration with August Denise and Joseph Anoma. The philosophical foundation of this African Agricultural Union does not reflect an orthodox and direct political direction. It was not revolutionary either. Members wanted equality of rights in economic and commercial domains. These planters, members of this union, wanted their products, in the national and regional market, to have the same commercial and financial values as those of the European planters. As noted elsewhere: "At the time of its formation, the intention of its members was not to challenge the existing power structures of the colonial administration nor to struggle for power sharing. Their goal was mainly economic; the SAA members wanted to sell their cocoa and other agricultural commodities at the same price granted to French farmers, (Lumumba-Kasongo and Assié-Lumumba, 1991, p. 261)."

Thus, this union paved the way for the establishment of the Democratic Party of Côte d'Ivoire known as *Parti Démocratique de Côte d'Ivoire* (PDCI), which was created in 1946.

Its members also wanted to have some control over what they produced. And they quickly understood that these economic rights would not be fully or adequately materialized without political rights. Some of the objectives of the party give some idea about how the questions of rights and citizenship, which are the main objectives in this chapter, were dealt with. According to Harshé (p. 24):

The P.D.C.I. championed the cause of the Africans in its manifesto. It advocated greater control of the administration by Africans, extension of suffrage, elimination of the system of dual college, and abolition of the practice of forced labour. It also demanded a radical revision in the taxation system. The P.D.C.I. was not fighting for Ivorian independence; on the contrary, it fully supported the Franco-African community based the principle of equality. The P.D.C.I. programme was essentially reformist in the sense it strove to improve the position of Africans within the framework of the French Union. Though it was the aim of the P.D.C.I to defend the interests of African planters, it championed at the same time the cause of socially downtrodden parts of the population.

In general terms, the post-colonial system that produced personalized politics can be called a totalitarian regime. This regime attempted in many forms to control and shape all aspects of the Ivorian political community. It was bureaucratically autocratic, economically peripheral capitalist, ideologically with a nationalistic flavor, and politically all-embracing. Some scholars tend to characterize it as a kind of "benevolent" totalitarian regime. Another characteristic of this totalitarian regime is that powers and sovereignty of the government were concentrated in the executive branch of the government where they were firmly in the hand of one person who had monopolistic decision-making power. It might be interesting to contrast and compare the characteristics of Félix Houphouët-Boigny's regime with other totalitarian regimes in the world. This totalitarianism can be appreciated in examining the nature of the state formation. The state formation in Côte d'Ivoire was articulated elsewhere as follows:

> State formation in Côte d'Ivoire must be viewed as legalistic and deliberate political effort of France to minimize any potential for revolution. The actual and potential progressive forces in Côte d'Ivoire were systematically crushed through the use of military force in the early 1950s, while a *rapprochement* was being undertaken by the Ivorian elite who survived. State building in Côte d'Ivoire was part of the general reforms undertaken in the French colonies in Africa and Asia. At the Brazzaville conference of 1944, where the representatives of the metropolitan French state and the colonial French administrators met, a new constitution was proposed that provided a certain level of autonomy for the colonies within the *Union Française*. This conference recommended representation of Africans in French political assemblies, access to all occupations by Africans, abolishing forced labor, developing education, and providing Africans with means for enhanced agricultural production (Lumumba-Kasongo and Assié-Lumumba, 1991, p. 260).

The *Loi cadre* was adopted in 1956 in the French National Assembly. It authorized in 1958 the constitutional referendum in which Côte d'Ivoire and other French colonies (except Guinea-Conakry) voted in favor of the *Communaté Française*, thus attaining a limited degree of autonomy from France (Lumumba-Kasongo and Assié-Lumumba, 1991, p. 260).

As part of *Loi-cadre* reforms, the recommendations of the R.D.A conference in Bamako in September 1957 may also clarify further how historically the question of constitution and citizenship, or the form of the state and political right, were perceived in the region in general and in Côte d'Ivoire in particular. Among the issues discussed were the questions of the nature of the R.D.A, the future of Franco-African relations, the issue of schism in the R.D.A. among many other themes. Rajen Harshé (p. 42) stated the recommendations at the economic sector as follow:

- To transform underdeveloped economies into modern economies;
- To liquidate the 'colonial Pact;'
- To take steps, gradually, for the integration of African economies;

- To develop production; and
- To liberate African masses from the perpetual exploitation of the colonial rule.

At the political level, the following recommendations were made:

(1) It declared the R.D.A.'s commitment to the struggle for political, economic, social and cultural emancipation of Africans.
(2) It declared that sovereignty was versed in people and independence was an inalienable right of the people.
(3) It supported the participation of elected African representatives in the functioning of the French Republic.
(4) It accepted Loi-cadre as irreversible.
(5) And it stood for the establishment of Franco-African community on a democratic base.

Although the conference did not solve the ideological and personal differences among the African leaders, for Houphouët-Boigny, the conference expressed firm attachment to the ideas of building a strong commitment of the Francophone countries with France. He was against the federalist constitution, which finally the *Loi cadre* did not envisage, as projected by the pro-federalism of Léopold Scdar Senghor of Senegal.

The result of a yes or no vote to Charles de Gaulle's referendum of September 28, 1958 on the question of Franco-African Community shows clearly where Félix Houphouët-Boigny stood on the issue of the nature of the Ivorian State that he preferred and opted for constructing in Côte d'Ivoire. There were 1,699,017 registered people of whom 1, 607,558 participated with only 224 voting no against the creation of the proposed Francophone community. The percentage of yes votes (more than 98 percent) was the highest in all Francophone countries both in French Equatorial Africa and French West Africa which, as indicated earlier, voted yes with the exception of Guinea-Conakry of Ahmed Sékou-Touré. This Ivorian record is essentially a political statement about the vision of Houphouët-Boigny of Côte d'Ivoire (*Bulletin de l'Afrique Noire*, p. 1958, p. 1210).

New Constitutional Experience in Côte d'Ivoire after Houphouët-Boigny

Historically, Côte d'Ivoire embodied various political and legal experiences which produced "liberal" constitutions, the French model, to a certain extent, before its independence and also in the post-colonial period. The experiences of party formations, national protests, and economic liberalism were firmly consolidated. However, Félix Houphouët-Boigny did not gain the political status of what he wanted for Côte d'Ivoire to be the French districts in Africa at the time of nominal political independence, like Martinique, or Guadeloupe. However, at the same time Côte d'Ivoire became deeply part of the Franco-African community under Houphouët-Boigny's influence and political disposition. Thus, as I tried to argue in this section, both elements of Houphouët-

Boigny's nationalism/patriotism or personal frustration for not being fully accepted as part of Paris' project of assimilation and integration into the French dominated Francophone African community schemes, did influence the nature of constitution-making in Côte d'Ivoire.

It should be noted that Côte d'Ivoire has historically inherited a strong presidential form of political regime, which was highly centralized on Félix Houphouët-Boigny. This system supports personalized or individualized politics that characterizes most aspects of the African politics. The military regime in Côte d'Ivoire also articulated the concentration of power on President Guéi, which he shared with few of his associates. What was new with this regime is the monopoly on utilization of the guns to enforce their rules and decisions.

The continuity in the new power arrangement is that there is no office of vice-presidency in the new Constitution (Law No. 2000-513) adopted on August 1, 2000. It contains 130 Articles and 15 Titles. In this kind of regime, the executive political power is not shared with any other political entity of the government. The description of the presidency alone, for instance, the nature of the institution of presidency, its role, and the conditions of being elected president are covered in 25 Articles (Title 3 Articles 34-57). The President is the Head of the State and the Incarnation of the "National Unity" (Article 34). He/she is the exclusive holder or keeper of the executive power (Article 41). He/she appoints a prime minister who is accountable to him/her (Article 41). Why is it that those who produced the 2000 Constitution did not make any effort to depart from this tradition? What are the benefits of this tradition to the Ivorians?

However, specific duties of the president can be delegated to members of the government by decrees (Article 53) in special circumstances. There is a Constitutional Council, a regulatory body with a regulatory power, to declare constitutionality or unconstitutionality of laws. It is composed of 6 members, three of whom are nominated by the President of the Republic and three by the President of the National Assembly for a term of office of 6 years. The President of the country also appoints the president of the Constitutional Council for a period of 6 years, non-renewable. As indicated earlier in this chapter, the preambles of the constitutions may reveal a great deal about the nature of the state and politics in most countries. However, one must also make a difference between theoretical elements of constitutions and practical elements.

The Preamble of the 2000 Constitution of the Republic of Côte d'Ivoire began as follows:

> The People of Côte d'Ivoire,
> Conscious of its liberty and its national identity, of its responsibility
> in front of the history and the humanity;
> Conscious of its ethnic, cultural, and religious diversity and
> wishing to build a united nation and prosper;
> Convinced that the union in the respect to that diversity
> ensures the economic progress and well social being;

Profoundly attached to its legal constitution and to democratic institutions,
to the dignity of human being, to cultural and spiritual values;
Proclaims its adhesion to the rights such as defined in the
Universal Declaration of Human Rights of 1948 and the
African Charter of Human Rights and the People of 1981;
Expresses its attachment to the recognized democratic values to free peoples
notably:

- The respect and the protection of fundamental liberties to the individuals as well collective,
- The separation and the equilibrium of powers,
- The transparency in the conduct of the public affairs,
- Engages itself to promote regional and sub-regional integration, in order to construct the African Unity;
- Gives freely and solemnly as fundamental law this present Constitution, which was adopted through the referendum.

As mentioned earlier, in terms of its sources, the 2000 Constitution embodies many elements of international conventions as, for instance, it cited the Declaration of Human Rights of 1948 and the African Charter of rights of man (sic) and the peoples of 1981 (preamble) that put emphasis on the universalism of the human being and his/her rights. It defines human being as sacred (article 2). However, this constitution, as compared to other constitutions, focuses on the presidency. It therefore articulates more the cult of a centralized and rigid presidential regime or power than this of citizenship. This constitution inherited this imbalanced dimension of power from the old Ivorian political culture and history.

It should be noted that this constitution also does not reflect the originality related to the Ivorian ideas of political struggles like the constitution of China, or that of Russia. It has a monolithic origin, which is the colonial history without the struggles involved. Thus, it does not embody elements of the Ivorian cultural diversity and pluralistic ideas. It is more a compilation of the existing liberal democratic ideas than being a product of how Ivorians would like to be governed or would like to govern themselves.

In short, the Ivorian state was conceived in this constitution as highly centralized, presidential, and unitary. In my view, given the fact that it did not touch on some important ideas such as the nature of the traditional power systems, local/indigenous democracy, and political culture, one would speculate that it was produced as a working document or tool, which could allow the dominant political parties or regime to eliminate Alassane Ouattara from possibly running for the presidential office in the future. However, the most important question is: Is this full ideal of what Ivorians would like to define their system of state power?

Constitutional Experiences in Kenya: A General Reflection

Introduction: Objectives and Issues

The inclusion of Kenya in this book is enriching to a political analysis and justified in many ways. In the December 27, 2002 elections, Kenya, a visible state in the international political economy and industry of world tourism, and a solid partner with the West, especially Great Britain and the United States, made a successful and smooth transition from the authoritarianism and totalitarianism of the ruling party to multipartyism. These elections occurred without any significant or reported disruption, which was not predicted by many people, given the history of political violence in Africa due to the tendency of the ruling parties to retain power by all means necessary in most African countries. President Daniel arap Moi's preferred and supported candidate, Uhuru Kenyatta of the Kenya African National Union (KANU) and the son of Jomo Kenyatta, the founding figure of Kenya as a postcolonial state, was defeated by Mwai Kibaki in a landslide victory under the banner of the reformist National Rainbow Coalition (NARC) party.

The new president immediately announced that he would change the constitution by creating a parliamentarian system and that he would undertake many other social and political reforms. But, taking a historical perspective still makes the discussion on Kenya in this section relevant even if the constitution change came late.

Kenya earned its political independence on December 12, 1963, after the actualization of the agreement of self-government in 1960. Some people tend to characterize this independence as the process in which the African elite had power without freedom. It was colonized in the nineteenth century by the then most powerful European nation, Great Britain. With its so-called indirect rule, anglophone Africa in general represents a different political tradition of political socialization and participation than the francophone Africa. However, direct rule as political strategy was also used in many parts of the British Empire, especially in Southern Africa and Kenya with their settler tradition.

Kenyan settlers' (white settlement) experience was characterized by a relatively large population of two major groups of immigrants, namely Europeans and Asians. For many people, the dominant ideology in Kenya, as articulated by Jomo Kenyatta and his KANU, was born at the Lancaster House Conference in London in 1960. In postindependence Kenya, it was either called "African socialism" or "African capitalism."

Although the Dual Mandate that Lord Lugard recommended for tropical Africa was generally accepted by the British imperial government in ruling the African land and dealing with the newly created conflicts between the Africans and Europeans, this government also promoted a "unitary system" of governance in Kenya, as Kamoche has indicated:

His (Lugard, sic.) view of the indirect rule and the development of African local government found some acceptance in Kenya through local governmental structures—one for the Africans and the other for non-Africans. The Imperial Government provided two structures within a unitary system, which was under the jurisdiction of the governor (1981, p. 196).

It is argued that at the philosophical level, a unitary form of government in Kenya would be constitutionally antithetical to the principle of Dual Mandate. As emphasized in this book, a constitution and the ideas that constitute its force are not produced outside of a given social context and within a historical vacuum. Constitutions are the products of various social struggles that should be reflected in analyzing them. In a study in which the author is inclined to be more philosophical in the analysis than legalistic in the argumentation, it is difficult to talk about the ideas of political institutions without relating them to the questions of their nature and their origins. The elements of political culture and major events shape the ways grand ideas are articulated, produced, and incorporated into the building of institutions.

In the case of Kenya, one needs to analyze these ideas within the framework of the rise of Jomo Kenyatta, his personality, the nature of the British colonial system and its evolution, and how major ideas or events and the dominant system influenced the institutions around Kenyatta. In many respects, the importance of Kenya in this section cannot be understated, as Malhotra wrote: "Kenya was the first of Britain's white settled colonies with white settled population to achieve African rule, a testing ground for the European's future in Africa" (1990, p. 1). Until recently, Kenya in East Africa and Côte d'Ivoire in West Africa were considered as the models of economic development or economic growth and political stability in Africa. In the case of Kenya, this stability was maintained due largely to the personality of Kenyatta, his liberal thoughts, and the national reconciliatory approach to politics that he undertook.

KANU's Manifesto for Independence, Social Democracy and Stability, which became the ruling party's doctrine for more than forty years projected the building of a democratic welfare state in which "all the privileges of colonialism will be swept away. " However, many have perceived the case of Kenya at the independence period as a kind of "freedom without the provision of the means for the vast majority of the people to enjoy that freedom" (Anonymous Authors, 1982, p. 17). Kiunjuri Edward Irungu characterized these forty years in illustrating this situation in *Machiavellian Art of Political Manipulation in Kenya* (1999). As Kenyatta stated after KANU's electoral victory in May 1963:

On this great day in the history of our nation, I pledge that the KANU Government, which is about to take the office will be guided in its task by the principles of democratic African socialism. We shall build a country were every citizen may develop his talents to the full, restricted only by the larger aim we have of building a fair society. The rights of all and of property will be fully protected. There will be no privileged for any minority. Equality, we shall see that no member of any group undergoes discrimination or oppression at the hands of the majority. The African people of Kenya have suffered under the yoke of colonialism, but now we are throwing off that burden we do not look to the past--the racial bitterness, the denial of fundamental rights, the suppression of our culture. Let us look instead to the new Kenya we are to create, where men and women of all colours, castes, and creeds will work joyfully together in unity. Let the experience of the past warn us of the misery of a land in which people are not free, but let there be forgiveness. We shall build ONE NATION in which every group will make its contribution to the creation of our Kenya identity (Gertzel, Goldschmidt, and Rothchild, 1969, p. 1).

How much has the optimism related to rights of citizens, their equality, and democratic practices of the nation-building process, as alluded to in the above quotation, been reflected in the constitutions and their amendments in Kenya? Kenya did produce a multiracial and multiparty liberal constitution in the 1960s, but then the government moved gradually, by means of amendments, toward a restrictive constitution, a one-party state; then with massive social movement, it moved back again to a multiparty liberal constitution, but the government, using its executive power, consistently and constantly violated constitutional rights.

One of the questions that guide my analysis of other cases is: How much have major historical events—which modernization school advocates have called political development, associated with political struggles be they are personal, social, or collective—influenced directly or indirectly the ideas of constitution making in states the world over? Why is it that the European settlers' colonies in North America, New Zealand, Australia, and Canada produced various forms of liberal democracies with their liberal constitutions while alienating the natives, yet the same European settlers' colonies in Africa did not produce any democracies, but rather the extreme forms of racist and fascist regimes of South Africa and Namibia, for instance.

Although each case that is included in this book is unique and relatively different from the others, as indicated earlier, I am chiefly interested in constructing a certain degree of regional and historical representation in this work. Still, it is not my aim to examine the colonial policy and politics in Kenya during British imperialist domination and administration in particular or in British East Africa in general, although one cannot completely examine the post-colonial constitutional experiences without touching on some central issues of British governance. I identified some of the key ideas and political institutions of decolonization that have finally governed Kenya for about forty years and, which have paved the paths for formulation of nation-building policies. That is to say, I am interested in selecting major elements of constitutions and their origins. In the case of Kenya, these key factors are intellectually, ideologically, and politically linked with the political personality of Jomo Kenyatta, his visions, and aspirations. This is similar to the case of Côte d'Ivoire and Félix Houphouet-Boigny, as Veena Malhotra stated:

But the Mau-Mau did not win the independence: independence was granted after the uprising had largely been suppressed and Kenyatta and his allies shaped a republic. Jomo Kenyatta led his country to independence in classic style of all freedom fighters under British colonial rule. With such origins, and given the personal appeal that Kenyatta was always able to exert in his speeches and writings, one might have expected Kenya to continue to represent the best hopes of new Africa (1990, p. xvi).

Before and during the struggles for independence, Jomo Kenyatta, after spending eight years in imprisonment and on restriction, came out like a hero, similar in some ways to Nelson Mandela. He always insisted on shaping his new governance on the simple principle that "We want to rule ourselves." He too, like Nelson Mandela, promoted forgiveness, unity, and reconciliation. However, it should be emphasized that he strongly believed in people's rights to run their businesses or affairs, though not necessarily in simplistic or egotistical capitalistic ventures. Thus, he encouraged and supported the Kikuyu's culture and rights to establish and run their own schools, which led to the establishment of the Kikuyu Independent School Association and the Kikuyu Karinga Education Association. They ran hundreds of schools for Kikuyu children. He believed in people's reassertion of, and faith in, their culture and themselves. People's right to govern themselves was perceived as an absolute right. It did not depend on any political theories originating from Moscow, Washington, D.C., or London. His role was central to the reconstruction of the contemporary Kenyan state and society, as Eric Aseka indicated:

> It is common knowledge that Jomo Kenyatta was a key actor in laying the foundation of the Kenyan State. As one of the most ardent promoters of nationalism in Kenya, he found himself steeped in the problems and complexities of a long historical event. This was the saga of the struggle for decolonization. It was part and parcel of a bitter complex and persisting struggle between imperialism and all those that were in contradiction to it (1992, p. 1).

The brief description above gives a framework for examining some key elements of constitution making in Kenya. The processes of political change, which were accelerated with the Mau-Mau movement, were centered on the question of land. This is why Mau-Mau freedom fighters called their organization the Kenya Land and Freedom Army (KLFA) (Wamwere, 1992, p. 1). In simple terms, the alienation of Kikuyu land, the imposition of various types of taxation, and the creation of the African or so-called tribal reserves leaning towards the practices of the United States, Canada, Australia, New Zealand, and South Africa were among the most important factors that led to the Mau-Mau uprising, which was transformed into national movement. Within the development of the nation-state, land has always been part of the constitutional debate. One of the characteristics of British policy in Kenya, as it was in most countries in Southern Africa, is that most of the fertile land was illegally, and by the use of brute force, appropriated and owned by the Europeans/British. Asians, for instance, were prohibited from acquiring land in the "White Highlands" and Blacks were forced off of their own land. This system exhibited a high level of racial segregation with its social and gender implications among Africans and Asians.

Considerations of the Evolution of Kenya's Constitution-making Experiences

It should be further clarified that the thrust of this section is to identify the significance of the postcolonial political experience in Kenya rather than to elaborate the political situation of Kenya under British rule. However, the situation and the ideas that led to political change did not just happen. Therefore, it is important to introduce this section with a description of some important historical elements in order to contextualize my arguments and point of views.

Kenya's transition to the independence before and after the Mau-Mau, which was mixed with gradual processes and rapid decisions resulting from the outcome of political struggles, reflected change in the number of the colonial legislations as Norma N. Miller indicated:

> The years 1959–1963 were turbulent politically as the early Mau-Mau period had been militarily. Influential Africans like Tom Mboya and Oginga Odinga, the Luo leaders from western Kenya, put themselves second to the imprisoned Kenyatta, arguing that his release was a precondition to negotiations for independence. Kenyatta continued to languish in jail as a series of constitutional meetings designed to edge Kenya along the pathway to independence began to unfold. In 1954, the Lyttleton Constitution, named for the secretary of state for the colonies, had opened the political door to African participation. Although still committed to parity between the races, that constitution did allow eight African representatives on the Kenya legislative Council and did establish a multi-racial administrative system. In 1958, the new Lennox-Boyd Commission raised African participation to fourteen seats (1984, p. 26).

Oliver Lyttelton was a Conservative Colonial Secretary at the time that Mau-Mau engaged in its struggles against the colonial policy as a determining step toward political decolonization. During this period, 64 Europeans held all the political power and excluded Africans from legislature and the government (Kamoche, 1981, p. 296). Based on the general objective conditions in the country, the nature of support that the Mau-Mau was enjoying from the ground, and its determination to change the political situation, he strongly opted for a political solution rather than a military one. This political solution supported the agenda of the East African Commission, which stressed the need for economic cooperation (Kamoche, Ibid, p. 299). Although they had common services under the aegis of the East African High Commission (Ibid, p. 298), Africans and Asians at that time had rejected the ideas of Federalist Constitution between

Kenya, Uganda, and Tanganyika territories. Members of the British delegation who visited Kenya and the government at war with the Mau-Mau recommended some of the following propositions such as the elimination of racial discrimination, the African rights to vote, the promotion of racial integration and Kenya as a multiracial society in education. However, they recommended centralization of the police forces on a colony-wide basis. The report of W. F. Coutts, a one-man commission, who was appointed by Governor Baring in February 1955 (Ibid, p. 305) contributed significantly to the lifting of the political ban on June 21 1955 and liberalization of political activities.

Concerning the characteristics of Lennoz-Boyd Constitution, Kamoche stated:

> The Lennox-Boyd Constitution, coming at a time when Africans had witnessed and suffered European intransigence in regard to power-sharing with the other races, did not significantly attract their support. In fact, the Europeans did not give it enthusiastic support either. Perhaps the reason was that none of the races saw the constitution as a permanent one. Africans, as Mboya subsequently explained, were no longer interested in the kind of multiracialism they had seen preached but never practiced. Mboya began in 1958 to talk in terms of "freedom now" (*uhuru sasa*) and "undiluted democracy" (1981, p. 311).

At the end of 1958, the European political parties and other groups generally opposed any constitutional arrangement which was likely to destroy the principle of multiracialism, which resulted in a quick change in favor of African independence (Ibid., p. 312).

The 1960 Macleod Constitution gave Africans a majority with sixty-five seats in the Legislative Council, and plans for internal self-government were also established. It allowed a majority of government ministers to be Africans. At this point, the British government surprised all the participants by announcing its intention to grant independence to Kenya within a short period (Ibid., p. 28). It was only in September 1963, after the elections of the internal self-government were completed, that a final agreement was reached in London on the Independence or the Republican Constitution in Kenya.

In the debates related to the creation of this new constitution, the Prime Minister of Kenya, Jomo Kenyatta, insisted in his political discourse that the new constitution should suit Kenya. What does that mean in relationship to his previous disposition concerning the respect, the restoration, and the need to promote African culture and unity? What about the place of cultural diversity that tends to reflect the Kenyan colonial society? What elements of the African socialism, if any, as defined by the ruling party, would be incorporated into this new constitution?

Debates on the first constitution of Kenya indicate clearly that the ideas of the new constitution derived from the combined elements of liberal constitutions of European nations, which were based on individual rights, racial equality, separation of power, strong role of the court, and many elements of welfare states. The ideas of welfare state, which were articulated both by KANU and most members in the self-government, were based on African socialism and inspired by the uprising that broke out in 1952 in Kenya, namely the Mau-Mau movement, as well as African traditions and cultures.

With Tom Mboya, a nationalist, as Minister for Justice and Constitutional Affairs, the new constitution in principle, was a product of the decolonization struggle, nationalistic ideas reflected in the structures of the Organization of African Unity (OAU), various universal declarations of human rights, and the dynamics of liberal European political thought.

One must note that the Constitution of 1960 in Kenya, which led to the independence of the country, gave Africans the majority in the Legislative Council. In this year, the Kenya African Union (KAU) split into two: the Kenya African National Union (KANU) and the Kenya Democratic Union (KADU) were established. Thus, two competing political parties were born.

Kenya is a republic, or *jamhuri*, which obtained its independence on December 12, 1963, under a new constitution that was promulgated the same year. However, by 1964, the KADU was dissolved. As discussed earlier, although the government was structurally parliamentary with a unicameral system (National Assembly), it functioned *de facto* as a presidential regime. In this regime, the executive power was central in the affairs of governance. It was legally a one-party state until November 1991. But it was not until 1992, when section 2(a) of the Kenyan Constitution was amended, that multipartyism was reintroduced into Kenyan politics. It should be noted that Kenya became an independent nation-state, in principle, under a multiparty system of governance. However, centralized decision-making was justified as a strategy to foster unity and quick development.

The Kenyan legal system is based on English Common Law, Islamic law, and "tribal" law, with a High Court and a Court of Appeal (Nations of the World, 2002, p. 760). It should be noted that through violent power struggles among the members of the political elite and President Moi that have occurred since the death of President Jomo Kenyatta, a constitutional amendment of November 1999 was approved to affirm the supremacy of the National Assembly (Ibid., p. 761).

To have a general idea of the content of the 1999 amended Kenyan Constitution, it is necessary to briefly provide the titles of each chapter. It should be noted that the Kenyan Constitution does not start with a preamble as some of other constitutions that begin with a statement such as: "We the people,...." It starts in Chapter I with the declaration of republicanism, for instance, "Kenya is a sovereign Republic," and "The Republic of Kenya shall be a multiparty democratic state. "

The Kenyan Constitution has eleven chapters that are divided into 127 sections. The titles of the chapters are listed as follows:

Chapter I, The Republic

Chapter II, The Executive

Chapter III, The Parliament
Chapter IV, The Judicature
Chapter V, Protection of Fundamental Rights and Freedoms of the
Individuals
Chapter VI, Citizenship
Chapter VIII, Finance
Chapter IX, Trust Land
Chapter X, General
Chapter XI, Transitory

It should be noted that one of the peculiarities of the current Kenyan Constitution is that, as in the case of Côte d'Ivoire, it does not implicitly mention some of its important historical moments that mobilized people's thoughts and ideas to redefine themselves, such as the Mau-Mau movement, Mwakenya, or presently the Mukingi movement. There are as yet no specific references to the demands of these movements in the constitution.

However, it should be emphasized that many other constitutions such as the French, the Chinese, and the American, have clearly articulated the dogmas related to some specific moments in the development or the evolution of their nation-states. These constitutions serve as collective memories in the history of state formation. Thus, for instance, the ideas of the French revolution, Maoist revolutionary ideas, and the ideas of the United States founding fathers (sic) are also projected into the centrality of the French Constitution, the Chinese Constitution, and the United States Constitution respectively.

A Reflection on Constitutional Experience in a Traditional Monarchic Society: The Case of Saudi Arabia

Introduction: Issues and Objectives

The question of examining cultural, sociological, and political elements that are associated with the constitutional experience in Saudi Arabia has been dealt with in broadly defined perspectives. Because of the author's lack of knowledge of the Arabic language, only secondary sources have been critically used to help make generalizations that were used comparatively in this book. In this case, I am not interested in analyzing the constitutionality of Saudi Arabia in its technical/legalistic and normative forms or political theology of Saudi Arabia. Rather, the issue is to investigate how the current dynasty captured power and restructured it to respond to the local cultural and political demands and international imperatives in relationship to contemporary claims related to democracy, modernization, industrialization, and development. Where is the state power located within the existing system of power? Or what is the nature of the authority and power in Saudi Arabia?

As compared to other Islamic, Arab, and Arabic speaking countries in terms of their religious dogmatism and ethical foundation of their societies, Saudi

Arabia is among the most conservative countries in the Middle East. It is also among very few contemporary welfare states, which are not localized in Europe and which have developed and promoted welfare programs not modeled after Europe. In the Saudian model, loyalty to the state is not necessarily associated with accountability as it is in the Western democracies. It is King Saud, who was born in Kuwait in 1902 and replaced his father King Abdul Aziz Ibn Saud in the late 1953, who firmly established the foundation of some welfare programs in the areas of education and health. For him, as it seems to be known, his father's reign was characterized by territorial conquests and the search for cohesion among clans, but he thought that his own was going to be remembered more in his social doing/performance than in military conquests.

In its diplomatic relations with the Western states, it is a controversial political actor, which combines elements of cultural rigidity and a commercial universalistic dogma known as the liberal market paradigm. Saudi Arabia is a visible state in the dynamics of the international political economy as the major member of the OPEC (Organization of the Petroleum Exporting Countries). As an essentially Islamic and Arab state, it is vocal in the debates on the Middle East political crisis and in Arab and Islamic affairs. It is also a non-Western and non-democratic society that has solid and predictable commercial, scientific, technological, and diplomatic relations with the plural and liberal democratic states and societies in the West. It is self-sufficient in food production. Furthermore, it is an autocratic political regime with a high level dictatorship. Incorporating it in this work is a comparatively enriching intellectual task. It also contributes to increase our knowledge of world constitutions and political leadership's efforts at constitution making.   ·

In Article 1 of the document promulgated by Royal decree of King Fahd on March 1992, The Kingdom of Saudi Arabia is described as "a Sovereign Arab Islamic State with Islam as its religion; God's Book and the Sunnah of His Prophet, God's prayers and peace be upon him, are its constitution." Arabic is its language and Riyadh is its capital.

Why is it that the dynasty of power in Saudi Arabia did not succeed or did not will to establish an absolute traditional Monarchy, which generally is associated with traditionally defined politico-religious regimes? What are the sources of its power?

Before Saudi Arabia became a traditional monarchy, the Ottoman Empire established a tributary structure that was common to all Islamic societies ruled by Ottoman polity. "All the land belonged to the state (*miri*). Peasant families with rights of access to land constituted the main units of production and consumption, and these were organized into wider village communities. Peasants farmed the land for tax payments to the state (Bromley, 1993, p. 382)." Bromley also continues to characterize the Ottoman Empire in the following manner:

> The Turkish overlords, whether state officials or military personnel, lived off
> the land and resided in the towns, and often did not learn the language of the

local nobility and peasantry. The tacit cooperation of urban forces, especially the merchant and *ulema,* was therefore necessary. Merchants required the over-lords to maintain order and the central tributary authorities, the *ulema,* were even more significant to social control than the merchants, for they provided more general social cohesion and regulation. They too depended on order and became dependent on state finance (op. cit., p. 383).

It should also be emphasized that traditional Saudi Arabia is composed of various "tribes" and clans, which historically had fought one another long before the coming of the Western powers in the region. Saudi Arabia is dogmatically an Islamic society. As a result of various political struggles, it produced relatively flexible political regimes based on different interpretations of Islam and Quran, and adjustment of the local traditions. But its political regime is not, as I insist, a theocracy like in Sudan under Bashir or Iran under Ayatollah Khomeini.

It should also be noted that although there is an old debate among Islamic scholars and some believers concerning the question of which country in the world of Muslims represents the centrality of the so-called pure Islam in its tra-ditions, dogmatic, cultural, and political values, Saudi Arabia is unique as it em-bodies the most important historical and cultural values related to Islam. The country is very important to include in this section for several reasons:

(1) It has the most important historical sites and cities in the Islamic world or civilization: (A) Madinah (Medina), the city in west Saudi Arabia where Prophet Muhammad was first accepted as the Prophet and where his tomb is located; and (B) Makkah (Mecca) is the birthplace of the Prophet Muham-mad, which is also the spiritual center of Islam.
(2) It is the largest country in the Middle East;
(3) It has the largest abundance of crude oil reserve;
(4) It was militarily the closest alliance to the Western Industrial countries, es-pecially the United States and Britain, in the Arab world until September 11, 2001.
(5) And it should be added that the British were militarily involved in support-ing the establishment of a non-historical dynasty, thus creating a new his-tory.

Whether Saudi Arabia does or does not have a written or concise Constitu-tion within the logic of the search for understanding the nature of guidelines and principles that govern peoples and societies is not my main concern. The main concern is to identify and discuss elements that have been the pillars or sources of the state formation and the forms of governance in the country since the Kingdom of Saudi Arabia was established in 1932. It was founded on the Wahhabi-Saudi movement

This current dynasty is different from the Constitutional rules of many European countries. The elements of its culture, religion, personality politics, and power struggles, and its role in the international political economy and foreign affairs, which constitute the foundation of the state power, are examined as part of "constitutional experiences." As previously stated, these experiences have not produced similar written documents the world over. However, each experience that is included in this work is worth analyzing in order to deal with the question of what constitutes power of the state.

In the study that examines power relations and citizenship philosophically and historically within a comparative perspective, it is methodologically justifiable to also include the discussion on a case that looks historically and culturally very different from other previous cases. This aspect of the study does not deal with the development of a systematic discussion on theological or dogmatic arguments related to the Saudi State formation. We need and have to identify some basic sources of the ideas of who and what govern in Saudi Arabia.

In the context of state formation or state building, the effort to include the case of Saudi Arabia should also help identify further what nation-states have in common, their particularities, and their differences. During and after the Cold War era, the Middle East region of the world has been, in most cases, perceived and defined with strong ideological bias lenses, as the most unstable, the land of terrorism, nationalistic Arabism and extreme Islamism, the oppression of women, deficit or lack of democracy, oil, and anti-West. From the views of mainstream Western scholarship and foreign policies, only the state of Israel created in 1948 is considered as exception to the general rules. The United States' foreign policy perception in the region, especially after September 11 2001, has not provided the basis for a much needed inclusive dialogue with nations in the region and a broad understanding and appreciation of political structures and personalities in the region. Despite all the efforts by enlightened people and the emerging global movements for peace, the Arabism strongly associated with Islamic fundamentalism is perceived in the West and especially the United States as a threat or a challenge to the Western power structures and civilization. Some aspects of this perspective have also been well articulated by Samuel Huntington in his book *Clash of Civilizations* (1996).

The inclusion of a country from the Middle East in this book provides an opportunity to de-mystify the politics of the region that has been studied in many ways by many scholars in religious terms and also to see what can be learned from the nature of the power relations in Saudi Arabia. In general terms, the study of politics in the region has been characterized in a simplistic manner as dictatorial, personal, clan oriented, traditional monarchy, oil politics, and permanent conflict with the State of Israel. Yet any critical and serious study of any state formation in the region reveals the existence of an historical, sociological, and political complexity that one can find in Côte d'Ivoire, India, France, Germany, Nigeria, Russia, or South Africa. There are power and class struggles, primordial conflicts, and the interventions of the Western imperialism as the cases in other countries. However, reactions to the European and the Ottoman imperialisms have been shaped by specific and unique local social, cultural, and physical configurations and traditions. As David Held states:

Saudi Arabia provides a striking contrast with the regimes dealt with so far. Three facts account for this: modernization and the state formation with rather than against, Islam; the absence of a landed notable class; and the huge abundance of oil in relation to population. Ernest Gellner has pointed to the important fact that Islam's traditional internal differentiation into the folk and scholarly variants was actually helpful in effecting adjustment. The folk variant can be disavowed, blamed for cultural backwardness, or associated with political machinations of colonial powers, whilst the "purer" variant can be identified all at once both with pristine origins and revived, glorious, modern future (p. 397).

Sources of Political Power and Elements of Its Law

It is appropriate to indicate both the uniqueness of Saudi Arabia in the sense that it is different among more than 190 nation-states, which are members of the United Nations, but it is also solidly a member of the larger family of the nations. Saudi Arabia is one of the ten countries of the world which do not have any "modern" constitution. It has often been stated that its Constitution is the Quran.

The contemporary Saudi political model of governing reflects a relatively high level of "consensus" between the opposing views within a larger web-type of political family relations. As it is articulated here, this "consensus," though it may be ideologically narrow, makes Saudi Arabia different from the tendencies of absolutism one can observe in other Islamic societies at certain periods. Its foundation is basically power struggle among members of the political elite as it was also taking into account some readings of the imperatives of the international political economy. A brief political history of the state formation presents a general picture necessary to contextualize the arguments concerning the nature of the political and policy consensus making in the country.

In an attempt to deal with the question of who and what governs in Saudi Arabia, two schools of thoughts have emerged within the Muslim societies and among scholars. There are those who closely examine the role of Islam as non-interpretative religion (traditionalists) and there are also those who advocate theological interpretation and the role of traditions. The debate is essentially on what constitutes the essence of the Shariah. What is peripheral to it and what is central or vital to it? According to Abdulmunim Shakir:

> Islam permeates all aspects of life and provides its followers with comprehensive concepts and delineated guidelines for their relationship with God and man alike. The believers in Islamic precepts do not separate the spiritual from the temporal, since both are considered integral concepts of the way of life they were taught to follow (1982, p. 1).

From the above belief, the Islamic law called Shariah, is based on five main sources:

(1) The Quran (Koran), which is the book God revealed unto Prophet Muhammad;
(2) The Sunnah, the words and deeds of Prophet Muhammad—complementing and explaining the teaching of the Quran;
(3) Qiyas, which is an analogy of the Quran and Sunnah to new problems not specifically stated in either source;
(4) Idjma, a consensus by Ulama who are the learned Muslims in religion and juridical matters;
(5) And the Idjihad, the use of independent reason and enlightened judgment within the Islamic context on issues and problems.

For the traditionalists, the Quran is literally the citation of Allah that should not be altered by human interpretations however. The modernists also tend to maintain that Islam and its Shariah are meant to provide viable socio-political institutions, which must fit and serve human beings at all times and all places. They believe that while the Quran and Sunnah are immutable, their interpretations by man are subject to change in proportion to the extent of knowledge and experience which man (sic) acquires through ages (Shakir, op. cit., p. 2).

It should be noted that both schools of thought recognize and respect the centrality of Quran in the lives of believers. The main difference is about the role of knowledge and experiences, which also are inspired by Allah and acquired by practicing Muslims through the centuries and generations.

Political reforms were introduced gradually by the Kings to consolidate their power base. Under King Faisal, for instance, who was born in 1904 and died in 1975, some "significant political reforms" were introduced in the country when he served as Prime Minister and then as King later. Before him, tendencies of a strong monistic patrimonial characteristic were more predominantly present and active in the Saudi's political behavior and political culture.

Abdul-Aziz, who defeated the Ottoman-sponsored ruler in Makkah, was crowned king of Hidjaz (Hejaz) in January 1926. He promulgated a set of principles called the Organic Instructions of the Hidjaz (known also as the Hidjaz Constitution of 1926). It is stated in this Constitution that "all administration is in the hands of His Majesty King Abd al-'Aziz Ibn Sa'ud. His Majesty is bound by laws of the Shari'a "(Bromley, 1993, p. 398). Article 2 of the Royal Decree of August 13 1927 declared that Hidjaz was an Islamic Constitution Monarchy. In January 1932, he unified the two parts of his newly acquired territories and was crowned in Riyadh as King of Hidjaz and Nadjd and their dependent territories. After his death on November 9, 1932, his eldest son, Crown Prince Abdul-Aziz Ibn Saud who was Prime Minister under his father regime, became the King. Under his reign, he introduced the concept of the Council of Ministers to assist him in governing the country, but that Council had only a consultative power.

It is the King Abdul-Aziz Ibn Saud who appointed his brother, Crown Prince Faisal Ibn Abdul-Aziz, to become Prime Minister. Faisal, as alluded to earlier, decided in May 1958 to revise the status of the Council of Ministers, from being a consultative body into a formal, policy-making body politics with both executive and legislative powers. However, the King retained the veto power. Other important changes he introduced include the formalization of the Monarchy and the production of the program called the Basic Law as cited by Abdulmunim Shakir:

> In order to achieve a unified system of government based on the principle of Shariah, a basic Law will be promulgated, drawn from the Quran, the Sunnah of the Prophet, and the acts of orthodox Caliphs. It will set forth the fundamental principles of government and the governed in order to provide the basic rights of citizen (op. cit., p. 6).

The common view has been that in order to achieve a unified system of government based on the principle of Shariah, a basic Law was drawn from the Quran, the Sunnah of the Prophet, and the acts of orthodox Caliphs. They were promulgated as the basis law. The fundamental principles of government and the governed were set forth in order to provide the basic rights of citizens.

King Faisal has had a reformist legacy in Saudi Arabia. The reforms he undertook included judicial, political, and social dimensions. He is known as the one who introduced far-reaching social reforms such as free medicines, free education (not compulsory), and free medical care for all citizens and foreign legal residents alike in Saudi Arabia, which characterize Saudi Arabia to be among welfare states. He abolished the post of the office of Prime Minister. But it should be noted that he worked closely with the *Ulama* and the Council of Elders to make the Shariah law uniform but at the same time adoptive to each province. There was also a division of power within the hierarchy of governance between the provinces, cities, and villages. Thus, in general, the judicial system consists of three levels of courts and a Judicial Supervisory Committee, which supervises all other courts. This committee is composed of three members and a president appointed by the king. The committee may review appeals of serious issues already considered by the Court of Appeals (Shakir, op.cit., p.10).

In short, the ideas and structural elements that govern the Saudi society can be summarized in three levels of Courts (Ibid.):

(1) Al-Mustadjalah—like the magistrates courts, deals with petty affairs, minor misdemeanors and small claims;
(2) Makakim Al-Shariah Al-Kubram—the high courts of Shariah—are found in larger towns;
(3) Mahkamat Al-Istinaf—the Court of Appeal, is the highest level to which decisions of the lower courts may be appealed. It is situated in Hidjaz.

Faisal was assassinated on March 25, 1975 by his nephew. Thus, the Crown Prince Khalid Ibn Abdula-Aziz was proclaimed King and his brother Abdul-

Aziz was appointed Crown Prince. They decided to follow, to a large extent, policy guidelines and philosophical principles undertaken by Faisal.

As alluded to beyond, it is difficult to characterize or to predict with a high level of precision the Saudi regime in comparison to other contemporary states. It is a totalitarian system of governance. However, from the above brief analysis, it is also clear that the system has some flexibility. It has the dynamic monarchic, personal, and religious elements, which can be generalized as being part of the Middle East politics. The system has promoted a systematic effort to look for a consensus between the influential members of the royal family, that of *Ulama*, and the notable tribal chiefs. According to the traditional Arab practice of personal and direct accessibility to the head of tribe, the Shaykh (Sheikh), and also to the king himself who is considered the Shaykh of the Shaykhs, does not allow the establishment of absolute ruling system. The society has many Madjlis (councils) found in every tribe, clan, municipality or region with the Shaykhs.

Finally, it should be added that the abundance of oil reserves, its management, its production, and its marketization have contributed to the consolidation of the power of the traditional elite in Saudi Arabia. Technologies related to oil and the foreign policy based on it and derived from it, has also contributed to some elements of political flexibility in the country.

As part of the above reform, the document that can be called Constitution was adopted by Royal decree of King Fahd on March 1992. This document contains 83 Articles and nine Chapters. The titles of the chapters are:

Chapter 1, General Principles; Chapter 2, Monarchy; Chapter 3, Features of Saudi family; Chapter 4, Economic Principles; Chapter 5, Rights and Duties;

Chapter 6, Authorities; Chapter 7, Financial Affairs; Chapter 8, Control Bodies; and Chapter 9, General Provisions.

Saudi Arabia should be, in principle, an absolute monarchy with its religious basis as it was the Japanese case or the European Monarchies such as those of Spain in the 15th and 16th centuries and those of France before 1789. But in practice, it is not functioning as an absolute system. This monarchy does not have a historically indigenous base. It was constructed as part of the global European expansionism and the interests of local dominant powers. As Richard Manbach rightly stated:

> The British waged war against the Ottomans in Palestine, Syria, and Iraq, triumphing every where. Among their local allies was Hussein, the governor sheriff of Mecca and leader of the Hashemite clan of Arab Bedouins, who, encouraged by British promises of national independence, launched an Arab revolt against the Ottomans in 1916. The revolt was aided by an adventurer of mythic proportions, T. E. Lawrence, known as Lawrence of Arabia. The Ottoman Empire collapsed in 1923 when the sultanate was overthrown by army officers led by Mustapha Kemal (Kemal Ataturk), who then established the secular Republic of Turkey (2000, p. 40).

In short, theoretically, the principles and the practices associated with an absolute power may not be operationally effective with the imperatives of the international capitalism, especially with the production, management, and commercialization of the most important raw material of the world economy, oil.

NOTES

1. Material from this section was drawn from the paper entitled: "Constitutional Experiences in Post-Colonial Central Africa with a Special Reference to the Case of the Democratic Republic of the Congo (DRC)," written for the Conference on Constitution-making in Southern Africa that was organized by SARIPS held in July, 2000 in Harare, Zimbabwe.

Chapter 3

ON CITIZENRY

Introduction: Objectives and Issues

In the West, two intellectual traditions, namely contractual and communitarian schools of thought, have dominated in the perceptions, definitions, and studies of citizenship (Conover, Pamela Johnston, Ivor M. Crewe, and Donald D. Searing, 1991). The contractual tradition can be characterized by its emphasis on individual rights while the communitarian tradition focuses more on citizens' rights to participate in the political affairs for the community's sake (Dagger, 1981). In this book, as indicated earlier, it was not my intention to analyze the debates on controversies related to the concept of citizens in various theoretical traditions. My contribution is mainly to discuss citizens as defined in selected constitutions, and I will also show how history and philosophy produced a concept of citizenship that cannot be rigidly fixed in a legalistic, "letter of the law" framework.

In its classical dictionary meaning, "citizenry" refers to the whole body of citizens. It can be understood better in terms of citizenship, which encompasses the status of being a citizen including the individual's response to membership in a community. Citizenship in general terms, as defined in this chapter, is one of the most important constitutive institutions of the nation-state, a core concept in international relations, which defines individual and his/her rights in a political basis. It defines an individual identity as well as a national identity. It provides a framework of social differentiation between those who belong in a given political community and those who do not. In this sense, it plays the role of a social categorizing force, a criterion for setting up social standards.

In contemporary world politics, the question of citizenship has always been important in debates related to the policies and politics of nation-states and their development processes. This question, in various ways, has also shaped the nation-states' perceptions of themselves as reflected in governmental decision-making processes and their perceptions of others. With the central notion of citizenship, the nation-states have claimed their "immortality." Nation-states have also used it to legitimize their aggressive behaviors, their militaristic motivation, and their economic expansionism.

As compared to the notions of regional, national, or international boundaries, government, ruling and social classes, political parties, and sovereignty, the notion of citizenship, as a legal political concept, is one of the most clearly and concretely defined attributes of the nation-state. Its definitions are less elastic and imagined than many other phenomena related to the studies of politics. The concept of citizenship is central to the intellectual debates in political science and related fields. Yet its significance and implications within the confined rules of the nation-states in changing world politics have been persistently ambiguous and controversial. Various social classes in different parts of the world have related to this notion differently.

Given the current trends of massive movements of people and labor, legally and illegally, from all directions crossing borders in many parts of the world, the repeated dismantling of some old nation-states and the emergence of new ones, the refugees question, civil wars, and the wars of invasion, the concept of citizenship—and its philosophical foundation—is likely to be one of the most important issues in international relations and world affairs in the twenty-first century. While the ideological conflicts directly related to the Cold War power struggles have significantly declined or diminished with the collapse of the USSR and its institutional socialism, in 1991 in most parts of the world, internal conflicts related to former mechanisms of state formation and their performances have dangerously increased, for instance, in parts of Africa and in the Balkans. Most of these conflicts and the ways they manifest or reproduce themselves are related to the question of citizenship. Thus, it is necessary that the concept of citizenship be further examined and clarified to allow the world to readjust or readopt it into new national and international realities and imperatives.

Is citizenship, or nationality as it is called in some constitutions and countries, the incarnation of the contemporary nation-state? How does this incarnation manifest itself in the real social life of people? And what does that mean in relationship to the efforts of defining the foundation of the citizens' power base and their rights? What does citizenship bring to humanity and society individually and collectively? How does it relate to nationality in a situation where citizenship is a distinctive phenomenon?

In this chapter, I will comparatively examine how nation-states define citizenship. What kind of political values are associated with it? What kind of political knowledge is linked with or derives from it? Few selected illustrations are used from the constitutions which were cited and examined in previous chapters. The main objective is not to formally examine the status of citizenship, but to identify and try to understand its meanings. Furthermore, I am not examining the nature of various claims that multiple social, ethnic, and political groups in different parts of the world have made concerning their perceptions and definitions of citizenship. Nonetheless, it should be underscored that the dynamics of the concept of sociological citizenship can contribute toward the understanding of the notion of civil citizenship. These two realms of power create their own distinctive identities. The conflicting nature of the relationship between these two concepts is due mainly to the uneasy marriage of thoughts and ideologies between the notion of nation and that of the state. In contemporary world politics, nations and states have historically claimed different rights, which reflect their different origins. Thus, the nation-state is, as articulated in contemporary politics, essentially a conflicting entity.

Thus the main emphasis here is on the examination of the concept of civil citizenship, to identify its general characteristics, and to contrast its various aspects as stipulated in several constitutions. Given the fact that civil citizenship has become a global claim and issue, and that the performance of nation-state is also partially evaluated in relationship to how this concept is actualized in pragmatic terms, another related objective is therefore to classify what these definitions may have in common.

In most countries, especially those in the developing world, the debates on the rules concerning statehood and its national policies have not yet solved the question of the nature of the relationship between nationality and civil or legal citizenship. In most pragmatic ways the historically dominant trend in the nation-building process has been either to fuse nationality or ethnicity and legal citizenship within the logic of nation-state building, or in the past, to attempt to dismiss the concept of nationality altogether as a "primordial" value. Thus, all French nationals are described constitutionally as French citizens. However, in some countries, like Canada, Canadian citizenship and *Québecois* nationality are still in conflict. The efforts to fuse them have created more conflicts than solutions in the process of defining the identities of the people. Furthermore, despite the fact that statehood remains an unsolved puzzle in many aspects of world politics, citizenship has been one characteristic of the state which has been relatively well defined, even though its content has not been agreed upon in practice. The definitions of citizenship have not been ambiguous as compared to other state characteristics such as sovereignty and territoriality. In fact, as argued here, the majority of nation-states have been attempting to reaffirm the status of their fragile social and economic basis of sovereignty through the re-definition and consolidation of citizenship. As articulated later, there are scholars who tend to perceive citizenship primarily as an ideological phenomenon. As such, it can be defined as a historical and social construct. In pragmatic and philosophical terms, and based on the dynamics of world politics, however, this historical and social construct contains a transcendent or international element in relationship to geophysical determinism, which defines a human being as a political animal. Second, another dimension for defining citizenship is the legal or civil one. This dimension is strongly associated with sovereignty of a given nation-state. But it should be added that the transcendent elements associated with citizenship as an international phenomenon do not totally negate the role of geography, as the "mother" of culture in the world of the states.

In the contemporary world, one may argue that the role of ideology rather than geography has been a greater determinant in defining the state. In fact, the colonial powers first mapped the globe combining an imagined world and a "missionary geography" dominated by imperial motives. The imperialist motives of exploitation and domination, the motto of a nation-state, were articulated without any intent for understanding or much appreciation for the imperatives of geography locally or regionally.

It should be emphasized that the notion of citizenship, its philosophical foundation, its attributes, and its practical values are currently in the center of controversial debates in the world of the states. Understanding its complexity implies an attempt to understand and appreciate the nature of the nation-state itself and how to deal with its decisions and policies in a more effective manner. In my view, this notion is among the most fragile; yet by international and regional agreements and conventions, it appears to be among the most respected attributes of the state, the other obvious attributes being (1) a defined territory, (2) a government, and (3) sovereignty.

Citizenship and constitutions are interrelated subjects. For the purpose of clarity, they are technically separated into two different sections. However, they are analytically complementary to each other in terms of understanding the nature of power within the parameters of the contemporary states.

Theoretically, it is argued that even if one were interested in studying power only in its institutional form, it would be difficult to demonstrate and maintain the view with convincing evidence that institutional power, in its technical perspective, can be fully comprehended without relating it to the question of the legitimacy and legality of citizenship. The questions of performance and expectations, which are part of the legitimacy question, can also be supported and promoted by the dynamics of a body of laws. The premise that is advanced and maintained in this book, and which also needs further comparative study, is that citizenship is the foundation of power in the world of the states. It is a legal/juridical question as well as a social and pragmatic issue.

How citizens are defined by the nation-states and by the people themselves in a given social and political context is a matter of power relations. The contradictory nature of this relationship (relations between people/citizens and states) is characterized by a permanent struggle between the state's claims of political knowledge and its perception of the world, as it uses control as a mechanism of insuring its legitimacy and citizens' expectations and rights. This struggle results from the fact that the state is a legitimized force and it uses its legitimate coercive power as a functional way of establishing its authority. Citizens tend to question the foundation of this legitimacy, even when they are protected by the state. Citizens' definition of themselves, regardless of the nature of political regime—be it liberal democracy in Europe, social democracy in the Scandinavian countries, or eclectical democracy in the transitional states in the South—is broad rather than legalistic. The definition of citizenship as a right is systematically articulated in the courts, for instance, in the case of the United States; or it can take place constitutionally on the streets, in rallies, for example in France, or in the claimed antagonistic ethnic and political debates of the opposition parties in Côte d'Ivoire.

In the contemporary world, the relationships between a state and its citizens have been, in most cases, problematic, as they tend to change over time. However, this has not stopped or impeded governments and people from continuing to redefine the phenomenon of citizenship, even when the claims, principles, and realities of globalization have challenged some of the key philosophical elements of the states.

The contemporary paradoxical situation has been that while the forces associated with commerce, communication and military technologies, and economic globalization have been systematically and dominantly weakening the domestic economic foundation of the states' policies in many countries, challenging therefore the functional dimension of the doctrine of sovereignty, many of the same weak states have become more nationalistic in re-conquering or reclaiming their autonomy by redefining citizenship. To a certain extent, the legalistic claim of citizenship has been expressed in nationalistic language rather than in the social and economic policies or the welfare programs of the states. In the post–Cold War era, while states have become more aggressive in specifying the defining criteria of their sovereignty through their thinking about citizenship, they have also adopted the dogmas and policies of global economic reform, which essentially counter states regulations. Thus, citizenship has become the incarnation of the state itself. It is the reflection of the claimed autonomy of the state. Within this contradictory relationship, how have citizens been treated by the states' institutions? How have citizens been able to participate in political processes? Is it possible to have citizens who behave like apathetic subjects when it comes to political participation yet who still consider themselves integrative citizens?

The question of citizenship is central to the very survival of the imagined or the real nation-state. Witness the following examples: In Côte d'Ivoire, there is the political determination to implement, maintain, and normalize the new constitutional law inspired by *"ivoirité"* and to exclude any naturalized or non-naturalized *"immigrés"* who have only one Ivorian grandparent from running for the office of the presidency. The Banyamulenge (the Congolese Tutsi), a name invented in the 1970s to identify the Tutsi of Kivu in the DRC who live on the mountain of Mulenge, have been struggling to reacquire their lost Congolese citizenship in the DRC in the post-Mobutu era in the face of the new, regressive law No. 001-2001 of May 17, 2001 concerning the organization and functioning of the political parties, which states that "only the Congolese nationals whose parents (father and mother) are originally from the DRC should form political parties." In Zambia there was President Chiluba's effort to redefine citizenship in order to exclude former President Kenneth

Kaunda from again running for the presidency. Albanians struggled for the independence of Kosovo and the new redefinition of their citizenship both in Kosovo and Macedonia. In Europe, debate surrounds the issue of regional citizenship in the European Union.

Despite the fact that the European Union is offering another approach to defining citizenship, it should be noted that this union is neither a state nor a legal entity according to Finer et al. However, although Finer et al. seem to envision that the processes of possible formation of the United States of Europe began with the treaties of establishing the European Community and later the European Union (1995, p. iii), the issue of relationship between "national citizenship" and "regional citizenship" is a subject that requires further analyses and debates. Will the French, the Germans, the British, the Italians, the Spanish citizens, for example, be willing to accept the weakening of, or to relinquish forever, the cultural and historical basis of their "national citizenship" in order to gain commercial and economic resources that might advance "regional European citizenship"?

In their December 2003's meeting in Brussels, Belgium, because of the implications to their national power bases, the 25 members of the European Union failed to reach a decision on the proposition of making a common European Constitution, a notion which has been previously referred to as a supranational constitution (Sweet and Brunnell, 1998). This constitution would produce some kind of a "unitary citizenship." The debate is now on what kind of consensus will be engendered between the federalist model of citizenship and the nationalist one.

The nation-state, the unit of analysis of international politics and the major force in international commerce and markets, is in the process of redefining its capacities and responsibilities, its obligations and duties, its moral and political domestic base, and also its relationship to the imperatives of labor and citizenship. As stated earlier, this process of redefinition is likely to be the most debated single issue in social sciences in the twenty-first century.

What does citizenship mean theoretically and empirically at individual and societal levels, and also at the levels of national and international politics? Does citizenship matter in rapidly changing world politics? What does citizenship mean in societies with a high level of social and cultural cleavages and with extreme or absolute poverty? What does it mean in relationship to the question of the permanent acquisition of property such as land? What does this specific social and political identity offer to individuals, societies, and the world?

What do citizens of Belgium, Bosnia, Brazil, Canada, China, Chile, Côte d'Ivoire, the Democratic Republic of Congo, France, Germany, Jordan, India, Israel, Kenya, Nigeria, the United States of America, Pakistan, and South Africa, to cite only a few countries, claim in common, if anything. What is their common denominator? Behind these questions, there are scholars who tend to advance the underlying position that, as the world of politics continues to change in order to respond to new social, political, environmental, and gender demands and challenges, the notion of citizenship is likely to become more fluid, leading to its increasing ineffectiveness if not its "collapse" in its current form.

However, it should be stated that despite the fact that the concept of "global citizenship" has been intellectually popularized and accepted among some scholars, from the practical legal point of view and in association with the notion of sovereignty of the nation state, there is no such thing as global citizenship (even within the current flexible regional framework of the European Union), a kind of internationally recognized status that transcends the parameters of national legalism and the sovereignty of the nation-state. Citizenship firmly remains one of the most important qualifications of the nation-state. Thus, it is still one of the most important topics in political and social studies. It is centrally related to state formation, constitution-making, social and political integration and participation, and political development at large.

People's claims and actions in the post–Cold War era in redefining their citizenship or political identity in countries such as Afghanistan, Bosnia, Canada, Côte d'Ivoire, the DRC, Eritrea, Ethiopia, Kosovo, Rwanda, Spain, Somalia, and Pakistan, have exploded in part because of judiciary activism, the dynamics of human rights' organizations, the visibility of the United Nations, and regional and local political and social movements. It would be important to ask if people in these different parts of the world are searching for the same thing, namely, the articulation of their rights to belong to a relatively coherent, functioning political entity. Although various actors have made those claims in various periods and for different purposes, it is historically clear that they do, in many ways, directly contribute to the questioning of the values, structures, legitimacy, and legality of the existing contemporary states.

Citizenship, one of the most important characteristics of the nation-state, is not a naturally fixed and absolute phenomenon. Even Aristotle, with his limited definition of citizenship, would not completely object to the simple reasoning that citizenship has meaning only in a descriptive sociological context. There is absolutely no need to speculate about citizenship in the Hobbesian state, a kind of "an organized contractual" state of nature. Citizenship is a fluid social concept that has always been created to actualize the specific interests of some social groupings. Thus it can be described as a constantly changing historical concept. Its meanings and its relevancy must always be sociologically, politically, and economically contextualized, although philosophical claims associated with it can be universalized or internationalized. It would be interesting to contrast the notion of citizenship at the period of colonization with the notion of citizenship in the post-colonial period and examine whether these two social contexts produced different philosophical meanings of the same concept. What does it mean in philosophical and pragmatic terms? Some generalizations are needed here before I identify some concrete definitions of citizenship in different historical contexts.

What Is Citizenship?

Etymologically, the word "citizenship" is more closely associated with the city-state (*polis*) than with the nation-state. Historically, citizenship as articulated in the Western traditions was essentially perceived as a functional, relatively harmonious, urban, monolithic phenomenon. In this sense, according to Aristotle, the city-state existed for the sake of the citizens' good life. This good life is referred to as a life of virtue. This city-state ought to provide the means through which this good life is actualized and protected. From this restricted angle and manner, citizenship can be depicted as a natural phenomenon rather than a social, historical one. However, historically, the city-state was built by diverse social groups, including women, traders, and slaves, all of whom were not entitled to become citizens regardless of their personal merit. Aristotle praised slavery as an instrument, a living tool, without which there would be no leisure for the activities that make life worthwhile (Politics, Sections 1253b32-41).

The first elaborated and documented city-states emerged in the Sumerian region (Mesopotamia and Babylonia), which is located approximately where today's Iraq is. They reached their peak in Greece in the fifth and the fourth centuries B.C.E. In ancient Greece, Italy, and the Mediterranean world, the city-state was an independent political unit consisting of a city surrounded by countryside. Its government consisted of an assembly and council; the former predominated in democracies and the latter in oligarchies. Various city-states combined into religious or military federations. Some of the last city-states in Italy after the fall of the Roman Empire were Florence, Genoa, and Venice until the nineteenth century (Chernow and Vallasi, 1993, p. 564).

Citizenship in its association with the nation-state has undergone a transformation since its usage in the ancient period. In ancient times, it implied municipality. "Citizen" originally meant "the inhabitant of a town." In Greece, for instance, property owners were citizens of a town. According to Chernov and Vallasi, in the Roman Empire, citizenship was first limited only to the residents of the city of Rome. It was extended in 212 B.C.E. to all free inhabitants of the empire. The expression disappeared in its political usage in feudal Europe. Then, it reappeared after the medieval era in Europe to mean "membership of a political community with republic forms of government, (ibid., p. 562). In some countries, such as the United Kingdom, citizens were defined as subjects until the British Nationality Act of 1981.

Historically, the concept of national citizenship, which first developed during the American and French Revolutions, spread all over the world. In this usage, it is associated with nationality. It describes nationals even of monarchical states. In its European usage, which became the dominant usage as it spread through massive migration and colonization since the fifteenth century, the notion of citizenship is determined by two concepts: *jus sanguinis* and *jus soli*.

According to the concept of *jus sanguinis* (law of blood), a legitimate child takes citizenship from his/her father and an illegitimate child from the mother (ibid.). Within this perspective, citizenship in the ancient Greece was limited to those born of citizen parents, meaning the fathers; and only citizens could and did participate in governmental debates. Participating in government was a process for an elected few, where decisions and elections took place. Slaves and women could and did contribute to build *polis*, but as instruments of exploitation, though they too had some limited rights (not political) to protect in a Machiavellian sense. This was the case in hundreds of city-states in Greece and Italy.

In other countries, depending on the histories of their state formations and the supportive ideologies behind them such as assimilationism and integrationism, national citizenship is also determined by *jus soli* (law of the soil), which refers to place of birth. This is the determining factor for defining citizenship. Over the years, these two concepts have been used either simultaneously or separately to deal with the questions of citizenship.

However, since the signing of the Peace of Westphalia in 1648 in Prussia, the general usage of the notion of citizenship has been strongly associated with the nation-state, an essentially multinational, historical, or imagined political community. It takes its simple philosophical origins from the city-state and its complexity from historical, political and economic meanings of the nation-state and international agreements. Thus, it is not a closed expression. Despite the fact that the nation-state has characteristics of being deterministic and rigid in its relationship to its surroundings, the struggles associated with colonialism, decolonization, and the politics of the Cold War support the view that nation-state is a constantly changing, self-defining phenomenon. From this point of view, citizenship is also a political entity that takes its strength from historical processes and power struggles locally and internationally.

By examining concrete illustrations, one can see that the logic and dogma of assimilationist policy and indirect rule produced various interpretations of the concept of citizenship. However, in most cases, the mixture of both kinds of rules was pragmatic and also used as a popularly applied method of ruling, naming the people, and classifying them.

Within the logic and dogma of assimilation, the French administration over the years put greater emphasis on becoming French through education and culture than on affiliation by blood or birth. It should be noted that the French colonial administration used also *jus sanguinis* in a limited selective manner for instance in the case of four communes in Senegal before World War I. The British, on the other hand, emphasized the legalistic and blood aspects of belonging to a country. Germany was the most radical, or the most exclusive, in defining citizenship. Until recently, with new political reforms after the collapse of the Berlin Wall in 1989 and the efforts of the new social democratic Chancellor, Schroeder, toward the end of the 1990s, blood origin as the criterion for German citizenship was not relaxed in comparison with the new constitution. Turkish people, who have lived and worked in Germany for a specific period, are now eligible to apply for dual citizenship. Some people have perceived the past German perspective on citizenship as the most racist approach. South Africa, with its apartheid system, an extreme case of social categorization and separateness, was closer to the German perspective of exclusion. The Liberian exclusionary definition, which at the same has a relative degree of openness, has basically been influenced by ethnicity and history. In principle, only people of African descent can become citizens of Liberia. Only citizens can own a piece of land. The United States has historically articulated citizenship in terms of a blood connection and labor. Thus, its notion of citizenship tends to be legalistic but sociologically and culturally less restrictive and diverse—at the least since former enslaved Africans became eligible to be citizens.

In short, theoretically, the common, generalized claims behind citizenship is the articulation of some kind of equality and rights, as Danilo Zolo stated:

> According to (T. M.) Marshall, the distinctive feature of modern citizenship that opposes it to status is its tendency towards equality. An image of 'ideal citizenship' always emerges where the institutions of citizenship develop. This 'ideal citizenship' operates as standard for measuring actual political achievements and as target of increasing social expectations. Citizenship rights, however, in spite of their pressure towards equality, cannot be separated from the rise and development of capitalism, and capitalism is a system not of equality, but in inequality (1993, p. 255).

How has this notion become central to the political struggles, the search for economic progress and power in contemporary societies at individual and societal levels? How is this element of inequality articulated among different states and citizens the world over? Although the issue of inequality is clarified further in the section on capitalism, it has also been included in the discussion of citizenship in each illustrative case.

Citizenship in the United States

What is the philosophical foundation of citizenship in the United States? Who should or ought to be an American citizen? What rights does he/she have? How was citizenship conceived? And how is it working?

As stated earlier, the main objective here is not to examine various people's claims of citizenship and how members of various social groups have defined themselves in or by the system. Nor is it to examine how they have been integrated into the system or how they have been accepted into the dominant system. As part of the comparative approach, the main objective is to identify and discuss some general characteristics of citizenship as articulated in the United States Constitution.

The concept of citizenship in the United States has been articulated mainly by the liberal school of thought and its contractual philosophical foundation. As Pamela Johnston Conover, Ivor M. Crewe, and Donald D. Searing argued:

> The contractual vision of citizenship, which forms the basis for contemporary liberal views, is rooted in the political philosophy of Locke and Hobbes. It tends to be legalistic and has at its core a strong conception of individualism and individuals" (1991, p. 802).

The United States of America is a country of immigrants. It was built principally with the combination of ideas and resources from the exploitation of the native Americans, labor from Africa in the form of slavery, and political and philosophical ideas of settlers from various parts of Europe, especially England, France, Spain, Germany, and the Netherlands. During what is known as the period of exploration in Europe, beginning in the fifteenth century, (especially after Columbus' adventurism and political end), Europeans gradually moved out of Europe for various historical reasons that can be summarized as "gold, God, and glory." This was also true elsewhere, especially in Asia and Africa.

The land that became the United States of America was colonized by the English as a settler's colony. The first and the oldest English settlement was established at Jamestown in Virginia in 1607. In 1620, other English people came to America on the ship Mayflower, on which they made a plan of government known as "the Mayflower Compact." These people settled in Plymouth, Massachusetts. The settlers produced the Pilgrim Covenant that is described by Breckinridge Long in this manner:

> The Pilgrim Covenant was signed and agreed to by the people, individually, who were to be governed by it. The community was small. There was no need to delegate to a representative authority to draw up and agree to it for them... as shall be thought most *meete* and convenient for ye general good of ye Colonie. This covenant was the constitution which bound them to observe the laws and ordinances which they foresaw would be passed, and was the authority which permitted the placing above them of some one, or more, in "offices," who should be the administrative means of effecting their desires as evidenced in such laws, ordinances...Their constitution was the foundation stone of democracy in America...The Pilgrim constitution implanted in America the principle of equality of men (sic) and of "due submission and obedience" to "all just and *equall lawes* which themselves should frame (1926, pp. 4-7).

It should be noted that not all the colonies belonged to the English settlers. There were also those that belonged to the Dutch, the Swedes, the French, and the Spanish, who struggled to obtain and retain in the battlefields portions of the "land of opportunity."

As compared to other European colonies in Africa and Asia, the colonists in the United States believed—even before the Boston Tea Party, a cartel of specialized interest groups—that they had the rights to govern themselves. The engraved philosophical notion of rights and elements of common history and culture between the ruling colonial powers and the colonists contributed, to a certain large extent, to making the English colonies in North America with those of India, Kenya, and part of China relatively different. Within the political economy and historical perspectives of the United States, the subjects were the slaves, who constituted what Abraham Lincoln once called the "peculiar institution." The above sections are intended only to provide a perspective and a framework from which one can discuss and project the question of citizenship in contemporary liberal democratic America.

The first ten constitutional amendments, the Bill of Rights, comprise the foundation of defining American rights of citizenship. They define the quality of what it means to be a free individual. Citizens of liberal democratic America are those individuals, born or naturalized Americans, who have rights as articulated by the Bill of Rights. They must exercise those rights justly and rationally, and they also must be protected by the constitution. The Bill of Rights is the most important part of the adopted changes that define the role of American citizens. They define the essence of what the American citizen is. The first ten amendments to the U.S. Constitution provide the following:

- The First Amendment defines four of the greatest rights (or freedoms): freedom of religion, freedom of speech, freedom of the press, and the right of assembly and petition.
- The Second Amendment is the right of people to keep and bear arms in a national militia.
- The Third Amendment stipulates that the government cannot make people keep soldiers in their homes except in time of war, and then only according to law.
- The Fourth Amendment protects people from arrest or search except by warrant.
- The Fifth Amendment is the rights of persons to due process of law.
- The Sixth Amendment addresses the rights of the accused in criminal cases.
- The Seventh Amendment concerns civil trials.
- The Eighth Amendment gives further guarantees in criminal cases and prohibits cruel and inhuman punishment.
- The Ninth Amendment is unenumerated rights (or rights retained by the people).
- The Tenth Amendment covers reserved powers (or, "the powers not delegated to the United States by the constitution, nor prohibited by it to the states, are reserved to the states respectively, or to the people." They are characterized as 'truism' (P. 1509).

In addition to the rights described above, the question of citizenship of the former slaves was taken as a special issue. Thus, the Thirteenth Amendment, which was ratified on December 12, 1865, was intended to address the particular issue, namely slavery, even after it had been officially abolished. On this concern, the Amendment (Slavery and Involuntary Service) states:

Section I. "Neither slavery nor involuntary service, except as a punishment for crime whereof the party shall have been duly convicted, shall exist within the United States, or any place subject to their jurisdiction" (U.S. Constitution, 1996).

Section II. "Congress shall have power to enforce this article by appropriate legislation" (U.S. Constitution, 1996).

On the question of citizenship, the Thirteenth Amendment was further consolidated by the Fourteenth Amendment, which is entitled: "Rights Guaranteed, Privileges, and Immunities of Citizenship, Due Process and Equal Protection."

In short, American citizens are defined as:

All persons born or naturalized in the United States, and subject to the jurisdiction thereof, are citizens of the United States and the States wherein they reside. No State shall make or enforce any law which shall abridge the privileges or immunities of citizens of the United States; nor shall any States deprive any person of life, liberty, or property, without due process of law; nor deny to any person within its jurisdiction the equal projection of laws (U.S. Constitution, 1996).

In 1866, Congress sought "to secure to all citizens of every race and colors, and without regard to previous servitude, those fundamental rights, which are the essence of civil freedom, namely the same rights to make and to enforce contracts, to sue parties, give evidence, and to inherit by white citizens."[1]

The Fourteenth Amendment was intended to use the word "person" to mean "natural persons." Natural persons protected by the due process clause, these include all human beings regardless of race, color, or citizenship (Killian and A. Costellio, p. 1567). As they cited, this amendment was going to clarify further the status of African Americans after slavery. As they state: "This Amendment was the desire to protect Negroes. This undeniable purpose of the 14th Amendment to take Citizenship of Negroes permanent and secure would be frustrated by holding that Government can rob a citizen of his citizenship without his consent by simply proceeding to act under an implied general power to regulate foreign affairs or some generally granted."[2]

Within the parameters of this Amendment, "the meaning of the citizenship of the United States must be natural and not artificial persons; a corporate body is not a citizen."[3] Philosophically, the American citizen is an individual with rights and freedoms. Given the centrality of these rights and freedoms, why is it that the United States has not established a solid liberal welfare state comparable to those in Western Europe to protect its well-defined citizens' rights? For further details on the question of citizenship see Amendments I through X, XIV, and XV of the U.S. Constitution.

Citizenship in France

"The Declaration of the Rights of Man (sic) and the Citizen of 1789" has been the philosophical and historical foundation of perceptions, definitions, and interpretations of French citizenship. This Declaration, in its seventeen points, has put emphasis on the centrality and sovereignty of citizens in France. For instance, it starts with the following statement that universalizes the humanity of citizenship: "All men (sic) are born and remain free and equal in rights. Social distinctions may be based only on public utility."

Who is a French person and who is a French citizen? The logic of these two questions can be expanded to any country. As theoretically alluded to earlier, a French person or a German person, for that matter, is an essentially ethnic phenomenon. It implies belonging to an ethnic group historically associated with, or part of, France or Germany. A French person also clearly implies French nationality.

There are ethnic Germans in France, Poland, Hungary, and Austria. But these Germans are also citizens of France, Poland, Hungary, or Austria. The French nationals, as other nationals, may choose to be citizens of other countries or states. While citizenship, as articulated in this section, is essentially ideological and legal, ethnicity is social and historical. In the specific case of France, Ehrmann and Martin Schain (1992, p. 4) state that "Historically, no such thing as a French race exists." They quoted a French historian, André Siegfried in his article entitled: "Approaches to an Understanding of Modern France," who wrote: "We are a race of half-breeds" and they added another portion of the quote: "mongrels are often more intelligent than purebred dogs (Earle, 1951, p. 4)." They also continue thus:

> Which of their gifts and deficiencies the French owe to the Latins, the Celts, or the Germanic tribes is far less significant than the fact that on a nation fashioned by a common historical experience, existing diversities have been encompassed by a strong national unity. Neither the survival of different languages (not just dialects) nor substantial regional differences were as divisive as they have been for all of France's neighbors, including Switzerland. Yet, the French often refer to their place of origin or of residence as *mon pays* (my country), one of the many indications that in modern France a variety of minicultures have survived (Ehrmann, op. cit., p. 5).

Wherever there are weak political institutions or strong economic cleavages in a given society, there are also possibilities of strong clashes between the manifestations of ethnicity, or nationality, and citizenship. In some cases, contemporary states have used citizenship in inclusive ways. For example, French citizenship has also extended to the nationals of Brittany and Corsica, which are composed of different ethnic groups from those of the dominant French social groups. However, one of the characteristics of world politics after the end of the Cold War era is that more nationals are struggling to reacquire their "national citizenship" or to have some kind of control over their own nationalities. As referred above, France is not an exception in this situation. Its relatively recent politics of regionalism has been used to solve or address the issues of conflicts between nationality and citizenship. This has become a generalized trend in several non-federalist European states.

The preamble of the French Constitution, which contains ninety-three articles and seventeen titles as amended on July 19, 1993, states,

> The French people solemnly proclaim their commitment to the Rights of Man
> (sic) and the principles of the human sovereignty as defined by the Declaration
> of 1789, reaffirmed and completed by the Preamble of the Constitution of 1946.

> By virtue of these principles and that of the free self-determination of peoples
> and that of the free-determination of peoples, the Republic offers to those
> Overseas Territories, which demonstrate the desire to join them, new
> institutions founded on the common ideal of liberty, equality, and fraternity,
> and conceived with a view to their democratic evolution.

After World War II, the French state became a weak colonial state, with a lack of any national integrity and confidence, which could contribute to its partial or total collapse as a result of several factors. These factors include, among others, Hitler's occupation, the existence of two weak governments, France's defeat in the Indo-China war, the Algerian war, and the rise of various movements of decolonization in Africa. All these factors caused France to become politically unstable between 1946 and 1958, with twenty-three governments in a period of twelve years. This situation did not result from a crisis of the French Constitution. Rather, the crisis was essentially geopolitical and international.

Thus, the French National Assembly invited General Charles de Gaulle, an older politician, the leader of the opposition movement against the German occupation and the Vichy government who was residing in London, to return and form a government of national unity which would save France from collapse.

Charles de Gaulle had some interesting characteristics as a leader that should be mentioned. He was charismatic, nationalist, populist, a good military strategist, someone with a spirit of reconciliation. Indeed, he was also a reformist political figure. He posed a major condition before accepting the new responsibility. He wanted to have a centralized government and executive power as compared to the decentralized form of government of the Fourth

Republic, which was characterized as parliamentarian, divisive, and relatively weak in addressing the national question. Thus, after the referendum in which almost 80 percent of the voters were in favor of amending the constitution in order to give more power to the executive branch even in the legislative branch of the state, the constitution was amended and the Fifth Republic emerged.

The French constitutions, including that of the Fifth Republic of October 4, 1958, are framed on the French Declaration of the Rights of Man (sic) and the Citizen of 1789. The representatives of the French people convened in the National Assembly declared seventeen Rights of Man (sic) and Citizen. A few rights listed below give us some general ideas about the philosophy of citizenship in France:

- All men (sic) are born and remain free and equal in their rights. Social distinctions may be based only on public utility.

- The end of every political institution is the preservation of the natural and indefeasible rights of man (sic). Those rights are liberty, property, security, and resistance to oppression.

- The source of sovereignty lies essentially in the nation. No corporation or individual may exercise any authority not expressly derived there from.

- Liberty is the power to do anything which does not harm another; hence the only limits to the exercise of each man's natural rights are those which secure to other members of society the enjoyment of the same rights. These limits may be fixed only by the statute law. It is commonly said within the above logic and premise that the freedom of each individual ends where the freedom of the others starts.

Concept of Citizenship in the Socialist Countries

Introduction: General Issues

In the contemporary world, socialism has been not only an ideological challenge to the dominant ideology, capitalism, but more important, it has produced different scientific and philosophical tools for defining political community, social relations of production and values, sciences, and nature.

In this section, I am making some reflective generalizations on the issue of how the socialist states, which claimed the articulation of the total emancipation of human beings in the twentieth century, perceived and defined citizenship. I will discuss some of the general characteristics of the socialist world, focusing on how constitutions define citizenship, with a few illustrations contrasting various types of socialist states. There is also an effort to identify and discuss some elements of both historical socialism and utopian socialism in their perceptions and definitions of the political being.

Have socialist states produced common or similar definitions of citizenship? Who were considered citizens in the socialist countries? What were the attributes of citizenship within the paradigms of socialism? What is a political being?

I start this section by articulating that there are scholars who argue that the concept of citizenship, whether sociologically based or by product of civil configurations of society and power struggles, and regardless of its historical and ideological context, is essentially imagined, utopian, or revolutionary. Those who support this view examine citizenship as being first of all, a philosophical concept. This position also defines citizenship phenomenologically as associated with the emancipatory politics of human society and conditions. The concept is also linked to reason and utilitarianism. The advocates of this proposition believe that, in principle, in socialism, a political human being should be totally freed and emancipated from the exploitation and alienation of the powerful social and political forces in any exploitative situation or oppressed society. As discussed in some parts of this book, however, it is not clear if historical socialism, also labeled "state socialism," as contrasted to utopian socialism, was able or well equipped to totally liberate the political human being from the contradictions of the nature and the society in which he/she is an integral part. Between the Russian Revolution of October 1917 and the collapse of the Union of the Soviet Socialist Republics (USSR) in 1992, although in a short period of time, the world knew one of the strongest ideological challenges to capitalism.

The Case of the Union of Socialist Soviet Republic (USSR)

It is argued that the concept of citizenship in the former Soviet Union was partially advanced by three main factors: (1) an attempt toward the "Russification" policies (term borrowed from Magstadt, op. cit., p. 166) of Eastern Europe; (2) cultural Russianization of the satellite cultures (for instance, the introduction of seven to eight years of Russian language instruction in the school systems); and (3) the dynamics of the Sovietization of former Eastern Europe based on socialist revolution as an international ideological movement. That is to say, citizenship was defined in terms of the capacities of various nationalities to assimilate into the dominant Russian culture and also the degree to which the acceptance, the adoption, the implementation, and the praxis of policies of socialist revolution were actualized.

Assimilationism, whether it is the French model used by the French administration in Paris since the fifteenth and sixteenth centuries as the dogma of advancing the so-called civilizing mission in France first and then elsewhere, particularly in its colonies, or the ad hoc Portuguese model used in the former Portuguese colonies, is based on notions of cultural superiority and political arrogance. In the case of Russia, assimilationism, especially the cultural dimension, met various forms of serious resistance in parts of Eastern and Central Europe. This assimilationism had its roots partially in what did happen in 1918 when the Russian Soviet Federative Socialist Republic (RSFSR) was adopted. As William B. Simons indicates:

> This 90-article document proclaimed the establishment of the dictatorship of the proletariat to be its fundamental task and that all central and local power in the new Federal Russian Republic belonged to the Soviets of Workers,' Soldiers,' and Peasants' deputies (1980, p. 344).

Citizenship was put into the large category of the proletariat, a newly defined ruling power. Citizenship in this case was more of an ideological renaming of the people than simply a historical and sociological categorization of belonging to the system.

Another new constitution of January 1924 put emphasis on the unity of the republics and equality of rights. Section II of this constitution addressed in particular the issue of the sovereign rights of Union Republics and Union Citizenship, and it also maintained the centrality of the dictatorship of the proletariat in changing society and defining citizenship. However, the 1936 constitution replaced the proletariat by "the socialist all-people's state" (Simons, 1980, p. 347).

In Section II of the 1977 Brezhnev Constitution, which contains 174 articles, thirty-six articles (between Article 33 and Article 69) clearly define the question of citizenship and associated rights. For instance, Article 33 states, "a single union citizenship is established in USSR. Every citizen of a union republic is a citizen of the USSR. The grounds and the procedures for acquiring and losing Soviet citizenship were defined by the Law on Citizenship of the USSR. Citizens of the USSR abroad enjoy the defense and protection of the Soviet State." Article 34 refers to equality before the law of all citizens of the USSR; Article 35 talks about the equal rights between women and men; Chapter VII describes the basic rights, freedoms, and obligations of citizens, which are literally, word for word, just like those of the Bill of Rights in the U.S. Constitution.

Who may be elected to public office? Chapter XIII (The Electoral System) describes the criteria for participating in the elections of deputies to all Soviets People's Deputies and the Supreme Soviet. Article 95 states that "Elections of deputies to all Soviets of People's Deputies are held on the basis of universal, equal, and direct suffrage by secret ballot." Article 96 states "Elections of deputies are universal: all citizens of the USSR who have reached the age of 18 years have the rights to vote and to be elected, with exception of persons who have, in the manner established by law, been declared insane. A citizen of the USSR who has reached the age of 21 years may be elected a deputy to the Supreme Soviet." Article 98 stipulates that "Elections of deputies are direct: the deputies of all Soviets of People's Deputies are elected directly by the citizens."

Finally, who governed in the Soviet Union? As articulated in many parts of this book, the question of who governs must be examined and understood historically and also in terms of identifying the relationships between the various units or elements of the state apparatuses and the society. A political elite does not function in isolation from the dynamics of society at large. And even within the parameters of the patron-client regime in the developing world, or regimented systems or transitional states, the capacity of the political elite to manage the resources and to deliver depends on the nature of its legitimacy, its commitment, its formal education, its ideological base, its professional experience, the nature of the institutions in which it functions, and the citizens' preparedness and expectations.

It should be noted that the relationships between the principles, the structures, and the praxis of governance tend to reflect social gaps and tensions if the rules of the game of governing are not well defined and implemented. In the case of the USSR, one can hardly claim that in terms of the principles and structures of its institutions, there was monopoly of power as articulated within the 1977 Constitution. The centralized democracy produced and supported an extreme system of concentration of power among key personalities or in key positions in central institutions within specific hierarchical political areas. However, this system of governance, in its philosophical sense, did not seem to create space for monopolistic power as some would claim. Maybe in other areas of politics such as the Soviet Communist Party or the structure of the military, the rules were relatively different. What is suggested is that the tendencies of power monopoly were related more to the praxis than to the governing principles of the state.

The organs of state power were constituted by the Soviets of People's Deputies, which included: the Supreme Soviet of the USSR; the Supreme Soviets of the union republics; the Supreme Soviets of the autonomous republics; the territorial and provincial Soviets of People's Deputies; the Soviets of People's Deputies of autonomous provinces and autonomous areas; district, city, city-district, settlement, and village Soviets of People's Deputies (Article 89).

In general terms, Article 93 gives only some general idea about the centrality of power in the former Soviet Union. However, this centrality of power may not reveal the whole story about how decisions could be or were, in fact, influenced by what considerations or forces. Article 93 of the constitution states: "The Soviets of People's Deputies, directly and through organs created by them, direct all branches of state, economic, and socio-cultural construction, adopt decisions, ensure their execution, and supervise their implementation."

Within a comparative perspective used in this work, it would be necessary to add another brief discussion on the citizenship in the new configuration, namely, in the Russian Federation, and to determine whether there were any historical memories or continuity in the ways states and people define citizenship even after the socialist states had collapsed. We have been arguing that political culture that does not provide a space for continuity of some kind in the realm of state or policy formation is not likely to have the solid and relevant cultural capital needed for resources' mobilization and trust and confidence building.

The definition of citizenship used here is drawn from the December 1993 Constitution of the Russian Federation. Article 6 states that:

- Citizenship in the Russian Federation shall be acquired and terminated in accordance with federal law and shall be uniform and equal irrespective of the basis of its acquisition.

- Every citizen of the Russian Federation shall possess on its territory all rights and freedoms and bears equal obligations laid down by the constitution of the Russian Federation.

- A citizen of the Russian Federation may not be deprived of citizenship or of the right to change it.

It should be indicated that a citizen of the Russian Federation has similar rights or freedoms as stated in Chapter 2 of Human and Civil Rights and Freedoms, as those of the Bill of Rights in the United States Constitution. Therefore, there is no need to repeat their description here.

Concerning voting rights, which is also part of the definition of citizenship in any form of democracy, Article 60 states: "A citizen of the Russian Federation may independently exercise all rights and obligations in full from the age of 18 years. Article 62 states that a citizen of the Russian Federation may hold the citizenship of a foreign state (dual citizenship) in accordance with federal law or an international treaty of the Russian Federation. Another important question related to the question of citizenship is the eligibility for the office of the presidency. Who should be the president of the Russian Federation?

The President of the Federation is the head of the state, the most powerful political personality and the guarantor of the Constitution of the Russian Federation. Article 81 states:

- The President of the Russian Federation shall be elected for four years by citizens of the Russian Federation on the basis of the universal, equal, and direct suffrage in a secret ballot.

- A citizen of the Russian Federation who is at least 35 years of age and has been permanently a resident in the Russian Federation for at least 10 years may be elected President of the Russian Federation.

- The same person may not hold the office of President of the Federation for more than two executive terms. The powers of the president are described in Articles 84, 85, 86, 87 88, 89, 90, 91, and 93. He/she is the central power and can challenge any other institutions in the country, including the Duma (the Parliament). In principle and within the hierarchy of the power system, the President of the Federation has far more power than the former president of the Soviet Presidium.

Citizenship in the People's Republic of China

Like the USSR, the People's Republic of China (PRC) was born out of the proletarian revolution, in which many elements were borrowed from Marxist-Leninist ideology and supported by the Russian revolution. But later, Mao insisted on a "people's revolution" to distinguish his revolution from the Russian one. Thus Mao himself became part of the state ideology (Article 16, 1978 constitution). In his brand of revolution, people were generally defined as peasants and farmers, and not working class in a classical sense.

Citizenship can be defined in terms of its rights, duties, and obligations. What are the citizens' obligations, duties, and rights? What should be noted first is that in the Chinese Constitution of 1954 and its amended versions of 1961 and 1978, citizens' rights are codified. Their rights are clearly articulated in legal and political terms.

Chapter 3 in both the 1961 (twenty-eight articles) and 1978 (fifteen articles) versions of the Chinese Constitution entitled "Fundamental Rights and Duties of Citizens," fully describes citizens' expectations. The description of a few articles is necessary to identify elements of the definition in order to allow an accurate comparison. In Article 85 (1961 Constitution), it stated that "all citizens of the People's Republic of China are equal before the law."

In Article 86, it states that "all citizens of the People's Republic of China, who have reached the age of eighteen, have rights to vote and stand for election, irrespective of their nationality, race, sex, occupation, social origin, religious belief, education, property status, or length of residence, except insane persons and persons deprived by law of right to vote and stand for election. Women have equal rights with men to vote and stand for election."

In Article 87, it is also stated that "Citizens of the People's Republic of China enjoy freedom of speech, freedom of association, freedom of procession and freedom of demonstration." To ensure that citizens can enjoy these freedoms, the state provides the necessary material facilities. In Article 46 of the 1978 version of the Constitution, it is also stated that "Citizens enjoy freedom to believe in religion and freedom not to be in religion, and to propagate atheism."

The question of the relationship among nationalities is relevant to the process of defining citizenship, especially in a context where there are regional and national autonomous areas as in the former Soviet Union and Russia. In Article 3 of the 1961 Constitution, it is stated that "All the nationalities are equal." The 1978 Constitution, after the passing away of Chairman Mao, contains an amendment which added to the principle of equality that "There should be unity and fraternal love among the nationalities and they should help and learn from each other (Article 4)." Article 38 of this Constitution states that "In autonomous areas where a number of nationalities live together, each nationality is entitled to appropriate representation in organs of self-government."

In short, all the universal rights, basic rights or freedoms described in the United Nations Covenant, the French and Russian revolutions, as well as in the United States Constitution and Bill of Rights clearly describe what citizenship is in the Chinese Constitution. However, while the United States Constitution emphasizes individual rights, the Chinese Constitution uses the expression the "citizens' rights." Both types of rights imply different implications in the context in which they are used. Thus individual rights tend to be more personal and atomistic while citizens' rights can be projected as being more civil and societal. The Chinese Constitution deals essentially with the division of powers and the articulation of "citizens'rights" based on Marxism-Leninism-Maoism.

Issues Concerning Citizenship in Africa

Introduction: General Context and Issues

Although the sociological classification of citizenship in Africa is an important element in finding or proposing solutions to the crisis of nationality and citizenship in most parts of Africa, in this book I did not expand on it. However, suffice to note that as the crisis of the political identity of the African state intensifies, the more the Africans define themselves essentially as members of their ethnic groupings. These functional forces become the exits from the dominant system as survival mechanisms. The value of sociological citizenship has been articulated by Mwayila Tshiyembe in these terms:

> Although colonial domination disrupted the process of state-building, African societies remain plurinational in nature. The pre-colonial nations that marked out the identities of these multinational states survived: even though they were parceled out and often dispersed among several states, it was not impossible to re-forge societal links. An unexpected consequence of the crisis in the nation state is that the concept of nation is no longer shackled by the law, or by revolutionary mystique. The break-up of the Soviet Union and Yugoslavia, the separation between the Czech Republic and Slovakia, the Tutsi genocide and the chaos in Somalia are all proof of that. From now on it will be possible to distinguish between the legal nation—the state—and the sociological nation— the ethnic group. The sociological nation is founded on shared language, blood ties, religion and a common history, and an evident desire to live together. It is the bedrock of nationality of origin. But the post-colonial state merely notes its existence, having no historical or administrative memory of the people and countries juxtaposed, because colonialism wanted it to be that way (1999, p. 1).

The above lengthy statement indicates how complex the question of citizenship is; it is legally and politically a byproduct of the machinations of the colonial political structures without the foundation of a broad historical and cultural collective consciousness. And yet, as elaborated elsewhere, this collective consciousness is responsible for forming the fabric of being a nation (Lumumba-Kasongo, 2001). However, in this chapter I am interested, in a broad way, in defining some general characteristics of citizenship and in identifying its political significance and implications; that is to say, the contradictions and functionalities of the contemporary state.

In the post–Cold War era, the African state's "obsession" to redefine citizenship has been highly disproportional as compared to its efforts and actual policies to deal effectively and efficiently with social and economic issues, which are needed for the collective and individual welfare of its society. The opposition parties and ruling parties have selectively used definitions of citizenship to challenge some candidates or to try to exclude other candidates from running for presidential offices. Thus, the citizenships of political personalities such as Mobutu of the Democratic Republic of Congo, Kamuzu Banda of Malawi, Dos Santo of Angola, Kaunda of Zambia, Tchiluba of Zambia, and Ouattara of Côte d'Ivoire have been challenged by politicians to stop them from running for the highest offices in their countries. In some cases, the challenges were real and fact-based, while in other cases they were either fictive or the product of wishful thinking or rumor.

In most parts of Africa, at the time of colonization in the nineteenth century, African people, kings, queens, slaves, free people, bureaucrats, and technocrats were turned into large classes of subjects with no or few rights. This also meant change in the nature of loyalty. Thus, obviously, they were forced to lose their traditional or national citizenship often across the new borders or social status. Within the class of subjects, there were also layers of many other types of subclass relationships such as caste, local slavery, and nobility, which will not be examined in this context. Nevertheless, it is important to state that the social hierarchy was decoded differently. On this specific aspect of class-of-subjects basis, many African societies were forced to move from being culturally and politically complex societies to becoming simple economic societies regulated by the laws of exploitation. Although the word "subject" does not necessarily mean pacifism, in general terms, the subjects were directly associated with forced labor and enslavement. It implies the negation of rights and humanity, exploitation, and subjugation.

Two dominant strategies or approaches, namely assimilation and indirect rule, which were used to colonize Africa, produced mechanisms that led to different human classifications in the colonies. Political decolonization through various forms and paths brought new constitutions and citizenship. In the postcolonial era, most African subjects were assimilated into civil citizenship without significantly changing the nature of their "sociological citizenship" status.

The Question of Citizenship in Côte d'Ivoire

The question of citizenship in Côte d'Ivoire has to be examined within the premiscs of French politics in Africa at large. As compared to Senegal, where four communes provided French citizenship to Africans with similar entitlements and rights as those of the French Europeans since 1875, in Côte d'Ivoire, which became a colony after the Berlin Conference of 1884–1885, all Ivorians were subjects like *les originaires* in Senegal. But it should be pointed out that the African-French citizens who fought in Europe alongside the French Europeans in World War II were not treated as equal to the French nationals.

On this question of French citizenship, Harshé made the following interesting observation:

> Africans steeped in the French educational system could acquire French citizenship and participate in politics. However, the political participation of Africans in the functioning of the Republic was negligible. The French rulers had divided Africans into two groups viz. Citizens and subjects. Only four communes of Senegal, (Dakar, Rufusque, Gorée, and Saint Louis) enjoyed the citizenship of France. The four communes sent one representative to the chamber of Deputies from 1875. The citizens of Senegal had been electing representatives to govern the four communes of Senegal since 1872. Citizenship also gave them rights to form political parties and other voluntary associations. In contrast to the four communes of Senegal, the rest of the people in West Africa were the subjects. They had no right to send representatives to the metropolitan institutions. They were victims of forced labour and *indigénat* (1984, p. 6).

It should also be mentioned that the opposition to, and the struggles against, French colonization were stronger and sharper in Côte d'Ivoire than in any parts of the former French West Africa. As Harshé noted:

> Ivory Coast's political history has a few distinct features. Unlike Senegal, a coastal state, which virtually became a gate-way of colonial expansion after the seventeeth century, the conquest of Ivory Coast was hardly an easy task. France established its presence in Ivory Coast by the turn of the nineteenth century but it was unable to consolidate its rule there due to a sustainable resistance of the Ivorians to the French advance. It took the French army almost six years (1909–1915) to crush the uprisings in Ivory Coast. No other West African state had resisted the French rule on this scale (1984, p. 19).

In the second period of colonization, after World War II, the resistance, which did not go away, reappeared in a more ideological form. Even after massive exile, brutal assassinations, and elimination of the radical national elements such as chiefs, the French colonial administration did not have any political and psychological disposition and means to transform this territory into either a *département* (district) such as Martinique and Guadeloupe, or an autonomous territory. Ivorians, like people in other colonies, were subjected to all the rules and conditions of colonized entities as elsewhere in colonized Africa. The status of Ivorians changed only toward the end of the French colonial experience. As Harshé indicated:

> The passage of *Loi-cadre* reforms in June 1956 changed the structure of relations between France and French Africa. They provided, as observed by William Zartman, the institutional stimulus to the formation of eight new states. *Loi-cadre* reforms granted universal adult suffrage to the Africans. The distinction between citizens and subjects was no longer insisted upon. Also, the system of double college was abolished and French citizens were placed on the same footing with the Africans (1984, p. 33).

In short, the issue of citizenship as Rajen Harshé indicated has to be localized within the logic and political philosophy of the P.D.C.I-R.D.A's opposition to the exploitation of black people and also within the personal ambition and vision of Houphouët-Boigny. He believed in maintaining a special political and economic space for Côte d'Ivoire and carving a particular relationship with France, after he de-linked from the metropolitan communist alliance.

Since the 1990s, the issue of citizenship has become central and potentially explosive in Côte d'Ivoire's political discourse and power struggle since Alassane Ouattara, the former deputy director of the IMF and the former Prime Minister of Félix Houphouët-Boigny in Côte d'Ivoire decided to run for the office of the presidency. He was constitutionally and legally disqualified from running because he was a Burkinabè citizen as evidenced by official documents dating from the 1960s. This issue has led to further segmentation of the Ivorian political elite, polarization of the society on a regional basis, and the brutal manipulation of primordial attachments among the leaders of political parties, especially Alassane Ouattara's political organization, with consequences that could lead to more violence and even to a future civil war. It contributed to uprisings, a military coup in December 1999, and the violent military coup of d'état attempt and the rebellion of September 19, 2002. It is this issue that motivated the military leader and the political oppositions to rally in making a new constitution in 2000. It is interesting to see how the previous constitutional provisions stand on this issue. However, it should be noted that this new constitution does not define who the Ivorian citizen is and what processes or mechanisms are to be used for becoming an Ivorian citizen.

The Constitution describes the rights of the "human person" and rights, duties, and liberties of the human being (Chapter 1) in universal terms. But it does not define in concrete and historical terms who ought to be an Ivorian citizen. For instance, in Article 2 it states that "the human person is sacred. All human beings are born free and equal in front of law…. and that the rights of human person are inviolables." It is probably assumed that the references to "human person" applies automatically to Ivorians as well.

It is only in relationship to the criteria of defining the qualifications of who should run for the office of the presidency that Ivorian citizenship/nationality is clearly referred to (in Article 35), as it states:

> The president of the Republic is elected for five years through direct universal suffrage. S/he is re-elected only once. The candidate to the presidential election has to be forty years more or less and not more than seventy-five years of age. S/he has to be of Ivorian origin, and born of a father and the mother both also of Ivoirian origin. S/he has never renounced his/her Ivorian nationality. S/he has never had another nationality.

The question of nationality and citizenship was fused in the common civil language of nationality. This fusion projects the assumption that all Ivorian nationals are or should be Ivorian citizens. This assumption must be clarified legally and constitutionally by defining, first of all, who Ivorian nationals are. In the current Constitution, Ivorian nationality is described only in universal, philosophical terms. Sociological and historical elements associated with nationality are completely absent. Yet, they constitute an important source of social and political capital in Côte d'Ivoire. Côte d'Ivoire, as in other African countries, is composed of many ethnic groups. People define themselves as being both Ivorian citizens and simultaneously as Agni, Baoulé, Bété, Dioula, Sénoufo, etc. Some of these groups and their subgroups are located in other neighboring countries and are citizens of those countries. What is the place of this element of nationality, which was not even mentioned in the constitution, in the formation of the state?

While in Western constitutions, including that of France, there is a cult of citizenship, in Côte d'Ivoire nationality is described only in relationship to the articles on presidency and indirectly in relationship to the vision of the international institutions. That is to say, the question of citizenship is still a secondary issue in the current national political discourse. Yet it is, in reality, central in the reconfiguration of the nation-state.

Law no. 61-415 of December 1961, modified the Ivorian Nationality code by the law no. 72-852 of December 21, 1972. Its Title 2, Article 6, providing the following:

- A legitimized or legitimated child, born in Côte d'Ivoire except in case his two parents are foreigners.

- A child born out of wedlock in Côte d'Ivoire except if his/her filiation is legally established vis-à-vis his/her two foreign parents, or one parent, also a foreigner.

Article 7 of the law of December 21, 1972, also continues to articulate that:

- A legitimate or legitimated child, born in a foreign country by one Ivorian parent.

- A child born out of wedlock, in a foreign country in which the filiation is legally established vis-à-vis the Ivorian parent.

In these two articles, the blood argument is central to the definition of Ivorian nationality. Further, the notion of legal claim is important in case one parent is Ivorian and another is not. Ivorian nationality is automatic if both parents are legally Ivorians.

In the same above law, it is stipulated that a child whose objective is for adoption acquires Ivorian nationality if one of the adopting parents is of Ivorian nationality.

Article 13 further stipulates that under dispositions of Articles 13, 14, and 40, a foreign woman who marries an Ivorian man acquires Ivorian nationality at the time of the wedding celebration.

Nationality can also be obtained by naturalization: naturalization in respect to specificity of steps and exigencies such as five years of residency for foreigners who do not have blood or marriage linkages or two years of residency (Article 27) for a foreigner born in Côte d'Ivoire or married to an Ivorian woman and for any one who has rendered special important services such as in the arts, sciences or literature, industries, inventions or establishment in Côte d'Ivoire's industrial or agricultural sector.

Nationality can further be acquired by reintegration, which is given also by decree after investigation. In addition, in all cases, Article 32 stipulates that none can have an Ivorian nationality if he/she does not have good customs or morals. It should be noted that according to Article 44, the naturalized person who rendered to Côte d'Ivoire exceptional services or the person whose naturalization presents for Côte d'Ivoire an exceptional interest, may be elevated in spite of the incapacities anticipated in Article 43. In addition to blood linkage mentioned earlier, imperatives associated with labor, individual achievements, and human character are among the criteria that support the acquisition of Ivorian nationality. On that ground, the Ivorian laws of nationality are not very different from those of other countries.

The question of citizenship has become central to the national political discourse in Côte d'Ivoire because partially Côte d'Ivoire is a country with a large proportion of migrants from throughout West Africa and also because of the unlimited ambition of Allassane Ouattara to become the president of Côte d'Ivoire. He intended to replace his boss, President Félix Houphouët-Boigny at his passing away in 1993, even if the law in the matter of succession of a deceased or incapacitated president presented no ambiguity, and thus disqualified him from holding that office. Social and political contradictions related to migrants and Allassane Ouattara's opportunistic perspective to use and manipulate the weak migrant factor contributed to controversy in the debate on citizenry. All sources point out, as indicated above, that Allassane Ouattara was from Burkina Faso at the time he was offered the position by President Félix Houphouët-Boigny. But after the death of the latter, he decided to become the president of Côte d'Ivoire without legally fulfilling the criterion of citizenship first.

The debate on citizenship in Côte d'Ivoire has been, for various purposes and ends, a political football for the national politicians, international human rights' organizations, and the so-called foreign donors. For the Ivorians, it is an emotionally charged issue partially because of the nature of the role of Côte d'Ivoire in West Africa in particular and in Africa in general. Because the sources of sociological citizenship are lacking in the Ivorian Constitution, there is a need to interpret universalism in the light of national perspectives.

Citizenship in Kenya

The discussion on the question of citizenship in Kenya will be relatively shorter than, for instance, that of Côte d'Ivoire or the United States. Even with the background of the presence of Somali, many of whom have lived as refugees in Kenya for many years and who should become citizens, the debate on citizenship has not yet provoked the same kind of emotions and anxiety as it has in Côte d'Ivoire or in the Democratic Republic of Congo. Kenya has also a significant population of Somali ethnic groups as part of its citizenry, which share similar cultural characteristics with the Somali groups in Somalia.

It is necessary to mention that there was no attempt by the British colonial administration to transform Kenyans to British citizens as compared to the so-called assimilation policy of the French, especially when the proposition of *communauté* was made. There was a sharp philosophical, political, and social difference between the subjects and the rulers. The notion of Black or African British was not quite envisioned and elaborated in this particular paradigm. That does not mean that individual Kenyans did not become British citizens. It means only that, in principle, according to the Dual Mandate dogma, which can be summarized by the so-called indirect rule, Kenyans were ruled only as subjects separated from metropolitan rule. However, it should be noted that Kenya was a settler's colony. Thus, direct rule was also effectively applied. Based on the dual mandate of Lugard, all the Kenyans were the subjects of Great Britain, having their protection from the colonial political structures and also the native laws that governed the colonial entities.

At the time of independence, citizenship in Kenya was obviously defined with respect to the colonial rules. This is so because the Kenyan revolution led by the Mau-Mau was halted. As it is articulated in Chapter VI of its revised Constitution of 1998, everyone who was born in Kenya before or on December 11, 1963, any citizen of the United Kingdom, British protected person or of the Republic of Ireland who was in Kenya became citizens of Kenya. Children of Kenyan citizens and spouses of Kenyan men are also qualified to become citizens of Kenya. Other lawful residents of Kenya can apply for naturalized

Kenyan citizenship. All the modalities and processes are clearly articulated in Chapter V of the Constitution. In Côte d'Ivoire too, at the time of independence, people who were not of the Ivorian origins but who were born in Côte d'Ivoire were given a timeframe in which to apply for their Ivorian citizenship.

As to the question of who is qualified to be a candidate for the office of the president, in Chapter 1 of the Constitution, it is indicated that the candidate shall be a citizen of Kenya and be also thirty-five years old. The candidate must respect many other rules regarding residency, domestic, and political requirements. As for legislative office, one has to be a citizen of Kenya, be twenty one years old, and respect other rules as stipulated in the constitution. In both cases, one must be able to speak the Kiswahili language. It should also be noted that in both cases, the issue of naturalization has not been posed. Citizenship seems to be the most important criterion whether one is naturalized or is Kenyan born. Kenya does not accept dual citizenship. Unlike the new Ivorian Constitution, the precedent does not matter. What counts is the citizenship at the time the person decides to run for the office of president. At the age of twenty-one, individuals who become of age with other citizenship must make the final decision on which citizenship they want to keep.

As in other constitutions, the citizen's rights in Kenya are fully described in Chapter V between Sections 70 and 85. They are articulated in the forms of universal and basic rights that one can find in such charters as those of the United Nations, the Organization of the African Unity (OAU), international conventions, the United States Bill of Rights, and the declarations of the French Revolution. Rights are set out in Section 70, which states:

> Whereas every person in Kenya is entitled to the fundamental rights and freedoms of the individual, that is to say, the right, whatever his (sic) race, tribe, place of origin or residence or other local connection, political opinions, color, creed or sex, but subject to respect for the rights and freedoms of others and for the public interest.

Kenyan citizenship is articulated differently from the definition of the so-called tribe, which is closely related to ethnicity or to nationality in some cases. It is strongly associated with the notion of the sovereignty of the state.

As compared to the Republic of Benin Constitution in which the traditional chiefs, as distinct political entities, play an important role in nation-building as articulated in the post-National Conference Constitution, in Côte d'Ivoire, the Democratic Republic of Congo, or Kenya although they also are plural societies, the concept of what I have characterized as national/ethnic citizenry or sociological citizenship is absent. If mentioned, it is not defined in the postcolonial constitutions as being an important factor in decision making or state building. It is simply instrumental to state building. Ethnicity is conceived more as an "inferior" concept in terms of the degree of power associated with it in contrast to the notion of civil citizenship.

NOTES

1.   "Civil Rights Cases," 109 U.S. 3, 22 (1883) as cited by Killian and Costellio, in the *Constitution of the United States*, 1996, p. 1553.

2.   "Afroying v. Rust," 387 U.S. 253, 262-63 (1967) as cited by Killian and Costellio, op. cit., p. 1567.

3.   "Insurance Co. v. New Orleans," 13 Fed. Cas. 67 (C.C.D. La.1870) cited in Killian and Costellio, op. cit.

Chapter 4

Democracy as a Global Force[1]

Introduction: Objectives and Issues

In its essence, democracy, like capitalism, is an ideology. That is to say, it is a belief system that contains great ideas, a guiding, systematic doctrine applicable to the individual, society, social groups, social movements, political parties, and political relations. It also has generally practical devices and internal and external mechanisms for producing and reproducing itself.

The main objective in this section is not to expand the discussion on the historiography of either democracy or globalization. Rather, the intent is to examine various elements that compose contemporary democracy in order to construct a broad definition and create intellectual consensus on what is being studied and claimed, with special attention to liberal democracy. In the twenty-first century, liberal or formal democracy (what Leon Trotsky earlier called political democracy) has become central in terms of its claims, the rise of the number of the electoral processes in the world, and also as a new prerequisite for access to corporate, global financial institutions.

This section examines the philosophical claims of liberal democracy with the intention of identifying its power base within the logic of the realist paradigm in political science. Thus, in order to accomplish the above purpose, the dominant general characteristics of globalization and liberal democracy are examined with the objective of discussing how they have been projected or incorporated into the dogma and power of the state and the corporate world. The discussion is mainly theoretical, but it contains some historical, political illustrations and also examines social implications.

In this introduction, the issues related to the meanings of democracy within the context of broad intellectual and political traditions are briefly explored. Thus, a brief discussion includes the views of Aristotle, Karl Marx, and a limited number of contemporary dominant political theorists who have made important contributions in the area of political development. Some of the author's previous works are used to contrast various perceptions and deduce general characteristics of this phenomenon.

Democracy is probably one of the most used and misused expressions in the post–Cold War era by social scientists, states, civil societies, political parties, social movements, and global institutions. Are all the social forces using it aware of its meanings? There is no definition of democracy that is likely to fit all the historical and sociological cases where the menus of democracy have been formulated and implemented. Regional and local particularities and differences have been accepted in a comparative study as a normal process, though in sciences the struggle is to produce theories that can be used to explain large samples and complex situations. However, despite diversity in defining various forms of democracy and its various sociological meanings, philosophically, all forms of democracy should share some common meanings.

A reflection on democracy is an enriching social and analytical exercise. It is partially so because the concepts of democracy are not only located in the domain of good or relevant ideas and theories; rather they are firmly actualized in the practical domains of society, namely in civil societies, social movements, and policy arenas. It is not only a reflective field. In some countries, it has become a "way of life": a civil culture. For the majority of people in the world, the expression "democracy" has become almost a magic word. It is expected to imply almost everything, from development, to rights, liberty, social justice, and access to power. But, it should also be noted that the more the word is used, the more confusion it seems to bring, especially to people whose conditions have been worsening as part of the adversity of the world economy. Thus, the necessity for debating the meaning of democracy is vital not only to this book, but also to the real world. Its meanings should be understood and appreciated within the larger context of the international, regional, and national political economies.

For Aristotle, democracy literally means "rule by the *demos*," which in Greek means "the whole people." The notion of the "whole people" implies "all those with rights of citizenship." For some, it is a rule by the majority and the poor. In this kind of democracy, the poor, who are generally the majority, should not be given special privileges, as Mulgan paraphrasing Aristotle stated:

> In such [a system] the law lays down that poor shall not enjoy any advantage over the rich, that neither class shall be exactly similar. For if, as is generally to be found in democracy, and also equity, this condition is best realized when all share in equal measure the whole constitution (1977, p. 75).

It should be noted that Aristotle treated democracy harshly because for him it was a pervasive system. He advocated polity as the best form of government because it is a mixture of democracy and oligarchy, which produces a moderate system.

In contemporary societies, the ideas of democracy in their various forms are central to scholarship in the discipline of political science and its related subfields. From Plato and Aristotle to de Tocqueville, Rousseau, Locke, Lincoln, Karl Marx, Madison, Gandhi, Houphouët-Boigny, Mandela, and Nyerere, the ideas of democracy have included some elements of universal suffrage, social justice, equality, participation, development, and fulfillment of human rights and human happiness. It is a philosophical and practical concept. Within the perspective of a critical theory (or praxis), in a democracy, the author argues, the unity of ethics and politics is likely to be finalized.

Karl Marx, who was not against the social idea of democracy, was very critical of bourgeois democracy, which he considered to be an instrument of class oppression, designed to reproduce the system of exploitation, as he stated:

> The large-scale industry and universal competition of modern capitalism created their own political set-up, the democratic republic: the unlimited despotism of one class over other classes, an instrument of exploitation of wage labor by capital, a machine for the oppression of one class by another. On this view, the liberal representative state serves its essential purpose by repressing threats from subordinate groups or classes (e. g. by the use of police and army to break strikes), by providing services to individual capitalists (energy resources, roads railways, subsidies), by arbitrating disputes between capitalists, by preventing unpredictable market fluctuations, and by securing foreign markets, through either diplomacy or military intervention (Femia, 1993, pp. 46-47).

Since the end of the twentieth century, especially after the Soviet Empire collapsed, liberal democracy as a powerful idea has reached most parts of the world. It has expressed itself differently but its claims have been generally . received as universal. In a book that is concerned about citizenship, power, and ideology and their implications in social development and nation-state building, it is important to elaborate on the role of liberal democracy in political and social transformation. As liberal democracy has been globalized, it is important before continuing further discussion on the subject to examine briefly the globalized dimensions of this kind of democracy.

Liberal Democracy and Its Globalization

A. General Issues Related to Globalization and World Politics

Globalization also means different things to different people. Thus, it should be emphasized that globalization is not a homogeneous and uniform phenomenon. As Shome and Hedge stated:

> It is uneven and heterogeneous in its workings and effects, its velocity and speed, its differential negotiations with structures of nations, economy, culture and international relations, in the unequal ways in which it is experienced by

people across different spaces, and, finally, in its complex and uneven productions of new forms, planes, and configurations of power (2002, p. 175).

Furthermore, also according to Hilaire French,

> To some, globalization is synonymous with growth of global corporations whose far-flung operations transcend national boundaries and allegiances. To others, it signals a broader cultural and social integration, spurred by mass communications and the Internet. The terms can also refer to the growing permeability of international borders to pollution, microbes, refugees, and other forces (2000, p. 4).

Furthermore, it should be emphasized that more and more on a daily basis we are wearing clothes or shoes made in China, Italy, Spain, or Hong Kong. We use watches made in Switzerland or France. We drive cars made in Japan or Germany. We decorate our floors with carpets made in Iran, Pakistan, or Bangladesh. We buy household tools, televisions, and stereo sets made in Japan or South Korea. Many people feed themselves with grain grown elsewhere. Many people drink coffee and tea cultivated in Colombia or Kenya and eat chocolate made from cocoa grown in Côte d'Ivoire, Ghana, or Peru. A computer virus created in the Philippines can reach where we are located in a matter of a few hours and disturb and disrupt our plans and work. The first atomic bomb that was dropped by the United States on Hiroshima and Nagasaki in Japan in August 1945 was made with uranium from the Democratic Republic of Congo. Are we more global today than we were yesterday? What does globalization mean in our understanding of world politics and in our relationships to other people that we meet only through their labor or products, the Internet, and CNN? Democratically, we have the right to know how these products, which have become part of our identities, are produced. What are the living conditions of the people who produce them?

As used in this context, globalization is a movement of goods, ideas, information, services, and political, cultural and economic activities (including production, distribution, and consumption, as well as trade and investment) and their implications at the individual and societal levels across political boundaries. Over the years, especially in the twentieth century, the movement toward globalization has been accelerated by the power of technology, for instance, improvements in aeronautics and communications, including the telephone and the Internet. Furthermore, the following questions are relevant if we want to understand the nature of the impact of globalization in our lives in general terms.

The core questions are: Is globalization real or a myth? How does it function? What are its structures and its agencies? What forms has it taken in different parts of the world? What social and cultural values does it represent? What factors, internally and externally, have shaped it and have been shaped by it? More and more people, including scholars and social agencies, talk these days about one world, the global village, only one earth, and vanishing borders. The right-bearing membership of an ethno-territorial nation-state has changed significantly over the last quarter of the twentieth century. However, after several centuries of triumph over other forms of memberships in the political community, the concept of citizenship, the most important political element of the nation-state, is still unsettled. Obviously, the challenges to the nation-state have become global.

Within the changes that are taking place around and in us, the "global village" is one of the most culturally intriguing, geopolitically challenging, economically pragmatic, philosophically multifaceted, and intellectually multidisciplinary concepts to be thoroughly examined and understood. From where people are located socially and economically, what do all the expressions mentioned above mean if they were to be translated into the imperatives of local politics and policies, international relations, and political economy? This translation is important in the domains of policy analysis and practices of the global commerce.

What were the structures of the states and the international political economy in the twentieth century that should be understood? As we embody the germ of the past and build the present on the past, understanding of that past must flow from a holistic inquiry. But the past, the present, and the future all have their own specific moment, space, and time. They should not be confused in an eclecticism and monolithicism of the 'romantic' globalization.

In this section I not only raise some critical issues concerning the nature of the dynamics of world politics after the end of the Cold War era—a major period in the twentieth century that rapidly shaped the global economy and world politics, but I also attempt to examine and understand the nature of some of its implications for national and international relations and politics. Although this discussion is generally conceived as an intellectual effort to search for elements of a new theory of international relations, it uses illustrations from various countries around the world to clarify or to support or contradict my propositions. And, it also has policy and political implications. Thus, my specific objectives are summarized as follows:

- to define and understand structurally the dynamics of globalization and its implications as reflected in international relations, and political economy, and the struggle for democracies;
- to identify and examine the possible or real contradictions and benefits within the system individually and collectively; and
- to project how societies, people, and states can invent new political and economic possibilities that can satisfy the claims and demands of emerging international and national popular and social movements.

There are several approaches to studying globalization. One may deal with it in terms of its effects or its behaviors or one may consider its structures and its composition as vital to an examination of its social and policy implications. As a structuralist scholar, I use a historical-structuralist approach with a dose of systems analysis as articulated by the advocates of the world system. The way social classes, states, and societies function in the world system is strongly influenced by the internal and external dynamics of their locations. But these locations are far from being historically fixed or static. The world is a system and an organic whole; its behaviors are conditioned by the actors' locations and how they came to be in the system (Lumumba-Kasongo, June, 2002). I am interested in the history of social production and the reproduction of world politics. It is argued in this book that how a social system produces and reproduces itself in a given physical and social environment and at a given time is likely to inform us about the nature of the system itself, its weaknesses, and strengths. That is to say, I am interested in studying contradictions in a dialectical manner, not necessarily as pathological tools of destruction, but as reflective tools of objective conditions needed for any kind of constructive discourse.

On the optimistic side, let me say that although world politics, which is composed of more than 190 states and thousands of languages and ethno-cultures, is in a slippery transition in which there is no collective philosophical consensus in terms of its direction. This situation has further created an opportunity or some social space that can be used to shape the world in ways one could not have imagined one hundred years ago or even forty years ago. In order to shape world politics in an economically productive way, so that it can be, on social class or gender grounds, environmentally sustainable and sound, politically responsible, and philosophically forward-looking, there is a primary need for a critical, comprehensive understanding of the nature of the world system itself. This thinking has two main methodological components, namely deconstruction and reconstruction of the world of the states, as we have known it—in some cases for less than one hundred years and in other cases for over five hundred years.

We cannot, however, deconstruct and reconstruct something that we neither fully or significantly know nor understand. This is where the role of further research and paradigm building become central in institutions of higher learning. Are we ready to accept the notions of deconstruction and reconstruction of world politics as part of the local/national · political processes, international coalition building, and learning processes? Are we ready to challenge our fragile yet accepted ethnic, racial, national, and political identities?

Most social scientists or politicians were not able to predict the collapse of the Berlin Wall on November 9, 1989. Many people also could not predict with a high level of certainty the violent collapse of the Soviet Union in 1991, despite the fact that there were many forces, both internal and external, working against the consolidation of its social base. With the exception of people like Winnie Mandela, most people could not imagine that Nelson Mandela of the African National Congress (ANC), who was considered a terrorist by the apartheid government in South Africa, would be the first elected president of a liberal democratic South Africa after spending twenty-seven useless years in prison and would now enjoy the status of the most respected statesman in the world. What do all these illustrations have in common? Without going into detail, it is clear that within these cases there is a high level of unpredictability. Further, there is the premise that nothing is impossible, or as Napoleon Bonaparte once said, "'impossibility' is not a French expression." These two dimensions are also part of globalization.

Do we live in a world of illusion or of reality? Let me note before further discussion concerning globalization and liberal democracy that historically we cannot construct the world without a utopia. Within the puzzle called the world of the states, actors have always played different roles in pursuing their 'national' interests and maintaining some equilibrium within the system. Although in 2004, the social forces and institutions of the functioning world appear, to a large extent, to be closer to one another in geographical, technological, and selected cultural terms, and in cyberspace politics, in reality, on political and economic grounds, those elements are distancing themselves from one another now more than ever in many parts of the world. In the past fifteen to twenty years, the gaps between poor and rich countries and between poor and rich social groupings within countries, have increased. The world system is not a natural phenomenon. We make it the way it is for given concrete social, political and economic purposes. In order to understand why states and people behave the way they do, we must examine the nature of the structures of the society-state relations. The manifestation of social gaps or social cleavages between the haves and the have-nots is another element to be examined as part of globalization.

One of the most important manifest characteristics of the end of the last millennium and the opening years of this new one, is the movement of states and struggles of people to redefine themselves. This redefinition takes place in different ways, sometimes tragically as in the Balkans and in many parts of Africa, the Middle East, Central America, and sometimes gradually and peacefully. Nonetheless, the substance of the content of this redefinition and its intellectual quality depends on the dynamics of local political configurations, how a given people and state have become part of the world system, the location of these actors in the international political economy; what they bring to the global market; who the actors are, and what alliances they form.

This process of redefinition is facilitated by several phenomena: (1) the level of solidarity, which has become anti-nation state, among institutions and professional organizations across nation-states, is increasing. This solidarity is in part caused by the relatively high level of consciousness or awareness on the relevant issues. This rising consciousness is the product of the level of interdependence among the actors. (2) The search for new identities: In most parts of the world people are struggling to redefine themselves by using history and culture, while others are attempting to reconstruct new ideologies or even mythologies through accommodation to the global system. This struggle and the processes it creates lead to clashes between what are perceived as nationalistic values and the values which are considered as chosen or imposed by global market forces. Since the Treaty of Westphalia of 1648 in Europe and the subsequent colonization of almost the whole world, the common policy has been to make and define national identities in ideological, geopolitical and ethnic-linguistic terms protected by the state. It has been state policy to systematically weaken individual cultural values, because they were perceived as premodernist and "irrational" primordial forces, impediments to nationhood and the strengthening of civil culture. This is also a significant problem faced by the European Union in dealing with the political relationship between European state's identities and national cultural and historical identities.

And (3) the nature of new information and communication technologies and the role of the media both challenge the old national and individual identities and they create new ones in the contemporary international relations' context.

One of the issues that has been raised in this work concerns the perceived meaning of the electoral democracies among various social groups, as these democracies have existed in more than 180 countries. This process started in the 1970s in South America. In the 1980s, the process was accelerated in other subregions and regions of the world, including Asia and Africa. Popular and social movements and states' reforms have exploded at different periods. Grassroots movements, representing the bottom-up organizations, and petty bourgeois intellectual movements of top-down organizations, have challenged the states; the bottom-up movements have demanded the redefinition of rights as an instrument of development, and the top-down movements have articulated the power-sharing model of governance. The most important issue that should be raised in this context concerns the legitimacy and accountability of the nation-state. Although it is still the most important agency of political articulation in international relations, the nation-state is not the only agency that has the power and legitimacy to bargain in international affairs. Thus, another important dimension of globalization is the proliferation of voices in international politics.

There is a multiplicity of actors in world politics. For instance, in 1909, there were thirty-seven intergovernmental organizations, and by 1994, the number had increased to 263. In 1909, there were officially only 176 international nongovernmental organizations. By 1994, the number had increased to 4,928. The challenges from multinationals, or multilateral and transnational organizations, to the state or to centralized authority have obliged the state to make accommodations in order to be more effective and remain relevant. In most cases, as in Africa, the state did not undertake reforms by its own volition; it was more or less forced to do so. The central political affiliation, for instance, the meaning and substance of national citizenship, among the peasants, farmers, the middle classes, and the petty bourgeoisie in different parts of the world, have been relatively affected by the dynamics of the international political economy and by the existence of challenging and functioning affiliations mentioned or alluded to in this section.

Globalization and Its Characteristics in the International Political Economy

As indicated earlier, globalization is one of the most complex and difficult concepts to define with precision. Indeed, there are many globalizations and many processes and mechanisms that produce them. According to Shome and Hedge,

> Globalization as a phenomenon produces a state of culture in transnational motion—flows of people, trade, communication, ideas, technologies, finance, social movements, cross border movements, and more. Globalization thus inevitably also has a material dimension to it (Giddens, 2000). Further, globalization is not just about "culture in motion." Rather, it is about what Appadurai calls relations of disjunctures (and conjunctures) that are produced by unequal transnational flows of capital and culture that precipitate new problems and planes of inequalities that challenge many of our theoretical frameworks for studying culture. Additionally, rather than just being a series of mere sporadic cross-national encounters, globalization refers to an entrenched pattern of world-wide connectedness (Held and McGrew, 2000) and disconnectedness (an issue that seems to receive less attention), caused by growing intensity of flows across national boundaries such that these borders themselves become a contested category as they are articulated in differential ways to the structures of the global (2002, p. 174).

However, structurally and historically, it is possible to identify its major characteristics and the processes of its reproduction. Globalization is not new. The contemporary form of globalization has its origins in the pre-nineteenth-century capitalist economy. Ted Lowi refers to globalization I, which roughly extended from 1880 to 1914 (2001, p. 133). This phase was supported by the dynamics of the Age of Reason in philosophy, the arts, and sciences, the end of mercantilism, and the adoption of the new dogmas of the Catholic Church. These dogmas, which were intellectually and politically revolutionary in the interpretations of human beings as freer animals, were known as part of the reformist movements in Western Europe. The movements systematically started in the sixteenth century in what became Germany. The protestant ethic and the spirit of capitalism were born out of these reformist movements.

Capitalism was developed in Europe after its inception in the Mediterranean region, not as a national force. It was after the industrial revolution in England in the nineteenth century, the American Revolution in 1776, and the French Revolution in 1789 that capitalism started to consolidate its mission of global exploitation. Its development was part of the rise of the new bourgeoisie in France that François Guizot, the leader of constitutionalism *à l'Anglaise* after the revolution, called, *"les capacités"* (Howard, 2002, p. 144). In France, political liberalism and economic liberalism developed as part of a monistic thought as characterized by the famous impérative attributed to Guizot: *"Enrichez-vous"* (Enrich yourself/selves) (p. 145). It should be noted that the combined values of labor and market made capitalism, from its inception, an international phenomenon and a potential global force. "Labor for sale" was its motto. It was built on the foundation of a slave economy and of power and class struggles. It was consolidated later by the enlightenment and liberalism. It entered its current global phase after World War II, when production systems, and even social classes, became transnationalized (Ninsin, 1998, p. 25). Since then, the world has been bound together by an unprecedented volume of trade, capital, and financial inflows (Amin, 1990, p. 85). As Hilary French stated:

> Growth in trade has consistently outpaced the global economy since World War II. The world economy has grown sixfold since 1950, rising from $6.7 trillion to $41.6 trillion in 1998. But exports increased 17-fold over this period, reaching $5.4 trillion in 1998. While exports of goods accounted for only 5 percent of the gross world product in 1950, by 1998 this figure had climbed to 13 percent (2000, p. 5).

In the past twenty-five to thirty years, globalization has been popularly used to depict the extraordinary scale and intensity of the world's economic transactions, aided by revolutions in science and technology. It is important to point out what happened at the beginning of the 1970s. Although the United States was still a superpower in the 1970s, it lost its status of hegemonic power, as Great Britain did in the 1870s. But, it should be also noted that toward the end of the nineteenth century, international relations and domestic politics were qualitatively different than those of the 1970s. However, between the 1940s and 1970s, various roles played by the United States government, United States–based multinational corporations and banks, its military science and technology, its foreign policy, and modernization school of thought after the end of World War II, were central to the process of defining globalization. The principles and policies used for the reconstruction of Western Europe after World War II, including the Marshall Plan (1947), the private U.S. banks, the formation of the North Atlantic Treaty Organization (NATO), and the creation of the International Bank for Reconstruction (the World Bank), the International Monetary Fund (IMF), and the General Agreements on Tariffs and Trade (GATT), testify to the vital role that the United States has played in reconceptualizing globalization. The "dollarization" of the world market, followed by "coca-colazation" of the world plays an important role in this new globalization, of which the United States is the major agent. Today, globalization has reached even the domains of social and cultural aspects of individuals and communities such as arts, popular music and culture, and food as its processes have also been facilitated by the liberalization of the world economy and financial resources, as van de Walle cited by Kwame Ninsin (1998: 26) stated:

> The growth of international trade has been particularly rapid; increasing on average at one and a half times the rate of growth of world GDP between 1965

and 1990 [...]. Foreign direct investment (FDI) rose at an even faster rate than trade during the 1980s. In 1990, the total stock of FDI exceeded $2,700 billion, roughly double the 1988 level and equal to about 10 percent of world economic output. [...] The most awesome growth has come in foreign exchange markets, where the daily transactions recorded by the Bank for International Settlements more than doubled between 1989 and 1995, to reach $1.2 trillion a day, in some 150,000 different transactions. Markets for other financial assets such as government bonds and various derivatives have also undergone strong growth, and have become seemingly impervious to effective regulation by national governments.

In this borderless dimension of globalization, Ted Lowi citing Eichengreen (1997, pp. 377-382) indicates that

> Annual turnover in global capital exchanges rose from an estimated $188 billion to $1.2 trillion in 1995, and is still rising. Cross-border capital transanctions in the G7 countries rose tenfold in that period, but more striking is involvement of the developing world outside G7. The biggest capital importers between 1990 and 1995 were, in descending order, China, Mexico, Brazil, South Korea, Malaysia, Argentine, Thailand, and Indonesia, and significant major newcomers are Bolivia, Poland, Russia, India, and Vietnam (2001, p. 133).

Two important aspects of globalization, which have been projected by the World Bank and the IMF as the forces of globalization in a complementary policy perspective are the privatization and the liberalization of the market and the public domain. These two dogmas have become the most important forces of globalization. The rules of the World Bank and the IMF have become the international rules or guidelines used by the local/national, regional, and multilateral financial institutions. Privatization and liberalization have become global not only in their content but also in their implementation.

The objectives and the mission of the IMF and the World Bank have already been well defined and established. Their main objective has been to restructure the world economy so that it can meet the requirements of capitalism. Restructuring is in fact another expression for deregulation, the movement that has been central to policy changes in regional economic organizations such as the European Union and the North American Free Trade Agreement (NAFTA). In developing countries, their programs have been called Structural Adjustment Programs (SAPs). Deregulation is defined as "the removal of controls on economic activity to allow the market forces to act unhindered by government intervention. A relative rather than an absolute concept—intervention is reduced rather than totally removed" (Hague, et al., 1992, p. 461).

Despite the claims of universalism associated with their programs, however, SAPs' objectives are diversified and their programs have not been uniformly adopted in all countries as has been claimed. They can only be summarized by the following points: to implement measures to stop economic decline and improve the general performance of a country's economy and to assist in assessing budget deficits and imbalances in import/export terms of trade through packages of corrective measures. Most of the adjustment programs in Africa and South America contain varying degrees of corrective policies focusing on devaluation of the currency, interest rates, reduction of government expenditures to line up with real resources, privatization, liberalization, and institutional reforms. Exchange rate policy is supposed to effectively devalue currency so that those export commodities can become cheaper and more attractive to foreign buyers. Terms of trade are expected to be fully liberalized and to improve the movement of goods and fiscal policies by removing tax and tariff barriers. Interest rate policies are undertaken to encourage the population to save money and to tighten credit so that people borrow less. The government is encouraged to cut spending on subsidies and other services. In short, adjustment programs in general include reforms to:

- establish a market-determined exchange rate;
- bring fiscal deficits under control;
- liberalize trade; and
- improve the financial sector, the efficiency of public enterprises, and the coverage and quality of social services.

Finally, what are the major attributes of the global system? Despite the inconsistencies and incoherence in the ways in which the global system operates, expands, and reproduces itself, the world has become a real, functional machine. This system is composed of many different parts and subsystems. But the system is larger than the sum of its parts. For the purpose of this discussion, the following attributes and characteristics of the world can be summarized thus:

- the growing interdependence and interactions among the actors;
- an explosion of the number of actors;
- a relatively high level of consciousness or awareness of the role of the actors;
- the diminishing classical significance of the meanings of systems of boundaries both at the state and international levels as well as at the personal level;
- a relatively high level of interpersonal and cross-cultural relations among people belonging to different orbits of powers and cultures;
- a tendency toward homogenization of cultures;
- the weakening of the notion of state sovereignty;
- liberalization of the market; and
- the privatization of the state.

In short, globalization in international political economy refers to:

A growing openness of national economies to economic activity by companies from other states, greater interdependence between different national economies, as well as the harmonization of what is produced, exported and imported within a nation with 'demands' of the international economy (also referred to as 'integration' into the global economy). Companies embark on the process because of the promise of higher profits and in response to competition in the market (Primo and Taylor, 1999, p. 11).

From policy points of view, globalization also means that more and more decisions made by governments, companies, trade unions, nongovernmental organizations (NGOs), learning institutions, and professional organizations in civil societies are influenced by events happening elsewhere in the world.

Democracy Factors That Have Been Globalized

What factors associated with the electoral democracies have been globalized? Have the demands of democracy and the processes of producing democracies become global? Through a new wave of democratization movements, though it is not ideologically coherent, democracy has been claimed by most people the world over. Theoretically, the demand for democracy has become global. In 2003, from the movements that started in the 1970s, the world over can be characterized by what Victor Hugo once said: "*On peut resister à une armée mais jamais à une idée dont le temps est venu,*" ("One can resist an army but never an idea whose time has come.")

After the end of World War II, many countries in different subregions of the Global South were still under the domination of the colonial powers. As indicated earlier, the new processes of globalization were set up with the creation of three major agencies of the United Nations, namely the World Bank, the IMF, and the GATT. In fact these new global forces not only produced undemocratic effects and behaviors, but they also functioned undemocratically. Thus, while there was strong economic growth between 1945 and 1960 as indicated in the first part of this book, democracy was not firmly a part of the economic equation as a global force. Even in Western Europe, the first priority of the reconstruction movement was based on economic determinism and military and security policies. In Western Europe, however, reconstruction was facilitated by the fact that it had relatively "mature states."

Although some countries in the Global South won their independence by borrowing from the dogmas of liberal democracy and building fragile institutions such as chambers of representatives or assemblies, in general, the struggle for democracy as an issue of political rights was not uniquely identified and distinguished from the overall strategic struggles for independence. The discourse of self-determination at the international level, which was articulated and promoted by the United States, was essentially adopted in many countries as a national liberation objective or nation-state building dogma. The priorities of most movements and political parties that led to political independence in the majority of countries focused more on building nation-states and promoting the ideas of constitutional rights and political sovereignty than on procedural democracies and the pursuit of individual political rights. The rights of the nation-state were perceived as more important and comprehensive than the rights of the citizens. It was assumed that the "immortality" of the states would later create the conditions for the institutionalization of democracy. However, the Universal Declaration of Human Rights, composed of a preamble and thirty articles adopted by the Third General Assembly of the United Nations on December 10, 1948, is one of the most important international elements that contributed to the rise of the struggles for democracy.

The polarization of the world by the ideological, military, and power struggles between the Soviet Union and the United States did not contribute to the development of liberal democracy. On the contrary, these struggles inhibited possibilities of the rise and expansion of both the centralized democracy (democracy as defined by the central political institutions and not by individuals) and liberal democracy models, by controlling the agencies of social change, including the people, in the name of the state's ideology and security. Wherever these models were experienced, in most situations, they were used as instruments of control and manipulation. During the Cold War era, states apparatuses, especially ruling political parties and executive branches of government, essentially served as national intelligence agencies for the superpowers, helping them to collect information, to recruit, and to intimidate progressive forces. Both categories of rights, namely social rights and political rights, which are considered to be the foundation of democracy, were limited and constrained by the dicta of the dominant ideologies. In fact, this international conflict created an undemocratic world, heavily armed and policed by the United States and the Soviet Union.

In 1999, there were electoral democracies in about 180 countries. This movement has swept over every region of the globe. In the 1970s, one-party regimes and military dictatorships of various sorts, supported by multinationals, the World Bank and the IMF, the U. S. and the Soviet Union, held power over Africa, South America, Asia, and Eastern and Central Europe.

These electoral democracies have produced new presidents and members of parliaments or national assemblies. Not only have the claims of democracy become global, but also democracy itself is being perceived and appreciated as a global value. There are high expectations about what these electoral democracies should do. For many people in developing countries, for instance, democracy is the savior. It is perceived either as another dimension of development or a complementary force to development. Its expansion between 1970 and the 1990s has been unprecedented in contemporary world politics. For instance, in just twenty-five years, since the mid-1970s, the number of electoral democracies has more than doubled. During this period, approximately seventy-four countries changed from undemocratic to democratic regimes. According to the survey conducted by James Holston of the University of California in San Diego, in 1972 there were fifty-two electoral democracies, constituting 33 percent of the world's 160 sovereign nation-states. By 1996, the number rose to 118 democracies out of 191 nation-states, or 62 percent of the total, for a net gain of sixty-six democratic states. Among the larger countries, those with a population of one million or more people, the number of democracies nearly tripled during the same period. Significantly, the number of undemocratic states has declined by a third since the early 1970s, after rising steadily from the beginning of the century. As Holston stated:

> If it took almost about 200 years of modern world history to produce fifty democratic states by 1970, it has taken only 10 years of political change since the mid-1980s to yield the same number of new democracies. .... In 1975, only four countries in all Latin America had democratically elected national leaders, namely Colombia, Costa Rica, and Venezuela. Of the 36 countries that gained independence in Africa between 1956 and 1970, 33 became authoritarian at the birth or shortly after. The exceptions were Botswana and short-lived electoral democracies in Ghana and Nigeria (2000, p. 4).

In the Asia-Pacific region, only a handful of countries, including Australia, Fiji, Japan, New Zealand, Papua New Guinea, and Sri Lanka had some democratic practices. Others such as India, Pakistan, the Philippines, and South Korea had suffered from democratic reversals in the 1960s and the 1970s. The recent military coup d'état in Fiji and the ongoing process of establishing some forms of the military control since May 19, 2000, and the declaration of a state of emergency on May 29 by the general of the army, have created a process of democratic reversal in the country, as it has been in Côte d'Ivoire since December 25, 1999.

By the end of the 1990s, among the thirty-five states that comprise the Americas, thirty-one had electoral democracies (89 percent). In South and Central America, of twenty nation-states, only Peru and Mexico cannot be clearly considered democratic despite some partial elections. Of fifty-three countries in contemporary Africa, the number of electoral democracies increased to eighteen (34 percent). But there are some democratic reversals in countries such as Côte d'Ivoire, Liberia, Niger, and Sierra Leone. The recent movement of Islamization of the state in northern Nigeria, for example, seriously threatens its electoral democracy. In the Asia-Pacific region, for instance, twenty-four of its thirty-eight nation-states are now politically democratic (63 percent). Within the new nation-states of the former Eastern Europe, out of its twenty-seven nation-states, nineteen have become formally democratic (70 percent).

Although democratic debates and local democratic projects are not absent in the Middle East, it is the only region of the world that has been comparatively stagnant in terms of engagement in the pursuit of liberal democracy. Only Israel and Turkey (14 percent) have had solid formal political debates on democratic and systematic elections and functioning democratic institutions.

We can make claims supported by Holston's survey, various world development reports, Carter Center's reports, etc., that electoral processes have been globalized. But we cannot make any legitimate claim that outcomes of these processes have produced similar behaviors. It is in discussing specifically how liberal democracy has been perceived and defined by the state that one can appreciate the practical and social meanings of this globalization, as the state is the major decision-making entity in which this phenomenon can be projected or reflected into people's lives.

Political or Liberal Democracy in the Realist Traditions

In the West, Machiavelli is known as the father of political realism, the figure who emphasized the emergence of the nation-state as an end in itself, the rules of power politics as the *raison d'être* of the state, the logic of political violence, and its theology of action. Since the eighteenth century in European scholarship, a realist tradition has produced the dominant political thoughts in the studies of contemporary states, international relations, and the world economy. They have focused on a state-centric perspective in examining the world. It is Montesquieu, the French philosopher, and Hegel, the German philosopher, who elevated the state to the level of a "divined and absolutist organization." Is democracy possible within the context of the traditions of absolutism and dialectical thinking? Or what kind of democracy is compatible with this kind of absolutist organization, which is the nation-state?

It should be noted that, despite the fact that globalization and democratization are "placing state sovereignty under real strain, as international rules and institutions appear to become more intrusive, transnational civil society more active, and unitary state control less pronounced" (Kingsbury, 1998), the international discourse is still essentially at the level of diplomacy and not about and/or on democracy. That is to say that the normative concept of sovereignty is still central in determining the nature of international relations.

However, political democracy, also known as liberal democracy, has become a global dogma. Universal suffrage, citizens' rights, and the struggles to form independent political parties have become the means through which demands for change are articulated. Although the values of these means are appreciated because citizens are participating in the political processes, it is argued that political democracy should be considered, especially in the developing world, an incomplete phase in the development of the whole society. As this form of democracy matures and people and citizens become more conscious about their social rights, it is hoped that this phase will lead to a higher, more sophisticated phase of development, namely social democracy.

One of the main differences between the realists and idealists in political science and their perceptions of the world is that realists tend to perceive and define world politics mainly in the state-centric paradigm while idealists maintain that although the state is vital to the management of world affairs, they also envision the establishment of some types of universal world (universal institutions) with common features. Idealists argue that in addition to the state as an important actor, there are other actors that should equally participate in the management of the world politics with legitimacy. As it is also called "power politics theory," and as it developed within many dimensions of European-American scholarship, the realist school of thought as reflected in the works of Thucydides, Hobbes, Machiavelli, Hegel, E. H. Carr, Hans Morgenthau, and

Henry Kissinger, for instance, is essentially a state-centric phenomenon. States are fundamentally self-interested and competitive phenomena (Newman, 1996: 17). As an irreducible element in international politics, the underlying condition for the state's development is conflict. In international relations, the state's expansionism is the motive for interactions among states and nations. It is in the name of national interests that states interact with one another. It is in the name of those interests that nation-states take up arms against one another. The so-called national interests are defined as natural and intrinsic. Humanity is secondary to the interests and actions of the actualization of state power. In classical Western scholarship, Aristotle fully discussed the conditions that ought to be conducive to the "immortality" of the *polis* (city-state). In this limited democracy, the citizens' participation in the *agora* was perceived to be the most important condition for advancing society while promoting the immortality of the state, even if women, slaves, and merchants were not qualified to be citizens. In this tradition, the state is then perceived as a rational political animal, despite any contradictions that emerge from its actions and means. As Ann Kelleher and Laura Klein state:

> While the state primacy perspective of the world does not define the superiority of types of systems, it does privilege a specific type of political organization: The state is viewed as the most important unit for both national and international interaction. According to those who hold this perspective, the primary political identity for all groups and individuals should be as citizens of the state of their birth or adoption. The state primacy perspective does not argue for universal similarity in cultures or centralized power between states. In fact, it gives states a tremendous amount of autonomy in deciding the nature of their realms (1999, p. 41).

Within state primacy, realists emphasize the sovereignty of the state. No matter how this state was created and whether it is located in the North or the South, as a reflection of human nature, the state must be a self-centered entity. As David Held wrote:

> Modern liberal and liberal democratic theories have constantly sought to justify the sovereignty power of the state while at the same time justifying limits on that power. The history of this attempt since Thomas Hobbes is the arguments to balance might and rights, power and law, duties and rights. On the one hand, states must have a monopoly of coercive power in order to provide a secure basis on which trade, commerce, religion and family life can prosper (1993, p. 18).

What does that mean in a competitive world economy? To be able to discuss how realists define and characterize some elements of liberal democracy, it is necessary to briefly cite the classifications of the functions of government as reflected in the structures of the industrial societies. Without examining the historical configurations of how a given government has been created and what the social forces behind its formation were, realist scholars (known also as "functionalists" and "neofunctionalists") have defined the role of government in a "perfect competitive society" in the following manner:

- to protect our freedom from the enemies outside our gates;
- to preserve law and order;
- to enforce private contracts;
- to foster competitive markets; and
- to undertake those few public projects like road construction, that are clearly of general value to the whole society and cannot be readily undertaken under private auspices (Franklin, 1977, p. 47).

First, it should be noted that the concept of "perfect competitive society" is ahistorical even in the United States. Second, I should also mention the idea of government functioning as a balance wheel through appropriate monetary and fiscal policies. This idea is important for the functioning of any government in the capitalist world as it also relates to another notion that realists, especially the mainstream economists, have produced, namely government as a neutral entity and impartial institution. Government can represent the general interest of society as a whole and hence steer capitalism toward the social interest (ibid., p. 48). In short, the best government should be the government that does not govern or that governs the least. In the United States, for instance, the ideas of "small government" or "take the government off the people's back" have been part of the lexicon of many election campaigns. However, despite controversies, the United States qualifies the notion of the strong government paradigm. Contrary to the arguments related to the *laissez-faire* principle of realists, the United States government, for instance, has significantly intervened in the mobilization of resources, sponsoring development projects including banking systems and the housing projects between 1944 and the 1970s.

What are the characteristics of liberal democracy from a realist's perspective? How does a citizen interact with the state? How should a citizen pursue his/her interests? How should his/her interests be protected within the framework of sovereignty of the state?

Citizens in this historical context are individuals who are born in a given country or are legally naturalized individuals who are part of a given society. They have obligations to the society and the state in terms of respecting its laws, paying taxes, and maintaining the equilibrium of the society. They also have rights (or entitlements) in their countries to pursue a good life and happiness as part of the sovereignty principle of the state. From a realist perspective, these individuals are also buyers and sellers, and producers and consumers. Within the logic of the self-regulated market or the invisible hand of Adam Smith, buyers and sellers are free to buy and sell whatever they have wherever they choose. What is important is that the quality of their goods should allow them to compete effectively with one another. The buyers and sellers (citizens) should be able to participate freely in order to sell and buy their services and labor according to their abilities.

Liberal democracy is the system of governance that, in principle, protects citizens' rights and the instruments of production (land, machinery, factory buildings, natural resources, and the like) that are privately owned by many individuals. The institutions of state should produce social equilibrium. This democracy is called procedural democracy. As Robert D. Grey, citing Joseph A. Schumpeter, states:

> The democratic method is that institutional arrangement for arriving at decisions in which individuals acquire the power to decide by means of a competitive struggle for the people's vote (1942). Scholars who adopt this procedural, or elitist, version of democracy tend to be concerned primarily with stability of the system. Once the rules are in place, is the system able to maintain itself without experiencing outbursts of violence or becoming oligarchies? Rule of law and constitutionalism help regulate both government and citizens activity to limit abuses of power and keep the system running (Grey, 1997, p. 83).

Do the people matter in this type of democracy? The question is complex but will not be expanded in this book. First, the expression "people" is ambiguous in the social sciences. In the Marxist traditions, it implies the proletariat, the working-class phenomenon. As compared to the elite, within the triangle of society, the people are the basis of the society. They form the majority. However, in general terms, it can be affirmed that in liberal market and liberal democracy, people as consumers and voters matter. The routine of elections brings political elite and electors closer for a short period of time. A fresh start can bring new possibilities for the ordinary people. But the mass values are articulated through elitist filters. And it is through them that important issues are selected and elevated from their individualistic origins to the local, district, prefectural, or national agenda. As Grey indicates:

> Central to procedural definitions of democracy is the free and fair competition among political parties for the power to make public decisions. This regular competition for power keeps conflictual groups from engaging in violence, much like individuals in conflict might "settle it" through a coin toss or an arm-wrestling match rather than in a fist fight. Hence, in a procedural democracy, conflicts are legitimate and adverse to public interest (1997, p. 87).

With its concern for reason, law, and freedom of choice that can only be upheld by recognizing the political equality of all mature individuals, this democracy limits the power of the state to a large extent (Held, 1993, p. 18). As David Beetham said:

> The definition of democracy in terms of the two general principles of popular control and political equality does in theory allow for institutionalization in different ways; and enables us to recognize democracy as an aspiration in many different societies and in various historical forms (1994, p. 40).

People's control over political institutions and the respect of their equal rights allow an effective participation in the decision-making process.

The question of whether liberal democracy effectively functions the way liberal theorists within the realist political thought tend to project is a very different matter, which is not the present object. In short, individualism or individual rights, free choice, freedoms or civil liberties, and democratic accountability are among the most important characteristics in liberal democracy. How have these elements of liberal democracy and the notion of a strong state been projected in the global economic reforms that have dominated the states in the past thirty years?

In the 1970s and 1980s, the reforms known as the structural adjustment programs (SAPs) of the World Bank and the so-called stabilization programs of the International Monetary Fund (IMF) were implemented in developing countries through a highly centralized political structure with a high level of technical secrecy. But even before the implementation of these programs in Africa, an anti-democratic formula was preferred in the name of efficiency and growth. As it is reported in *World Development Report*:

> Authoritarianism often has been seen as a useful, if regrettable, expedient for effective policy-making in the face of political instability. A strong held view from 1970 through the 1970s was that development policies took time to bear fruit, and that this was inconsistent with the politics of short-term electoral cycles. Democracies were seen as having a built-in inclination toward populist policies (1991, p. 132).

In most cases where the SAPs were adopted, in their initial stage there were no serious debates on how to implement them and what the long-term consequences of their implementation were likely to be. Even when they were wrapped in the symbolism of African policy, their content had "universal" tendencies or they were Americo-European oriented. It was essentially a technical operation of highly selected members of the political elite in the ministries of finance, economy, planning, and in some cases, the office of prime minister. As Ali Mazrui indicates:

> When I served on the World Bank's Council of African Advisors, I repeatedly asked the Bank to devise a calculus of democratic indicators by which an African country would be judged democratically before a loan was granted. Vice-President Edward Jaycox of the World Bank repeatedly protested that it could not be done. Partly because market ideologies have been pushed with greater vigour and consistency than has liberal democracy, the market is almost

triumphant by the end of the 20th Century. There are more countries which have been forced to privatise and adopt structural adjustment programmes than there are countries that have been penalised for not democratising (1998, p. 2).

Although the political situation in the world has become relatively different since the 1990s and there is a space for political debates in most countries, the SAPs are still very much elitist programs in many parts of the world, including Africa, Asia, South America, and Russia. That is to say, the majority of people, especially those who live in the countryside, have not been able to participate in their formulation and implementation.

However, since the early 1990s, as a result of popular movements, intellectual critiques from both liberals and organic intellectuals, and the brutal end of the Soviet Union and its socialist bloc, the World Bank was obliged to revise some of its requirements for granting access to its financial resources and to those of its affiliate institutions. In the process of producing new reform guidelines, the technocrats and policymakers at the World Bank started with what they called "rethinking the state." Thus, the World Bank started to insist on "good" governance as one of the prerequisites for approving loans and lines of credit. As it stated in its report, "The agenda for reform that emerged in the course of this Report calls for government to intervene less in certain areas and more in others--for the state to let markets work where they can, and to step in promptly and effectively where they cannot (*World Report Development*, 1991, p. 128)."

The notion of the strong state, which was defined by the militaristic and personalistic power structure that prevailed throughout the 1970s and 1980s, is no longer a rigidly defined central dogma of the World Bank. The state that can maintain "law and order" is the one that the Bank can do business with. "Law and order" is a legalistic expression that has been articulated in the literature of the modernization of school of thought as the state's coercive power. Even Léopold II of Belgium used it to govern the Congo as his personal property.

It should be noted that despite the fact that the World Bank has started to engage nongovernmental institutions, it still believes in the power and organization of the state in the process of implementing its programs. It should also be emphasized that the notion of "law and order" does not necessarily imply liberal democracy—or any type of democracy for that matter. Another notion that has been central in the discourse and lexicon of the bank is "good" governance. Projected in normative terms, this term includes building states, institutions, and accountability.

It has been clear that liberal democracy within the SAPs entails periodic elections at most levels of the societal organizations within a framework of multiparty politics, as well as political stability of some kind. Concerning elections and multipartyism, the rules have not been generalized throughout Africa. Some countries with limited democracy, such as Egypt, and the non-party politics as in Uganda, are still considered, despite recent debates on their performance and possible calls to stop pouring money into Kampala, for instance, as *les enfants chéris* of the Paris Club and the World Bank. The point is that multipartyism and liberal elections are still used as ad hoc principles within the World Bank.

In a situation where multipartyism has become almost routine in some African countries, the World Bank does not seem to care much about whether this multipartyism is autocratic or democratic. I define "multiparty autocracy" as a system of governance with more than one political party in which the ruling party has monopoly over political and financial resources; it controls them to advance its causes, and it also determines the direction of discourses of other political parties and those of national politics at large (Lumumba-Kasongo, 1998, pp. 22-23). In countries such as Côte d'Ivoire, Cameroon, Togo, and the Democratic Republic of Congo, for several years before the end of the 1990s, multiparty autocracy was confused with liberal democracy. The ruling party was still the engine of policy formulation and implementation. It also attempted to provide the guides for the behaviors of other parties.

The presidential election in Togo of June 1, 2003, in part reflects my definition of multiparty autocracy. President Étienne Gnassingbe Eyadema of Togo, Africa's longest serving ruler, won a further five years in power in an election which was denounced by the opposition as being riddled with fraud (IRIN, June 5, 2003). He arrested members of the opposition parties, released them at his will, and he used the military and police apparatuses to control the so-called democratic elections. Eyadema has ruled Togo with an iron hand for thirty-six years. The National Independent Electoral Commission announced that he won with 57.22 of the votes cast in this presidential election (June 1, 2003).

Characteristics of a Welfare State as a Democracy

As indicated in the section on capitalism, the current dogmas of liberal globalization in their economic, market, technological, and information forms were strongly articulated and organized by President Ronald Reagan in the United States in the 1980s and Margaret Thatcher, the former Prime Minister of Great Britain, in the 1970s and the 1980s as combative ideological instruments. They were effectively used as instruments of struggles against any forms of socialism. These dogmas have been fully incorporated into the principles and policies of the structural adjustments (SAPs) of the World Bank and stabilization programs of the International Monetary Fund (IMF) and those of the Maastricht Treaty in Europe of 1992. The forces associated with global liberalization and their social contradictions are partially responsible for the rise of the movements against welfarism as it has been taking place in France and Germany.

So far, based on comparative social and political indexes between social welfare states such as the Norwegian states and liberal states such as the United States and Australia, it can be stipulated that the differences between liberal or representative democracy and social democracy are primarily based on their philosophical foundation. Their differences, however, are not abstractions. Second, perceptions of human nature within these political systems are also different. Third, the differences are historically and socially rooted as well. The origins of their ideas, their social agencies, and their defined visions of society are qualitatively different from one another. Thus, they produce different types of societies, democratic processes, citizens' behavior, expectations, and political participation.

In this section, the focus is on the origins of the ideas of welfare state at large. I will identify its major characteristics, and explore how these ideas define and support democracy.

The main objective is on how we can understand what constitutes the uniqueness or particularities of a welfare state and what we can learn from it. How do citizens participate in these states? What are the economic and political benefits citizens gain as a result of their participation in the welfare states' political processes and institutional building? The effort is basically an attempt to make a theoretical contribution in the search for alternatives to liberal democracy.

It is argued in this section that the functioning of the welfare state has to be essentially democratic. That is to say that the welfare state in its contemporary form whether it is a liberal, a nationalist, or a socialist/social oriented system in terms of its philosophical foundation, embodies some general elements of "social" democracy. As Robert Elgie stated:

> The welfare state is more than just a set of static institutions. It takes potent political forces to create and maintain it. In the Western European context, one of the major political supporters of the welfare state has been social democracies (1998, p. 78).

It is the activism of labor parties, socialist/communist parties, leftist groups, and unionists at large that promoted the welfare state. There are various views in the ways the welfare state have been perceived, defined, and also in the way it performs and reproduces itself, its political claims and intellectual arguments. In contemporary societies, these arguments touch more directly on human, individual, or collective rights than in any forms of states among the industrial nations. However, the analysis of concrete policies based on the welfare principles needs to be further explored. No attempt is made in this section to universalize the characteristics of the welfare state. Its achievements/performances will not be assessed by some universal ethical norms.

Many contemporary nation-states and governments in various periods of their development or evolution have produced various forms of welfare states and programs to deal with the inclusiveness of their citizens, to address the questions related to social distribution of resources, and to solve social 60inequalities at a given time. For instance, the formal discussion on the welfare state in India goes back to the writings of Kautilya in his theory of prince as the safeguard of the social order based on the *Varna* and *Ashrama* system (Kohli,

1995, p. 36). In many parts of Africa, the philosophical idea of the welfare state can be located in the notion of "harmonious" organized or divine cosmology and communal ethos. However, as stated earlier, in this section, I am interested in what we can learn from the contemporary debates and policies of the welfare states and not in prescribed science.

Within the current logic of liberal globalization and its mandate to liberalize, privatize, and universalize the markets, the concept of a welfare state has been seriously challenged in many parts of the world, as reflected in recent years in Western Europe and North America. Welfare reforms in Canada and Western Europe were the central policy issues in the past decade. In developing countries, especially in many African countries, most of the partial welfare programs associated with the euphoria of political independence were dismantled as results of various economic crises of the 1970s and 1980s, for instance, indebtedness, inequalities in the market place of the primary commodities, oil crises, mismanagement, etc. It should be emphasized that many African leaders and their political parties in the 1950s and the 1960s strongly articulated elements of welfare states in their political ideologies such as the African socialism, African humanism, Afro-Marxism, African capitalism, and African nationalism including pan-Africanism. To a certain extent, the struggles for independence embodied, in theory, some ideas of making the state the major agency of social change. In addition to the question of the degree and the nature of the state's intervention, in Africa as well as in Europe, within the perspective of global economic reforms, there is a declining interest in the part of the nation-states to promote and sustain the ideologies of welfare states.

However, it should be noted that the civil societies in many European cities have been waging multidimensional wars against their governments over the question of the welfare state and programs and the possibility of dismantling them all together based on the cost analysis, the profit arguments, and free market premises. These struggles, in different forms, are also taking place in popular movements in the developing world.

However, despite the continuous organized global protests in the past several years (1999-2003) in Seattle-Washington, Washington D.C., Prague, Quebec City, and Paris against policies and politics of the global institutions such as the World Bank, the IMF, the WTO, and the summit of the Americas, some scholars argue that this "war" has, to a certain extent, been partially and legally won by the states with the establishment of the European Union and its common currency, the Euro. The 27th summit of the G-8 (highly industrial nations) that took place on July 20-22, 2001 in Genoa, Italy was also met vigorous protests by thousands of people who represented hundreds of organizations the world over. It should be noted that the European Monetary Union, set up in a motion by the Maastricht Treaty in 1992, is perceived by the forces of liberal democracy and free market as the victory of global privatization. For the advocates of this view, this union is likely to accelerate the mechanisms of global regionalization of world politics, given the historical and commercial importance of Europe, which has previously had solid trade relations with about 130 countries in the world as of 2000.

The concept of the welfare state in its most current popular usage was born out of the liberal philosophy in Europe. It was in the 17th century that the philosophy of liberalism appeared in England and it dominated the thought in Western civilization by the late 19th century and early 20th century. While European nations were pursuing their interests in Africa and other regions through colonization, in Europe itself the debate on the liberal philosophy, which is the foundation of welfare states, was emerging. As Sankhdher and Cranston state:

> In explaining the liberal concept of the welfare state in England during 1889 and 1914, we should begin by a precision of its symbolic representation at the point of culmination in Lloyd George's mind. The Liberal philosophy, which had its origin in John Locke's ideas, was given a new turn by the philosophical Radicals and the Utilitarians. In practical politics, however, liberalism in this period, though rooted in individual liberty, extended the meaning of liberty to incorporate the idea of welfare state (1985, p. 245).

This is to say that political representation as the key characteristic of liberalism has been one of the most important forces of welfare state. After the French revolution and industrial revolution, the attributes of liberalism were expanded from individual quest for freedom to societal struggle against "undemocratic parliaments" and despotic monarchs. Of course this was not done without the bourgeois power struggles and proletarian struggles as well. As stated earlier in the 19th century, both the classical liberalism and later Marxism were distrustful to the state. The classical state was conceived as an instrument of coercive forces and thus it was perceived as anti individualism. In England, liberalism was articulated by such philosophers as Edmund Burke, Herbert Spencer, T. H. Green, William Berridge, J. M. Keynes, Ludwig von Miesses, etc. In my view, none of them paid sufficiently any attention to the gender issues in the development of rights and capitalism. However, they were against the exercise of unlimited power by the state and monopolistic law of capitalism. The main characteristics of liberalism include: the ideology of representative democracy, based on the Rule of Law, the notion of limited government, and the concepts of individual's rights of life, liberty and property (Sankhdher and Cranston, 1985, p. 245). As Mimi Abramovitz said:

> Classical liberalism originated in seventeenth-century England, took root in the eighteenth century, and with the rise of industrial capitalism, became the dominant political theory of twentieth century Western societies. Reflecting new views of human nature which placed selfness, egoism, and individualistic seif-interest at the center of human psyche, liberalism held competitive pursuit of individual self-interest in a market free of government regulation would maximize personal and societal benefits (1989, p. 14).

Struggles against the feudal economies, monarchic and strong states in their militaristic and personalized forms contributed to the creation of the welfare states in Europe. The industrial revolution of the 1700s and early 1800s led to the development of social insurance in many parts of Europe as most of the workers received low wages and were also working under hazardous conditions. Thus, many workers did not and/or could not afford to live a relatively productive life. For instance, in 1883-1889, Germany was the first nation-state in Europe to institute national welfare programs, mandatory workers' insurance. Chancellor Otto von Bismarck, who instituted the welfare programs, was trying to accomplish two objectives: (1) to remove the workers' impetus for a possible revolution and (2) to ensure that the cost burden of the programs would not be borne by the local governments. Even during the years leading to World War II, social welfare programs continued to expand, as it is stated in Article 20 (1) of the Basic Law that Federal Republic of Germany is a "democratic and social federal state." The nature of the relationship between other nations has partially been determined by the effort of the government to provide the basics for all Germans. As Krasner indicates:

> In addition to attempting to control the flows of capital and ideas, states have long struggled to manage the impact of international trade. The opening of long distance trade for bulk commodities in the 19th century. Depression and plummeting grain prices made it possible for German Chancellor Otto von Bismarck to produce the landholding aristocracy into a protectionist alliance with urban heavy industry (this coalition of "iron and rye' dominated German politics for decades (2001, p. 24).

In France also since the pre-revolutionary times, entrepreneurial timidity was partially compensated for by the role that the French government played in technological innovation and economic development as indicated by Erhamm that the royal *fermiers,* Jean-Baptiste Colbert's merchantilism, and the way in which Napoleon III's entourage interpreted the doctrines of Claude-Henri Saint-Simon created the traditions.

In Britain Keith Windschuttle stated:

> The reforms Bills of 1867 and 1884 extended the franchise to males in virtually all social classes. The new concept of the state sanctioned the existing political parties to abandon laissez-faire and to appeal to these new voters with the promise of social legislation and welfare reform. Whereas classical liberal regarded the state as necessary evil, the new liberalism saw the state as a necessary good that was capable of removing or alleviating the insecurities and misfortunes of newly enfranchised lower orders. It was the Liberal Imperialist governments of 1906-16 that went furthest in delivering tangible legislation to back these ideas: the Workmen's Compensation Act of 1906, the Old Age Pension Act of 1908, the Minimum Wage Act of 1909, and the National Insurance Act of 1911. The welfare state of the later twentieth century was

largely an unfolding of principles and measures introduced in these years (pp. 82- 83).

Welfare states in the 20th century sought to limit the power of the ruling class. And it promoted the intervention of the state on behalf of individuals as to create the conditions that should allow individual's ability to maximize self-interest and to secure liberty, equality, and justice. Most of the welfare programs or packages that were produced in Europe include laissez-faire doctrine that restricted the responsibilities of the state without eliminating its regulatory role as protector of capital, property, and national security (Abramovitz, p. 15). Pragmatically, Sankhdher and Cranston describe the welfare functions in the following:

> The key functions of a welfare state were, in addition to police responsibilities, promotion of economic development and social welfare by providing full employment, equal opportunity, social security and insurance of a minimum standard of living for those downmost of the social ladder. Such an idea materialized largely in the Beveridge plan which prescribed, within a liberal democratic framework, provision of basic needs, as also remedies for problems of disease, ignorance, squalor, and idleness. It was the application of collectivist methods for the individualistic aims of laissez-faire (1985, p. 246).

Theoretically, how have the European welfare states perceived and defined social inequality? Firstly, it should be emphasized that each state has produced its own welfare programs based on its social, historical and political specificities, and needs. And secondly, the formulation and implementation of the welfare programs should not be generalized. The success of each welfare state depends on the political culture of the country, the nature of its leaderships and that of its state. Thus, the Nordic countries in Europe (the Scandinavian countries) have produced stronger and more elaborated welfare states than the countries in continental Europe.

However, the idea that the government ought to protect minimum standards of income, nutrition, health, housing, and education assured to every individual as a political right, not as charity (Abramovitz, p. 16), can be generalized as the universal claim of a liberal political thought. Within the Marxist traditions, the welfare state is to use the state power to modify the reproduction of labor power and to shift the costs of socializing and maintaining workers from the private capital to the public sphere (p. 17).

The concept of justice that has been the philosophical and social engine in welfare states can be summarized in the following statement of John Rawls:

> Justice is the first virtue of social institutions, as truth is of systems of thought. A theory however elegant and economical must be rejected or revised if it is untrue; likewise laws and institutions no matter how efficient and well-arranged

must be reformed or abolished if they are unjust. Each person possesses inviolability founded on justice that even the welfare of society as a whole cannot override. For this reason justice denies that the loss of freedom for some is made right by a greater good shared by others. It does not allow the sacrifices imposed on a few are outweighed by the larger sum of advantages enjoyed by many. Therefore in a just society the liberties of equal citizenship are taken as settled; the rights secured by justice are not subject to political bargaining or to the calculus of social interests (1971, pp. 3-4).

In addition to legalism, other related notions developed in the welfare states are those of equal citizenship and equal participation in the political affairs of the states.

Before concluding this section, it is important to mention some differences between the welfare states and programs that have strongly been promoted by the liberal political thought as described above and those developed out of socialist traditions. The liberal theory of politics allows social changes through legalistic reforms with the focus on individual rights. But not all legalisms can promote social justice as Alan Wolfe said in the case of the United States, for instance:

America's failure to contemplate, let alone redress, social injustice and inequality is another indication of its impasse, a backhand confession that ills are beyond the reach of human action to remedy them. For a "can do" culture, such an intimation of impotence was found relatively easy to accept (1989, p. 81).

A selective approach to welfare programs puts the case of the United States neither on the liberal crusade against injustice nor on a stand-pat preference for the status-quo especially during the New Deal era (Wolfe, Ibid.). But the social cost in choosing this approach has been heavy with the long-term impact that is extremely difficult to deal with for many generations in the era of globalization. The principle of each according to her/his merit has retarded the discourse on the pursuit of social equality, including the gender relations in the U.S.

As I stated earlier, different states have formulated different policies at various periods to address the issues related to social inequalities, for instance. The major distributive principle that socialists used was "each according to her/his needs." Whether factually all socialist welfare states or welfare states within social democracies attempted to transform the social relations can be questionable, their principle of each according to her/his needs is worth pursuing.

In short, the socially defined welfare states, until recently in Northern Europe, had a strong base for collective citizenship perspective in dealing with needs and progress as contrasted to the liberal democracy in the United States where individual rights and personal hard work ethic (the Weberian Protestant ethic) are promoted as the most important means to social progress. In this kind of situation, the origins of social inequalities are not relegated to the so-called personal choice and motivation.

NOTES

1. Many parts of this section were published in the author's article "Capitalism and Liberal Democracy as Forces of Globalization with Reference to the Paradigms Behind the Structural Adjustment Programs in Africa," *Politics and Administration and Change,* No. 34, July–December 2000, pages 23–52. I thank Dr. Habib Zafarullah, the Editor of this journal, for granting me the permission to use this article. For further information on this topic, see also Tukumbi Lumumba-Kasongo, "A Theoretical Perspective on Capitalism and Welfare States and Their Responses to the Question of Social Inequality with Particular Attention to Gender Inequality: What Lessons for Africa?" The paper was prepared and read for the Fifth General Assembly and Seminar of the Association of the African Women Researcher in Africa (AAWORD) held on July 19–24, 1999 in Dakar, Senegal.

Chapter 5

Ideology: What Is Its New Role in the Twenty-First Century?

Introduction: Objectives, Issues, and Definitions

Does ideology matter in the process, mechanisms, and politics of governing and governance? There are people and scholars who stipulate that the decline in party politics as was very much documented in Western Europe and North America between the 1970s and the 1990s is a reflection of substantial disinterest in ideology and in coherent thinking among political elites; and that this fact would be one of the reasons why most parties' leaders were not capable of making persuasive arguments in the process of recruitment and mobilization of new membership to support their platforms. They alienated constituents and thus contributed directly or indirectly to the development of the apathetic political behavior among the majority of social groups. While the above statement may be partially relevant in political and social realities in some countries and in some periods, in relationship to the place and role of ideology in politics at large, it cannot be generalized. The causes of the apathy are sociologically and economically complex. They cannot be reduced or simplified to a single factor of the weakening of an ideology.

As a coined word, the term ideology has a precise origin in the era of the French Revolution. The decisive shifts in its meaning, moreover, have been associated with some of the most colorful and influential figures in modern history—Napoleon Bonaparte (1769–1821), Karl Marx (1818–1883), Friedrich Engels (1820–1895), and V. I. Lenin (1870–1924). From its very inception, in fact, ideology has been associated with highly abstract philosophy and forceful, even brutal political repression (Terence Ball and Richard Dagger, 2001, p. 4).

This chapter on ideology does not necessarily focus on Karl Marx's thoughts and the origins of both his ideology and his social and political philosophy, which have become an alternative intellectual tradition. However, as a thinker who put socialist ideas and ideology upon a sound basis and who also called into question the whole tradition of Western social and political thought (Nelson, 1996, p. 327), many parts of the discussion touch on elements of his theory of ideology. This theory is used to clarify my conceptualization of this complex phenomenon. My interest is to construct a broader political and intellectual framework that may help define ideology as a social and intellectual force and identify further its role in the process of governance.

Ideology as a societal phenomenon has been enriched over time by the nature of state-society relations and various contexts of power and class struggle. As such, it should be added that during the past hundred years or so, the concept has been, in its various practical and interpretative uses, influenced by national and international politics and the policies of many political figures other than the classical ones (Marx, Engels, and Lenin). Some of these figures include Amilcar Cabral, Félix Houphouët-Boigny, Fidel Castro, Ayatollah Khomeini, Charles de Gaulle, Mahatma Gandhi, François Mitterand, Rosa Luxemburg, Patrice Lumumba, Nelson Mandela, Winnie Mandela, Pierre Mulele, Kwame Nkrumah, Julius Nyerere, Ho Chi Minh, Ronald Reagan, Margaret Thatcher, and Mao Zedong. These figures, despite serious moral grounds that separate their actions, have believed in different ideas/ideals in their perceptions of the world and in how to organize it, understand it, and change it. Factors that are common among them are not about their efforts to make the world a better place to live. Rather, it is about their vibration to see the world in a monistic way and also their determination to try to convince the rest of the world, with or without historical and sociological evidence, that their perspectives are functionally more relevant than others. Some of the above figures even became apologists in this process of communicating with others or the society at large about the validity of their points of view.

In general, the main objective in this section is to reflect theoretically and philosophically on the kind of role ideology has played in the processes and mechanisms of state formation and development paradigms during the colonial and post-colonial periods and during the post–Cold War Era. Further, we consider the role it might play in this twenty-first century. In order to reach this objective, I intend first to define the general, dominant elements and characteristics of ideology and second to compare and contrast its embodied intellectual components. In so doing, I hope to justify how and why I think that the twenty-first century is likely to be a century of more intensive ideological struggles. This projection is supported by identifying and examining the role that dominant ideological elements have been playing in politics and policies of the world, the world over. I am distinguishing, but at the same time trying to find implicit relationships, between ideologies as intellectual systems of thought and the analysis of phenomena and ideologies as platforms for social changes.

Thus, in terms of using some illustrations, which may help to broaden our horizon concerning studies on ideology, I briefly revisit a discussion of the old and well-established forms of ideologies, namely capitalism, imperialism, liberalism, nationalism, and socialism. My specific intent in identifying the elements and values related to some of these dominant ideologies is to raise the critical issues and pose questions concerning their political and social significance and policy implications in world politics in this century and beyond. This section thus reflects on the nature of the initiatives and projects of the agencies that have constructed ideologies and also those that have been constructed by ideologies. Will the world (nation-states, private corporations, citizens, and social movements) continue to use ideologies effectively even if and when we are being told that world politics has become less ideological?

It is argued that the twenty-first century is likely to engender more ideological debates than the Cold War produced, despite the emergence of a unilateral re-alliance of power after the United States was attacked on September 11, 2001. This re-alliance is based on what President George Bush has characterized in terms of "either you are with us, or you are on the side of our enemies." The reactions to this dictum will be basically ideological oriented. As has become obvious, this re-alliance is essentially militaristic, politically, and intellectually unidimensional. Efforts toward revival of rebuilding the United States military bases in each region of the world have re-emerged. These efforts are fully supported by the United States Congress and by United States public opinion, with the exception of the active voice of a small movement of resistance against this new trend. But this movement, in its infancy, is still very much academic in nature.

For many people, especially in the West, the age of ideology stretched from the French Revolution (eighteenth century) to the collapse of the USSR in 1991. Within this reasoning, logically then, we should be now in the post-ideological era. What does that mean? One thing that should be recognized is that the ideological dualism which characterized post–World War II politics for more than fifty years has ceased to be considered as a source of systematic and viable guidelines for consistently shaping the actions of states, citizens—or any political force for that matter. Furthermore, the proposition of limiting the dynamics of ideology to a strictly fixed historical period does not seem to be able to take into account the dynamics of the nation-state, which in my point of view, is essentially an ideological institution, and the dynamics of social movements.

Between the end of the 1980s and the end of the 1990s, many scholars and activists, given the intensity of the degradation of social conditions in the Global South, started to discuss vigorously possible shifts in the dominant paradigms in the international political economy and the possibilities for projecting world politics in the direction of de-linking and multipolarity. They imply the possibility for articulating and validating the existence of several axes of power. Scholars associated with world systems, the dependency school of thought, and third world forum, including Immanuel Wallerstein, Samin Amin, and Claude Ake, have been among the leaders at this position. However, these new paradigms that deal with de-linking and multipolarity in a systematic manner have represented only a minority position. In light of historical evidence reflected in world politics, replete with contradictions, this position will continue to provide different ways of thinking and of analyzing social phenomena.

In social sciences, particularly in sociology, political science, and political economy, ideology is a dynamic concept. In principle, an ideology has an intellectual capacity for clarity and a claimed moral/ethic base for its supported political actions. Its evolution and meanings cannot be understood outside of a given historical context and social origin. Ideology has an epistemological basis in real society, and it embodies some higher ideas or principles. Thus, it is a social knowledge. As discussed further, for Karl Marx, for instance, it was a science. From the above perspective, ideology is also perceived as a superior force.

Within the logic of this new international political order (NIPO), which sharply delineated world politics at the "complete" end of the Cold War era, will ideology still matter in shaping people's opinions, views, and values and states' policies related to social progress in areas such as development, gender, technology, political stability, nation-building, and democracy? How will ideology manifest itself in newly emerging alliances of power, economic relations, and the dynamics of new orbits of power?

The failures of global capitalism throughout the world, the intensification of intrastate and transnational conflicts, and the continuing militarization of world politics have been at the core of the rise of new waves of ideologies. However, the forms that these new ideologies are likely to take and the envelopes in which they will be embodied are likely to be very different from what was known as the "science of ideology" for the past half-century. The behaviors of world politics and its multiplicity of actors and organizations were more predictable in this recent past because in this science, the elements of ideologies were more or less tangible, quantifiable, and controllable. The historical role that various elements/dimensions of ideologies have played in contemporary nation-state building cannot be denied. Nevertheless, that role has also been politically, sociologically, culturally, and economically controversial in its attempts to define and promote uniformity.

It is further argued in this section that one cannot fully or comprehensively understand the dynamics of the nation-states, their policies, politics, and their international relations without linking them theoretically and empirically to their ideological base. As defined in this section, the nation-state is essentially an ideological construct and a self-motivating entity. The successes of the claims of its mortality or immortality as reflected in its national policies and politics depend very much on the dynamics of its ideologies.

In general terms, I also argue that nation-states that have collapsed unpredictably faster toward the end of the 1980s and in the 1990s did so in part because either they, in their internal power struggles and structures, lost their ideological base, or because this base became either extremely weak, or segmented, or unsustainable. Some of these nation-states include Czechoslovakia, Liberia,

Somalia, Zaïre (the Democratic Republic of Congo), Sierra Leone, and Yugoslavia.

In comparison to other studies such as development, industrialization, market, trade relations, class and gender relations, social movements, and globalization, the studies of ideology during the Cold War era were elevated to almost a science of struggles and conflicts. Some of these conflicts, as reflected in the nature of the relationship between research, knowledge, education, and power, were well articulated in books such as Claude Ake's *Social Science as Imperialism: The Theory of Political Development* (1979), Michael Apple's *Ideology and Curriculum* (1980), Carnoy's *Education as Cultural Imperialism*, Chinweizu's *The West and the Rest of US: White Predators, Black Slavers and the African Elite* (1975), Samir Amin's *Eurocentrism* (1989), Paulo Frerei's *Pedagogy of the Oppressed,* and E. Y. Mudimbe's *Invention of Africa.*

World politics was also defined as a world of sharply delineated ideologies. In most cases, especially in the literature of Marxist paradigms, ideologues in Communist parties were considered planners and philosophers, central forces in the maintenance of the power system. The struggle of the proletariat against the petty bourgeoisie is ideological. However, from the end of the 1970s, with the support of economic reforms, state ideology was reduced to the level of what can be characterized as "propagandist" studies. As the state became weaker and more disengaged, so did its ideological foundation. The mobilization of global economic reforms to support uniformity contributed significantly to the attacks against systematic ideologies. Furthermore, after the end of the Cold War, especially with the propaganda associated with the Fukuyamaist end-of-history paradigm, the study of ideology continued to acquire a lower intellectual status in the social sciences. Generally, it was degraded to be part of the past policy and political failures of the so-called evil empire and its associates. In this case, it was associated mainly with communism, which was perceived as morally evil and an inferior phenomenon.

But, as further discussion will show, it is important that we distinguish between state ideologies, the constructs of political elites, and societal and people's systems of beliefs. State ideologies can be characterized as constructive in the form and the linear logic of nation-state building. The societal ideologies can be described in many ways as constantly de-constructive. They can be defined in terms of their efforts to challenge the state apparatuses and their policy foundation. In many forms, the nature of their relationships appears conflicting. While state ideologies have recently been forced to retreat somewhat by global forces and neo-liberal policies, societal and people's ideologies have been gaining momentum and increasing. In the absence of total or partial security articulated and offered by state apparatuses and supported by formal or systematic ideologies, people have been using what is called in this context "informal ideologies" as a means of searching for security. These informal ideologies are formulated in social movements, grassroots movements, cultural values and means, and are written in local initiatives. For the majority of people, known as "ordinary" people in developing countries, these informal or nonsystematic forms of ideology have become the most important sources of inspiration, raised expectations, actions, and survival. The majority of people's loyalty to the formal ideologies has been quite limited, if not completely absent.

Furthermore, the tragic events of September 11, 2001, in which the United States military power base and international capitalism were furiously attacked by "international private terrorists," most of whom have been identified by the American intelligence establishment as nationals of Saudi Arabia, have changed the perceptions of ideologies. After these events, which were characterized by a high level of banditism, as these individuals transformed commercial air planes into missiles, the studies of ideologies, both systematic and informal, are acquiring new momentum and attention, new academic space, and new international status. The continuous efforts, both intellectually and from intelligence agencies, to explain what happened, from various perspectives, and the people's positions around the world on, and about, what to expect or to prepare for next, have been creating a space for further critical ideological discourse. Linear logic and arguments are not sufficient tools to provide fully intelligible and intelligent explanations of these events. In my view, it is in the world of ideologies that one may be able to identify some elements of the explanations of this tragedy and its relations with other, broader international and national events and issues.

Perhaps, one of the questions people might ask is, "if the United States, the most powerful country on the face of the earth, could be savagely attacked in such a way, who is not subjected to similar anger? Logically, no one can hide from any well-defined or programmed violent actions or terrorist attacks any longer. No one or no society has the full intelligence and technologies that can predict and deter these types of violent actions. Thus, since September 11, 2001's events, the meanings of ideologies have become different from the classical expressions of the bipolar world. But ideologies still continue to be used as instruments of national, ethnic, gender, and class struggles dynamically related to primordial forces. The pursuit of multipolarity, which was attacked and which stalled during the 1970s, 1980s, and 1990s by the forces related to global economic reform programs, is likely to re-emerge with force. Though less ideological in their nature, various processes of multipolarity will continue to attract people and mobilize constituencies because of the high level of national anxiety, poverty, social injustice, disillusionment, political instability, and powerlessness of both citizens and states to change the world around them.

It can be generalized that from the views of many people that, following the collapse of the Soviet Union, or institutionalized Marxism-Leninism, which was one of the most dynamic characteristics of contemporary world politics in the twentieth century, the role of political ideology must be redefined. This characteristic has been among the most visible elements of any social dominant paradigm (SDP) and state building in the nineteenth and the twentieth centuries. Although this phenomenon can be described as being as old as any political community, its instrumentalization of power in contemporary world politics in shaping governance systems and principles is relatively new.

Since the enslavement of Africans on a large scale by Europeans in Europe and the Americas and the European colonization of the world, the appropriation of formal ideology by the nation-state, individuals, and social classes, and the ethos of expansionism and consolidation of the nation-state became sharper in the twentieth century. The two belligerent dominant military powers, the superpowers, the USSR and the United States, and their allies advanced their ideological struggles the world over, which characterized post–World War II poli tics. Most of the major revolutions, starting with the overthrow of the Russian czar in 1917 by the Bolsheviks (the Bolshevik Revolution) and including the various types of national liberation movements in the developing world, were based on some revolutionary or national ideological paradigms.

As already indicated, the evolution of European types of nation-state testifies that the foundation of their roots can be historically located in the doctrines of "God, Gold, and Glory." These doctrines have promoted and supported imperialist and neoimperialist projects. Forces of both imperialism and decolonization have defined themselves and defended their actions and policies on ideological terms. In most parts of the world, even without necessarily being part of well-defined political and social organizations, people and citizens have reacted to the states' actions and behaviors on ideological bases.

Is it possible to study world politics without examining its ideological foundation? It is likely that if one studies the world of the states quantitatively, in terms of finding only causal relations between the actors' actions to explain their behaviors, it will be possible to isolate faith, beliefs, cultural dispositions, or "bias variables" from facts and vice-versa. But the explanations might be segmented at the best. What can or should one do with the explanations of facts outside of their political and economic base? Can facts be complete, functional, and understandable without being wrapped in worldview perspectives and in people's convictions? Can a given social context exist without a system of beliefs?

Even with the best minds and the best available technologies based on correlative facts, no one is able to predict with precision what direction the world of the states is likely to take twenty or fifty years from now. This is why it is appropriate and logical to talk about social progress, development policies, technological innovations, and the like in terms of identifying its dominant trends and characteristics or the dynamics of the context.

Based on the existing social, environmental, and economic indices, the world is more socially fragmented today than it was thirty years ago. The gap between the haves and the have-nots has been constantly widening across social classes, gender lines, countries, and regions. The pyramid of wealth, ecological conditions, and the emergence of new diseases—in the 1990s there were about twenty-nine (Brown, 1999)—all testify to the various forms of segmentation. Have world politics become less or more ideological today than thirty or forty years ago? What does less or more ideological mean in relationship to people's and states' struggles to redefine themselves? What has been or should be the role of ideology in class and state formation or the choices of policy or developmental paradigms? Has ideology become less attractive today than thirty or forty years ago? In short, does ideology matter in evaluating or assessing social projects and developmental progress or in formulating and implementing policies? These questions are used as an analytical framework, which enables me to define ideology and its political and cultural significance.

At the end of the confrontational politics of the Cold War in the early 1990s and the disappearance of institutional Marxism-Leninism or socialism, many people started to see the end of ideology or "isms." This view tends to reduce ideology to a tool of the dominant state for controlling resources or affairs.

The majority of nation-states and their ruling elites, especially those of the Global North, believe that ideology is either dead or has become totally dysfunctional with the end of the institutional Marxism-Leninism and the Cold War era. I agree with what Terence Ball and Richard Dagger stated:

> That ideologies and ideological conflicts have persisted throughout modern history should come as no surprise. Ideologies are born of crisis and feed on conflict. People need help to comprehend and cope with turbulent times and confusing circumstances, and ideologies provide this help. An ideology does this by performing four important and perhaps indispensable functions for those who subscribe to it. First, it explains political phenomena that would otherwise remain mysterious or puzzling. Why are there wars and rumors? What causes depression?...Second, an ideology provides its adherents with criteria and standards of evaluation—of deciding what is right and wrong, good and bad. Are class differences and vast disparities of wealth good or bad? Third, ideology orients its adherents, giving them a sense of who they and where they belong— a social cultural compass with which to define and affirm their individual and collective identity....Fourth, an ideology supplies its adherents with a rudimentary political program (2002, p. 1).

Since the expansion of the European empires (the Dutch, English, Italian, French, Portuguese, and Spanish) outside of Europe, which started in the late fifteen century, their imperialistic ideology has become central in the dominant social paradigm (DSP) of the world system. Nation-states that were established on imperialist objectives and incentives continue to produce various conflicts, most of which can be traced to a crisis of legitimacy, confusion of identity, and lack of national vision. Historically, the military power that was used to conquer territories for commercial gain supported scientific innovations (Kegley and Wittkopf, 2001, p. 128). In this first wave of European imperialism, its economic strategy can be described as follows:

> The economic strategy underlying the relationship between colonies and colonizers during this era "of classical imperialism" is known as mercantilism: an economic philosophy advocating government regulation of economic life to increase state power and security. European rulers believed that power flowed from the possession of national wealth measured in terms of gold and silver and

that developing mining and industry to attain a favorable balance of trade (exporting more than they imported) was the best way to accumulate the desired billion (Kegley, op. cit., p. 129).

What do the first and the second waves of European imperialism have in common ideologically? Can they embody ideological elements or dynamics that may help one understand the explosion of ideologies in the post–Cold War era? According to Kegley and Wittkopf, the second wave of European imperialism began in the 1870s and extended until the outbreak of World War I. This wave of imperialism washed over the world as Europe was later joined by the United States and Japan, which aggressively colonized the new territories.

Finally, what is ideology in practice? First, the term ideology, as indicated at the beginning of this section, was coined by one of the French enlightenment philosophers, Antoine Louis Destutt, Compte de Tracy (1754–1836) during the French Revolution. In his approach, as also reflected in the *Institut de France* that he and other philosophers founded in 1795, ideology was rationalism. The problematics or their approach was how to find the truth. The main focus of the *Institut* was to find the relationship between ideas and power. Their final concern was, using rationalism, determining how one changes the structures of power. Destutt's thoughts can be summarized in the following points, summarized by Terence Ball and Richard Dagger:

> There are three important features of de Tracy's conception of ideology: (1) the explicit linkage between logic, psychology, and politics, set down in a "table" of simple propositions and backed up with more extensive observations; (2) the assumption that intellectuals discover the truth and that well-advised political authorities implement policies to match; and (3) the claim that logic, psychology, and politics, as linked, are coincident with science and history, properly understood (p, 4).

From the above perspective, ideologies are scientific materials, which can produce predictable precision similar to the calculations and results of mathematical or physical science. Despite various struggles the Catholic Church waged against rationalism in France and Germany, ideology kept its intellectual force until Karl Marx and Friedrich Engels. They internationalized and popularized the concept through their critique of its previous usage by the German intellectuals. Karl Marx introduced material interest and its control. As Teresa Ball and Richard Dagger indicated:

> Ideologies and ideologists arise in class divided societies, according to Marx. In particular, "the class which has the means of material production at its disposal consequently also controls the means of mental production." Thinkers are "producers of ideas, in other words, while ruling classes regulate "the production and distribution of the ideas". Thus "the ideas of the ruling class are in every epoch the ruling ideas: i.e., the class which is the ruling *material* force of

society is at the same time its *ruling intellectual* force." Within the ruling class,
the division of labor divides mental from material tasks (2002, p. 5).

Marx considered ideologies as advanced by the German intellectuals as "il-
lusions and distortions," while Engels defined ideology as "false consciousness." Although Marx rejected "rationalistic ideology" as a system of bourgeois
ideas, in his work with Engels entitled *German Ideology* (1846) their usage of
ideology was perceived as scientific and historical. Marxists later constructed
and elaborated on the notion of scientific ideology, a comprehensive system that
has clearly articulated laws, agencies, and material interests. It became an instrument of social change of the proletariat.

In contrasting ideologies of the modern period to those of the classical tradition in Europe, Brian Nelson stated:

> Now let us apply this general view of modern thought to analysis of modern
> ideologies. It immediately strikes the attention that ideologies seem to be char-
> acterized by their attempt to reaffirm the unity of ethics and politics, but in a
> radically new way. In the classical tradition, the unity of ethics and politics pre-
> sumed the existence of the morally autonomous individual. This is why classi-
> cal thinkers assumed that human beings possess by nature a social and ethical
> capacity. Ideologies, on the other hand, tend to replace the idea of personal
> moral autonomy with a "higher principle of moral progress" beyond the indi-
> vidual, a principle to which the individual is to subordinate him or her. Unlike
> the higher principles of the classical tradition, such as natural law, which in-
> clude the individual as a moral agent, the higher principles characteristic of
> ideologies tend to subordinate the individual's moral agency rather than to actu-
> alize it. Marxism is one of the clearest examples of this tendency. The Marxist
> revolutionary does not choose communism as a moral ideal, but as the dictate
> of the higher principle of historical necessity. To be sure the necessity involves
> praxis, that is, the revolutionary action of the individual. Action, nevertheless,
> flows not from the impetus of ethical ideals but from a realization of a necessity
> transcending such ideals (1996, p. 360).

As indicated above, ideology was part of the movements of ideas associated
with rationalism; hence it is important to define rationalism and its basic arguments.

An ideological assessment may create an opportunity to state some prob-
abilities in human and state actions and behaviors, which may embody elements
of scientific reasoning. People believe in things and they act consequently. If we
study elements of those beliefs structurally, it may be possible to understand
them and also to make some predictions about what some people think, why
they think the way they do, and why they behave the way they do.

It should be reiterated that this concept has had various meanings over time
depending on who used it and the nature of the cultural, economic, and political
factors that influenced the user. Thus, ideologies can be revolutionary or they

can be conservative, reformist, reactionary, violent, or peaceful. I believe that in trying to show how the concept of ideology is used in the context of this book, it is possible to identify some of its common characteristics so as to comprehend its dynamics at the global level. According to Charles W. Kegley, Jr. and Eugene R. Wittkopf, "ideology is a set of core philosophical principles that a group of leaders and citizens collectively holds about politics, the interests of political actors, and the ways people ought to ethically behave (op. cit., p. 12)." It is a significant part of the political process.

Naomi Chazan, Peter Lewis, Robert Mortimer, Donald Rothchild, and Stephen Stedman define political ideologies in the following manner:

> Political ideologies, as distinct from policies, are systems of beliefs that serve as a standard of evaluation and a guide an action. They give an indication of the preferences of rulers, of their reasons for acting. In a very real sense, ideologies attempt to grapple with tangible problems, describe and explain existing conditions, and prescribe desired courses of behavior. In this respect, they encompass the conceptual, and hence the subjective, principles of political action (1999, p. 160).

Thus, from the above statement and the previous discussions, one can affirm that ideology effectively matters for citizens and states. What is more important, however, is its functioning context, its content, its social and political implications, and how it shapes people's and states' behaviors.

Socialism as an Ideology of Social Construct

Its General Definition and Its European Origins

As indicated earlier, since it was promoted during the age of reason and appropriated by intellectuals and transformed by Karl Marx and Friedrich Engels in the nineteenth century, ideology has played an important role in the definitions of the behaviors of nation-states, social classification, and intellectual categorization of social phenomena. In the twentieth century, in many countries in Europe, socialism was used and promoted by various social classes and social movements as an instrument of power and class struggles. These movements were to define history as a moving force. What we have in mind is to pursue questions such as: What do all forms of socialism have in common, if any? What are the political and economic meanings of their commonalities?

Like the concept of liberal democracy, the concept of socialism as developed in Europe did not come from only one source. It was shaped over time by various social forces and cultural, political, and intellectual ideas. Elements of its content were borrowed from many traditions, which make its current content complex. However, the main objective in this context is not to review its historiography but to identify and examine its main or primary characteristics. As Alan O. Ebenstein, William Ebenstein, and Edwin Fogelman have indicated:

Socialism, like many other movements and ideas, has no bible or single manifesto because socialists do not have one set of beliefs or doctrine. Moreover,
socialism had developed in a variety of countries in accordance with different
national traditions, and has thus taken on different meanings for this reason.
Further, as a democratic movement, it has never had a central authority to lay
down a party line (2000, p. 6).... The complex, and frequently self-
contradictory, elements of socialist thought and policy, reflecting the complexity of the societies in which they exist, are well-exemplified by the British socialist movement. While not all of these elements are as prominent now in the
British Labour party as they once were, their historical importance serves to
enlighten roots of current socialist thought (2000, p. 1995).

For instance, while the British socialist tradition embodied the four elements of religion, ethical and aesthetic idealism, Fabian empiricism, and liberalism, the Russian socialist movements were anti-religion. United States socialist
movements from the nineteenth century have been dogmatically religious. For
example, in the United States, Norman Thomas, who symbolized the cause of
socialism in the twentieth century, had been a Presbyterian minister. The United
States has a stronger tradition of the religious left than any other industrial country. In Germany and France in the nineteenth and twentieth centuries, socialists
were essentially anti-clerical. In most countries that were colonized by the European states, their socialist traditions were strangely nationalistic and traditional.

With Marxism first, and second, Leninism and third, their advocates, socialism in Europe was elevated to the level of a systematic science with a clearly
articulated method and approach (dialectical materialism), and it was decidedly
secular. While in terms of principle of how to change societies, reli-
gious/Christian socialism focused on enlightenment of the mind, charity, humil-
ity, and democracy, scientific socialism underlined the understanding of social
conditions of the working classes and the power relationship between those who
own the means of productions and the laborers. As Nelson indicates:

> Marx's scientific socialism is based upon what he terms the materialist concep-
> tion of history. To assert the possibility of communism is by definition to assert
> a historical possibility. This requires, Marx argues, a scientific understanding of
> history, an understanding that he claims the materialist conception provides.
> This materialist view conflicts with concepts of Hegelian philosophy, which in
> Marx's time, and particularly in Germany, influenced historical studies heavily.
> You will recall that Hegelian philosophy is based upon idealist rather than a
> materialist metaphysics. In Hegel's view, therefore, history involved the work-
> ing out of a spiritual principle and as such, it was to be understood in that light.
> Marx insisted that such a perspective was only leading historians and social
> theorists further and further from the truth (p. 328).

His socialism promotes the discourse of social contradictions that may lead to the social emancipation of the proletariat through class struggle. We have to study individuals and society as they really are.

In order to be consistent with the spirit of the comparative approach used in this book, a different kind of socialism articulated outside of the European historical context and development models is also projected into the study of ideology at large.

In Africa, for example, in the continent and around the world, the best-known form of socialism was the African socialism of Mwalimu Julius Nyerere of Tanzania. This is known as a homegrown form of socialism based on the ethos and the values of the African communitarian systems of production, consumption, and social management.

Socialism as a Development Paradigm in a Non-European Context: the Case of African Socialism

During the Cold War era, African socialism as articulated by Mwalimu Julius Nyerere of Tanzania was probably the only brand of socialism that was internationally accepted and that was also supported by the countries in the North and their developmental programs and foundations. Other types of socialism, such as those developed in Eastern Europe, China, Cuba, and North Korea, were perceived and defined as the enemy of liberal democracies and free market dogmas.

Social progress is a multidimensional phenomenon, but one must choose or select among diverse theories to account for all sides of a complex process to provide for a balanced treatment. Socialism as perceived by Nyerere was a combination of multiple approaches unified on one philosophical ground.

African socialism is a political ideology that guided agricultural policy in Tanzania. Starting in 1962, Nyerere conceived a general African socialism based on the village setting as an alternative to European capitalism. But it is only in the Arusha Declaration (1967) that the Tanzanian socialism became a more or less official and public political guide and a systematic way of thinking of the society, state, policy, and development. The decision was to take an evolutionary revolution path, rather than the classical revolutionary concept of Karl Marx or the class struggle advocated by Kwame Nkrumah. Two major ideas are crucial to this socialism: (a) development of rural areas in the scheme of the communitarian village systems; and (b) the idea of self-help, which means the willingness of Tanzanians to count on themselves and on their own energies, forces, self-sufficiency, and self-reliance.

Ujamaa, which is ideologically translated as "familyhood" in Kiswahili, was chosen as the model of Tanzanian socialism, which involved building a new society on the foundation of the Tanzanian past and which was based on African-ness (Nyerere, 1968, p. 2). This socialism was designed to create a society based on justice, power, and love, the three essential features of family life in Nyerere's reasoning and philosophy. As an ideology, a mode of thinking, and a belief system, it encouraged the willingness of Tanzanians to create something uniquely Tanzanian with the support of the traditional patterns of living (ibid., p. 3).

Ujamaa was also defined as a communitarian and egalitarian society in its opposition to private land titles and to the private ownership of the important sectors of the country's economy (ibid.). Its objective was to limit the force of selfish acquisitiveness and to promote communal activity and a greater sense of mutual responsibility. It was conceived as an egalitarian society to limit differences income between the rich and poor and to avoid the emergence of dominant economic classes in the countryside. It was also intended to be democratic: leaders should be electorally responsible to the people and should limit themselves to persuasion, encouragement, and example. This system is "rational" and could be used only among equals (Nyerere, 1963, p. 16).

This socialism was conceived as unique in its foundation, methods, and philosophical and historical roots, but it was also an international phenomenon. According to Nyerere, this universal concept should relate to the people of Tanzania as they were. That is to say, this kind of socialism had to take into account the peculiarities of the history, culture, and resources of Tanzanians. All this implied that while the Tanzanian socialism was part of international socialism philosophically, it was not an extension of any other forms of socialism. For Nyerere, geohistorical and cultural elements should determine the form and the content of a given social formation (ibid., p. 3).

The common characteristics of the different forms of international socialism are not clear. Are the organization and management of labor, or the productive and distributive mechanisms, or the control of means of production, common characteristics to all varieties of international socialism?

Nyerere believed that social progress could be triggered through serious peaceful discourses. Kwame Nkrumah of Ghana, Nyerere's contemporary, for example, believed that it was only through some forms of class struggle that social progress was possible: proletarians, revolutionary intellectuals or organic intellectuals, and other progressive social classes should take arms or form a vanguard class against the oppressive social formations in the formal and neo-colonial contexts. However, Tanzania was a peasant society and as such, the peasants, rather than proletarians, should take initiatives for changing their own social environment by the means they possessed and which they controlled. All this should have led to the establishment of a system of governance compatible to their needs, culture, and history. This resembles some of the paradigms developed by E. F. Schumacher in his book entitled *Small Is Beautiful: Economics as if People Mattered*, 1973.

In recent years, before the collapse of the Marxist and socialist regimes in the world, there were debates from the left on the issues of whether revolutionary policies were possible and consistent without class struggle or some form of "modified" social struggles. Another aspect has been whether such policies can be revolutionary if inequalities rather than conflicts are the bases of their practices. In my view, there cannot be any revolutionary policies without revolutionary ideas, principles, and thoughts that reflect and challenge the social conditions of a given milieu. The current popular movements show that things cannot change without some form of struggle. Nyerere's model of revolutionary change was conceived as a synthesis of international socialism and African social systems. This synthesis provided the basis for organization and social action (Nyerere, 1961, pp. 30-32). For Nyerere, ideology is an instrument of social development. As Chazan et al. state:

> The African socialism of the 1960s was nationalist in orientation and evolutionary in thrust. Although encompassing quite divergent stands, all early socialists, from Nyerere to Sékou Touré, proclaimed a commitment to the creation of an egalitarian, just, and self-sufficient polity. The mechanism for the attainment of these goals was the state, which would furnish the pivot of critical identities, organize the economy, and supervise the second, societal, phase of decolonization. Although differing substantially in the degree to which they relied on precolonial values and traditional institutions to promote these goals, African socialist worldviews extolled political centralization and mobilization as the vehicles for real transformation. Socialism at this juncture was hence both Afrocentric and non-aligned: It shunned to unselective transfer of socialist terminology (such as the class struggle) to Africa and at the same time laid claim to a universality of political ideals (1999, p. 161).

To not recognize the role and the power of ideology in a social science analysis would lead to ignorance of the essence of understanding the factors that shape the process of building social life, which is based on convictions about power of the belief systems in Weberian or Marxist perspectives. But not all ideas can form or can constitute the foundation of an ideology. Ideology is rather a conscious defined expression than a collection of some general and vague ideas about the self, collective self, society, and others.

Chapter 6

Theories of Corporate Power

Introduction: Objectives, Issues, and Framework of the Analysis

In contemporary world, the area of corporate power is a contested domain of control between the state and private corporations, the economy and the public, and the management and ownership (O'Sullivan, 2000). The main objectives in this chapter are to identify and raise theoretical, ideological, and social issues associated with the contemporary elements of the corporate world and to discuss their policy assumptions and implications both at the domestic and international-relations levels. I define corporatism and the major arguments the discourse on it has produced; I also identify and discuss the foundation of corporate power and its general policy and philosophical claims. In an effort to define corporatism, I further examine its main characteristics. One cannot fully comprehend the significance of private corporate power as an ideological phenomenon without defining what capitalism is and what it represents in political relations and policy discourse. Thus, there is a brief discussion of capitalism and the privatization of the state as another dimension of the corporatization of world politics. The discussion is essentially theoretical.

However, to balance my arguments between claims and assumptions associated with social sciences' theory and practice, and also because the question of foreign debt is clearly part of the global discourse on corporate power, I also touch on, albeit briefly, the question of debt and debt relief as an issue currently debated in the African region.

There are some theoretical, ideological, and political disagreements on what constitutes corporate power in a broad sense among various social classes, nation-states, scholars, and people the world over. Furthermore, many scholars and policy makers from different perspectives, with different objectives, and for different reasons have characterized the end of the twentieth century and the beginning of the twenty-first century as the century of global corporatism. In dealing with this subject, one should try to identify the common and consistent characteristics that these two centuries share relative to global capitalism. What are those dominant characteristics and how are they different from other centuries? Although my interest and focus are on the concept of private corporate power, I have also touched on corporate power in general.

At this stage of the development of international capitalism, with its technological innovations and its expanded market and basis of communication, giant companies without necessarily respecting the principles of the "rational" competition, comparative advantage, and the free market are aggressively buying other major companies, especially in the United States and Western Europe. This complex mechanism of accumulating surplus is leading, once again, to the articulation of monopoly capitalism in which mega-companies, as the central actors or the dominant powers, are guiding and shaping the direction of the international capitalism. The corporate oligopoly, which was broken in the 1960s and 1970s by new firms and other economic actors entering the market, and the growing power of the oil-producing states (Mansbach, 2000, p. 201) have come back with force.

Within the logic and the functioning of the international political economy and the failures of the nation-states and the global institutions to systematically contribute towards the improvement qualitatively and quantitatively of the living conditions of the majority of people in most parts of the world, there is a need to critically review, redefine, and reconceptualize corporatism. What are its values and how are they maintained and distributed?

Some scholars have argued that in order to understand and appreciate the dynamics of any phenomenon—in this case, corporate power, its social base, and its causal relations with other phenomena in a given environment—one must be able to measure its presence and activities and to assess its consequences with precision in utilizing quantitative methods, that is the science of numbers (statistics, econometrics, and other social science research methods including the qualitative method). In support of the above view, A. T. Kearny cites the Scottish physicist Lord Kelvin who indicated:

> When you can measure what you are speaking about, and express it in numbers, you know something about it. But when you cannot measure it, when you cannot express it in numbers, your knowledge is of a meager and unsatisfactory kind (2001, p. 56).

Although the above principle is central to any research inquiry, however, the studies of its social ramifications and the consequences of its actions should go beyond its simple logic. In studying corporate power, the nature of the structures of state-society relations and their historical and cultural development should also embody valuable factors, which can enhance understanding of state-society-corporate partnerships. Thus, there is a need for continuously and systematically considering qualitative typology as an important analytical perspective in this section.

Although some scholars think that the intensity of private corporatism is declining in the advanced capitalist states, as well as within the major institutions that have promoted it, at the end of the twentieth century in part because of the strength and interests of regionalization and democracy movements, its universal and/or international claims and energies have become more part of the DSP today than ever before. It is not clear which dimensions or levels of corporatism have been declining, if any. Thus, it is necessary to define and reconceptualize corporatism and clarify how it is used in this context.

I am specifically interested in the dynamics of state-centricism, or what may also be called the concept of the corporatist state, the domination of the state in governing, governance, social or class relations, and also in private corporatist practices and politics, as articulated by global financial institutions such as the World Bank and the IMF.

Furthermore, I have identified elements of corporate power and examined their political and social implications rather than focused on the organization theory of the corporate world, despite its importance in the way corporate power operates. I did not focus on the neo-Weberian institutional structure of interest intermediation. Rather, my focus is more on the ideological aspect of corporatism, which is related to a Marxist social class and policy analysis.

Private corporations in general are interested in growth, namely surplus accumulation and productivity. To understand the nature of their power base, one needs to examine how capitalism works and how the surplus is produced or obtained. And states, in principle, are interested in the questions of control and distribution of resources, people's participation, and security/protection. How do states and corporations engage in dialogue with one another?

The role of private corporate power as an agency of international relations, national development, and international political economy is politically and philosophically perplexing and controversial. Some scholars have argued, especially dependency theorists, that this type of corporate power has been one of the major causes of underdevelopment in the developing world. To put it simply, the movement of private capital and the mechanisms of producing the surplus lead to rapid overexploitation of labor and raw materials, and capital flight, the factors which have accelerated underdevelopment. There are others who have also advanced the views that no country or nation in the world of the states can survive without integrating the culture and identity of private corporate power. From this perspective, corporate power provides the necessary prerequisites such as liberal and free marketing, competition, foreign investment, and accumulation, which are important for economic development and perhaps for political pluralism as well. This proposition, in light of historical conflicts or contradictions between the free market and political development or economic reforms and political change in developing world, has led to building a lower degree of intellectual consensus concerning the role of corporate power.

What authority and legitimacy does the private corporate world have in influencing domestic and international affairs? Is its power real or myth? How does it function within the logic and structures of the sovereignty of nation-states? It should be noted that within the Western-dominated paradigms of economic development and political democracy, there is normatively and philosophically antinomy between the state and the private interests and markets. The public and the private sectors, representing the state institutions and the free market respectively, function within the logic of "dichotomous" and dualistic "irrationality" versus "rationality." How can the contemporary states and economic forces work to decrease this unnecessary antinomy? This is one of the underscored objectives behind the arguments articulated in this section.

Historically, some nation-states have succeeded in decreasing the aforementioned level of tension in favor of human and social progress by constructing mitigating mechanisms or instruments between the state and the market, while in other countries and regions of the world this antinomy has engendered more misery and poverty. The states and the private sector have interestingly developed positive dialogues in some countries, such as the Scandinavian countries, Switzerland, Austria, and some other Western European countries. Until recently, Japan, for instance, has been perceived and defined by many people as an example of a "perfect" corporate state in which the state and private corporations harmoniously work together in rigid hierarchical structures to promote and protect state-societal interests. In the case of Sweden, for instance, Kunkel and Pontusson pointed out that: "Sweden's claim to rank at the top of the corporatist league hinges on the highly centralized system of economy-wide wage bargaining that came into being in the 1950s (1998; p. 2)." In post-Franco Spain, for example, Heywood indicates that "Social pacts in Spain have been used as temporary adjustment measures rather than as a long-term policy instrument, reflecting the lack of entrenched social interests with privileged access to the policy arena (1998, p. 226)."

As mentioned earlier, the antinomy, which is not a natural phenomenon, has been better resolved in some countries, such as Sweden, than in others. In other countries, it has been consolidated through economic reforms to limit the state's authority and power to adopt any restraints against the dogmas of so-called free trade. However, as elaborated elsewhere in this book, despite this antinomy, the laws that regulate and protect the market forces are not natural laws or laws of economics. They are state laws. Thus, despite real or possible tensions, the market is *de facto* under the political determinism of the state. It is important to search for theoretical elements that can help create a balance in terms of actions, policies, and behaviors among the state, the community, and the market. I argue that development and underdevelopment can be studied by examining the nature of this balance. Countries, which have historically had a lower balance in actions among the state, the community, and the market, are societies with a higher level of economic and political difficulties. Where can this balance be placed among these three sectors of human life and experience? Who should articulate this balance?

Why is it that some corporations have contributed significantly to social and economic progress in some countries, especially in Western European liberal and social welfare states, while in many other countries in the developing world, for instance, corporations have been perceived as the agents of underdevelopment and consequently detrimental to the well-being of the societies and citizenry? Do the origins of financial, economic, marketing, manufacturing, or industrial corporations as defined in classical terms, matter when examining the nature and the quality of their impact on social classes, gender relations, state sovereignty, public policies, and the physical environment in a given country or a region of the world? Why is it that private capital from the United States, an important part of corporate power, through the Marshall Plan, has had a long-lasting positive impact on the devastated economies of the Western European countries which were involved in World War II? These questions are not dealt with in this section; they do, however, help to focus on and to be critical toward the objectives as described above.

The role of corporate interests or well-organized private interests in state formation or in the public sector of the contemporary world of the states has been more than controversial, as alluded to earlier. It has been so in part because of the individualized and privatized nature of those interests in the process of profit-making, managing labor, distributing goods, and consumption patterns. The political and social contradictions related to the processes of production and accumulation make corporate power very suspect in terms of its real or possible positive contributions to the improvement of the well-being of citizens and their political participation.

Since the end of the 1980s, with the intensification of the level of poverty in many parts of the world, especially in Africa, the generalized analytical observation has been that corporate power, with its profit-making motive and its general hostility to democracy and social progress, is the single most important factor contributing to the degradation of life in social and environmental terms. An important question is: As people and societies search for new paradigms of social progress and new policy alternatives to improve their social conditions, can we continue to consider corporate power as a "permanent evil," which should be permanently excluded or alienated from policy possibilities or options in political debates? Or, what kind of role, if any, should corporate power play in political and social progress schemes?

Since the corporate debates of the 1970s, as reflected in the works of well-established scholars such as Philippe C. Schmitter, G. Lehmbruch, and D. Brand in their studies of South America and Western Europe, the interest in social sciences in theorizing about the nature of the relationship between the state (public) and corporate world (private interest/profit) has grown. Philippe Schmitter's article entitled "Still the Century of Corporatism," in *Review of Politics*, 36, 1 (85-131), provided a solid intellectual reference in the discourses on corporatism. Undeliberately, using European and South American cases, he paved the ways toward its universalization. Several combined factors make the studies of corporatism vital or central to international political economy and comparative politics since the 1970s: (1) efforts toward the Europeanization and popularization of Margaret Thatcher's policy (Prime Minister of Great Britain in the 1970s) to dismantle the welfare state in Britain; (2) the collapse of the Soviet Union; (3) the adoption of the Maastricht Treaty in 1991 for creating a common European currency (Euro) in the European Union; (4) the universalization of the structural adjustment programs (SAPs) of the World Bank and the International Monetary Fund (IMF) and their failures; and (5) the recent global mobilization or global protest against the principles and policies of the global financial institutions.

Clearly, there are emerging intellectual and public policy interests in social sciences as reflected in many studies of globalization in political science and environmental and development studies to analyze the philosophical nature, the policy implications, and the sociological and political significance of corporate power in a slowly changing world. Yet this world is still, in terms of resource allocation and distribution, firmly and structurally unequal. Corporate globalization also comes with balkanization and marginalization of some states, citizens, and their economies and markets. What has been the nature of the relationship among the community, which is characterized as spontaneous solidarity, the market, which is identified and analyzed as dispersed competition, and the state, known as hierarchical control (Schmitter and Streeck, 1985, p. 1)?

The role of the corporate world in international relations and national economies and political affairs is not new. However, the nature of its impact and its patterns of growth are new. The colonial European states, especially the the Dutch, the English, the French, and the Spanish in the early colonial period, were created as extensions or expansions of private corporate power or as political entities with solid alliances with private corporate power. For instance, in the Caribbean, the Dutch West India Company, chartered in 1621, aggressively took the struggle to the Spanish Indies and destroyed the Spanish Atlantic fleets. Thus, the Dutch became the most successful traders in the Caribbean (Knight, 1990, pp. 50-051). *Compagnie des Indes Occidentales*, the Royal African Company, and the Company of Merchants operated the slave trade, which was known as the triangular trade, which for many years became the foundation of colonization. The French also advanced their settlements under the auspices of the *Compagnie des Iles d'Amérique*, which was chartered by Cardinal Richelieu in 1635. "The company settled in Martinique and Guadeloupe, and thus gave France a permanent interest in the Caribbean (op. cit, p. 52)." In most cases, as is well known, states and cities were established by corporations with the exception of the models of the classical Mediterranean city-states, like Sparta and Athens in the fifth century B.C.E., most of which were organizationally militaristic.

The making of profits and exploitation of labor and resources were the first motive for the establishment of colonies. This was the cases with the East Indian Company (India), the Virginia Company, known also as the London Company, (Virginia), the Massachusetts Bay Company (Massachusetts), Lord Baltimore (Maryland), Group of Nobles (North and South Carolina), the Duke of York (by conquest of the Dutch, New York), Berkeley and Carteret (by purchase from the

Duke of York, New Jersey), and Oglethorpe and the Group of Trustees (Georgia). It was for the main purpose of profiting from farming, gold mining, and trade that the above colonies articulated their nondemocratic forms of governance that allowed them to advance their commercial and economic businesses. States were, in fact, institutions for advancing and protecting private rather than public interests.

Between the seventeenth and nineteenth centuries, the political structures in Europe during the mercantilist era can be described as semi-private and semi-public, fully supported by the power and the blessing of the Catholic Church as Franklin W. Knight stated:

> The organizational structure which Europeans fashioned for their empires responded to their perceived needs as well as the actual circumstances of the seventeenth century; but it prevailed, with only minor modifications, until the nineteenth century. The structures did not vary greatly among imperial divisions, having been conscious imitations of the most successful aspects of the expansive empiricism of the age. The basis of these schemes rested on the delegation of public functions to private corporations or associations of merchants such as the Dutch West India Company, Richelieu's *Compagnie des Iles d'Amérique,* or any of the numerous charters given to Roger North, William Courteen, or the Earl of Carlisle. All charters and companies involved in American exploration, trade, and colonization at that time blended political activities of the medieval guilds and corporations in Europe with the cooperative stockholding concerns of the Italian and Dutch cities. They therefore possessed three characteristics: financial support through joint-stocks, with shareholders receiving a share of the profits; political supervision in their sphere of operations; and some form of economic monopoly from their chartering government (1990, pp. 56-57).

In Africa, the case of the Democratic Republic of Congo (Belgian Congo) is an eloquent illustration in which the country was first of all given to Léopold II as his personal property (a personal domain) between 1885 and 1908 (the so-called Congo Free State). In order to obtain material resources and labor from this private estate, about ten million Congolese were killed. Because of strong intervention by France, the United Kingdom, and the United States, this property was given to the Kingdom of Belgium, as a result of extreme mismanagement and atrocities that were committed by the corporate power and the political authority. This property was transformed into a colony between 1910 and 1960. The colony was ruled by the trinity of three forces, namely the Church, representing the power of God; private companies, representing the power associated with the exploitation of gold; and the Belgian State, searching for glory. The management of these colonial states by the representatives of the corporate world was essentially dictatorial and authoritarian.

In the twentieth century, the corporate world has also been known as corporate globalization, global capitalism, or corporate capitalism. Immanuel Wallerstein and Samir Amin, as recalled earlier, have referred to it as "the world system." Although there are perhaps some nuances distinguishing the above concepts, depending on the context and the ideological disposition and intellectual rigor of the user, they also refer to a system of rules whose power is determined by the laws of accumulation of surplus, the dynamics of the free market economy, privatization, the *laissez-faire* principle, and restructuring or economic reforms. Thus, aspects of the theories of the corporate world can be discussed in terms of its organization, the processes of production, consumption, growth, marketing, dependency, and political influence and control. I am very much interested in the impact of the corporate world on the society-state's relationships and on its policy implications within the framework of the structures of state power. According to Hilary French,

> The world economy has grown sixfold since 1950, rising from $6.7 trillion to $41.6 trillion in 1998. But exports increased 17-fold over this period, reaching $5.4 trillion in 1998. While exports of goods accounted for only 5 percent of the growth world product in 1950, by 1998 this figure climbed to 13 percent. In recent decades, international investment by multinational corporations has also exploded. Over the 1980s, foreign direct investment flows grew twice as fast as trade—increasing 15-fold between 1970 and 1998, from $44 billion to $644 billion. The number of transnational corporations (TNCs) has also soared in recent decades, increasing from only 7,000 in 1970 to more than 53,000 in 1998. And not only companies are investing abroad... Some 44 million U.S. households have at least some money in mutual funds, up from only 4.6 million in 1980. Their dollars are increasingly invested overseas: the assets of U.S.-based international and global mutual funds climbed from just $16 billion in 1986 to $321 billion at the end of the 1996 (2000, p. 5).

In the statement below, Mansbach indicates the complexity of private corporate power and its international ideological contradictions as he states:

> Even when they have no political intent, corporate decisions may have important political consequences, over which governments have limited control. IBM, for example, illegally exported advanced computers to a Russian nuclear weapons laboratory, causing one observer to declare. "This shows that one of America's leading corporations has been undermining national security because it was willing to take risks in entering the Russian market." Swiss, British, French, Italian, American, and most important, German firms aided Iraq and Libya efforts to make weapons of mass destruction. German companies such as Karl Kolb, Rhein Bayern Fahrzeugbau Thyssen GmbH, Gildermeista projecta, Inwako, and Messerschmitt-Boelkow-Blohn are accused of providing Iraq with lathes and presses to enrich uranium, plants and equipment to produce poison

gas, equipment to make bottling toxin and myco toxin weapons, and equipment for improving Scud Missiles (2002, pp. 201-2).

What are the theoretical, policy, and political issues involved in examining the nature of the practices of the corporate world and its growth in relationship to its power and the power of the states?

Since the end of the Cold War between the Soviet Union and the United States and their allies, political activism against the corporate world has emerged. For instance, since the meeting of 135 trade ministers in Seattle, Washington, in the United States in November 1999, where tens of thousands of demonstrators with different social, political, and ideological backgrounds from all over the world protested against the World Trade Organization (WTO), many other similar meetings have been challenged by massive protests, which, in general, have been met with strong violence by state security forces.

What are the main reasons for this activism? Is it possible for contemporary states to organize societies and manage their resources alone without corporations? Do states have enough resources to govern without cooperating with corporations? How does the power of corporations manifest itself, in a short and long run, in the world of the states? What mechanisms does the corporate world use to control or negotiate with the states?

Indeed, corporate power has become an important part of the lexicon of protests. Thus, there is a need to continue to intellectually and socially redefine it in order to understand its complex dimensions, its implications, its impact, and its power base in the world of the states.

World politics in its complex dimensions is increasingly defined in terms of "vanishing borders" (Hilary French, 2000) from the point of views of the principle of international trade, environmental impact and assessment, and communication technology. As pointed out earlier, however, the world of the states is still articulated in terms of territoriality, physical or imagined borders, citizenship, and sovereignty. Within the framework of so-called security factors, state nationalism is constantly challenging many aspects of the theory of "vanishing borders." The concept of security is still very much a militaristic one. How much can the "vanishing borders'" theory help us understand the nature and the role of corporate power in the world of the states with their market protectionism? How do states interact with the corporate world?

It should be mentioned that there is a corporatist state model, as in Japan, where the politics and policy of allocation and distribution of resources and policy formulation are determined by well-articulated, negotiated schemes between the state and the corporations (or the private sector of the economy) from the bottom up to the highest level of government. There is a constant effort to balance policy between the corporate interests and those of the public/state. There are also Western European models, where corporate power and interests, despite their importance in influencing policy and politics, are theoretically subordinate to state power in terms of decision making, with the exception of perhaps some welfare states such as the Netherlands. In this case, corporate interests must simultaneously serve the public interests. There is the United States model, where the corporate interests (with perhaps the exception of security interest in a technical sense) are perceived by many segments of the United States political elite as superior to those of the state. In this case, the interests of the corporate world, such as those of corporate industrial companies which fabricate arms and own military technologies, are the determining factors in foreign and domestic policy making. For instance, George Walker Bush's cabinet (2001–2004) is called "Corporate America." Fifteen members of his cabinet have been leaders in corporations in areas such as oilfield services, banking, transportation, technology, food and trade, agribusiness and biotech, and real estate. With their public base of power, they articulate public policies that support corporate interests. The United States has a stronger, better organized, better financed, and thoroughly professional lobbying system than any other country in the world. Then there is the case where the state is a client of transnationals and powerful states. This model was adopted in many developing countries, such as Liberia with Firestone and mining companies like LAMCO, and the DRC under Mobutu with *la Companie Minière du Haut Katanga* (Lumumba-Kasongo, 1992).

In real or pragmatic terms, especially toward the end of the twentieth century, it has become clear that the politics and policies of the world of the states are essentially shaped and determined more by economic forces, military and communication technologies, and their markets than by the so-called primordial factors such as ethnicity, religion, and family relations, despite the fact that these factors still play an important role in the unwritten aspects of national and global policies. It is the level of economic development and political stability related to the dimensions of the military organization of a state that bring respectability and energy to the global negotiations in which states are engaged. They ensure that states will create alliances, develop puppetism, and advance their policies.

In most of the issues raised in the above section, corporatism tends to be perceived as a force external to the state structures, an independent entity with which the state must engage to promote specific interests and objectives. These interests and objectives can fluctuate depending on the modes of both states and the corporations and the conditions of their reproduction. There is, however, another form of corporatism, which is known as an internal structure of the state, or an arm of the state. It has also flourished in many parts of the world since the nineteenth century. States have also produced and maintained their private interests. These private interests can support political parties, public policies, or class interests depending on the nature of the political configurations in a given country at a given time.

It should be emphasized that all contemporary states possess their own enterprises or corporations, which are, in principle, sponsored largely by public money and investments. They are called *les sociétés d'État*. These state-owned enterprises, although politically the instruments of the national power elite, have objectives similar to those of private corporations, namely, to make a profit or surplus. Do the differences between the first kind of corporatism and the second kind exist only in terms of the social usage of their profit, or are the differences also a result of the mechanisms of how the profit is produced? Are, for instance, the Chinese state-owned enterprises within their new ideological base of "socialism with market economy" different in their mechanisms of production, operations, and their management from the privately owned enterprises located in the free-zone areas?

After World War II, the liberal welfare states in Western Europe firmly expanded this type of internal structural corporatism. Until recently, in developing countries nationalization, in some of its extreme forms, has been one of the means through which political elites created state-owned corporations. In many African countries, nationalization took names such as "ivorianization," "liberianization," "togolization," and "zairianization." In Tanzania, under Mwalimu Nyerere, for instance, it implied the consolidation of self-reliance and *uhuru* (independence). Although the outcomes of these nationalizations vary from one country to another, their generalized common feature and claim has been the effort of the states to create extra and relatively guaranteed sources of revenues for the state in appropriating foreign or private companies. But for a state that was born through national revolution, the production of state-owned corporations should be considered as a normal outcome of the history of state formation. Corporations must serve the public, as this is the ultimate purpose of being a revolutionary state. It would be interesting to discuss theoretically what these two types of corporatism have in common and how they can or might contribute to providing, capital, human, and material resources to a given society at large.

It should be indicated, however, that the fascist dictatorships or regimes guided by extreme nationalism in Europe in the 1940s, Mobutu of Zaïre (DRC), or Bokassa of Central African Republic, were also supported by modern corporatism. The association of this kind of nationalism with the negation of the state defined in the form of citizens' rights and the raw physical and military appropriation of the public domain makes the concept of corporatism controversial.

Toward Conceptualizing and Theorizing Elements of Corporate Power

General Issues

The activity of theorizing involves an initial process of conceptual mapping (Steals, 1998, p. 61). As indicated previously, it is difficult to define the concept of corporatism with precision. In terms of organization and relationshipz between agents within a given organization and how interests are negotiated, nation-states also are characterized, to a large certain extent, as other forms of corporate power as economic and financial corporations are. The state is also very much a money-making machine and a power-control entity in its own name. Based on its coercive power, it appropriates, relocates, and distributes material resources and social values to enforce its own legitimacy. What happens to societies when and if states behave like private domains?

The main intention is to conceptualize the economic and political aspects of corporations, to identify their main theoretical components, and to discuss the nature of their power base. The major components of the theoretical dimensions of corporate power include the major arguments concerning capitalism and the privatization of the state.

I partially agree with Stan Luger, in his review of Mitchell's book, *The Generous Corporation: Political Analysis of Economic Power* (New Haven, Yale University Press, 1989), as he indicates that political scientists have usually ignored the corporation as a proper area of study, although it exerts enormous power, for instance, in the case of the United States (1990, p. 972). Nevertheless, it has also been argued historically that there is no period in the contemporary world of the states during which corporatist interests, that is to say, private, organized interests, were developed and managed without some support from the public sector, the governing elite, or the ruling class, such support being legal, political, cultural, or social. As Ted Lowi correctly indicated in the case of the United States and other states, for instance, "The States continue to provide virtually all the legal support systems of American capitalism, despite the constitutional revolution of the 1930s. Even in countries with classical European-type states, a similar legal support is provided (2001, p. 135)."

Within the same issue of identifying the nature of the corporate governance's relationship, from which one can define its power base and its complexity, Jane Collier and John Roberts wrote:

> Beyond these conceptions of governance, there is yet another set of issues revolving around the concerns of the indirect stakeholders. The focus here is on the effects of corporate activity in the communities within which a company operates. The basis of these wider relationships is tacit: "license to operate," the granting of rights and associated obligations to the corporate entity by wider society. The state and legal institutions play a key role here in setting the ground rules within which corporate can be expected to operate, and in enforcing sanctions where possible (2001, pp. 67-68).

This support can, in many forms, alter the notion of "pure" corporatism or the "pure" state that some scholars have used in defining these concepts. The concept of pure types (Hempel, 1952) is a problematic notion in terms of theorizing a complex notion such as corporatism, unless it is reduced to a formal concept or a mathematical or econometric formula. For this author, formal conceptualization can only be understood as a limited methodology to be used toward the understanding of this phenomenon and solving its internal contradictions. In order to understand it, the greater part of the efforts should be put into the dynamics of political sociology and the political economy of the corporate world.

In social sciences, in general, the notion of "purity" is exclusively unscientific and ahistorical, and thus is epistemologically absolute, dangerous, and limited as part of an explanatory tool. Therefore, the focus in discussing corporatist interests and their ramifications has been to identify the nature of the causal relationships among phenomena, to discuss the dominant classificatory elements of the corporate world, for instance, class, gender, state, business, and market, to explore how these elements interact with one another, and to assess the nature of the impact of the power of influence between states and corporations. This is what we call "power relations," the relationships that can significantly influence the directions, structures, and intentions of the actions of some individuals and their history at a specific time. Power relations are the dynamic relations that move things according to some specific intended and predictable objectives of the most powerful entities within a given social or physical arrangement. These exchanges can be described as correlations, which are simply the predictable or anticipated relationships between and among variables. Another way of assessing the nature of correlations is to examine their outcomes, or what the mainstream economists call the "end product."

It is difficult to find a nation-state that emerged after the 1648 Peace of Westphalia in Europe without the involvement of some private interests or business classes, be they individual citizens or private corporations. But the level and the quality of the interests involved and their management and organization informs the role corporations have effectively played in such state formation.

It is also important to make a brief distinction within the parameters of state formation between corporatism and voluntarism, which has been part of liberal democracy in the West. Corporatism, in its classical usage and as it is used in this context, implies entrepreneurial profit-making of individuals or groups in the marketplace. It is an organization with paid agents and the mechanisms of production. In a modern society, it is generally a planned organization. Voluntarism, on the other hand, can be defined as part of civic duty; it implies civic consciousness. It is a not-for-profit and philanthropic activity. For instance, the United States' political development has been partially supported by individualism and philanthropic activities, which are the elements of voluntarism. As Kenneth Newton states:

> Voluntary organizations are a special kind of social organization because they are neither family, nor work, nor state: we are born into families; we cannot avoid the state; and most us have to work. Voluntary organizations, clubs, intermediate voluntary and collaborative activities we are involved in. Membership is entirely up to individuals who engage in a set of cooperative activities to achieve their mutual goals, whatever these may be (2001, p. 206).

Voluntary organizations can play a role in the socialization process and in developing social capital and political trust (Ibid; pp. 201-202). But the above organizations lack the competitiveness, rigidity, profitability, and organizational complexity associated with the corporate world as advanced in this book. Thus, voluntary organizations, as part of the arguments of corporate world, were not explored here. The focus is to reflect further on the nature of the relationship between the idea of profitability and the public.

Conceptualizing or Theorizing Corporate Power

According to Kevin Keasey, Steve Thompson, and Mike Wright (1997), there are four competing theories concerning corporate governance. The question is, Where is the power located within these theories? The first is the "Principal-Agent or Finance Model," which is the most prominent of the four. The second is the "Myopic Market Model," which focuses on the managers' short-term orientations. The third model holds the view that the main problem of corporate governance rests in the abuse of power by corporate elites, hence the name "Abuse of Power Model." The fourth model embodies the view that "the purpose of the firm should be defined more widely than the maximization of shareholder welfare alone. There should be some explicit recognition of welfares of other groups having a long-term association with the firm such as suppliers, customers, and particularly, employees" (Gong, 1998). This last model is called the "Stakeholder Model." For the purpose of this book, we put more emphasis on the last model because it focuses on some aspects of "dependencies" between the state and society in the form of "welfarism," which are important in the relationship between the state, citizens/customers, and the corporate power. Is it possible to develop a win-win theory of corporate power?

As indicated earlier, the concept of corporatism is multidimensional. In this section, I clarify its usage and the arguments concerning power relations. As Gerhard Lehmbruch states: "We may understand 'corporatism' as highly complex phenomenon (or a set of phenomena) of which different dimensions are covered by diverse conceptualization" (Lehmbruch and Schmitter, 1982, p. 3).

I examine some general conceptual elements of this phenomenon in identifying its common or di-similar characteristics. Lehmbruch cited the theory of "modern" corporatism first developed by American authors of the New Deal era. Within this sense, it designated an economic system opposed to market liberalism and having strong connotations of managerial bureaucratization and state intervention in the economy and planning (Ibid). However, he also recognized that:

> The concept of corporatism was first developed by French theorists referring to a quite restricted concept of 'corporatism,' namely a functional association comparable to the estates and guilds of the Ancient Regime. The equivocation with the business first is excluded in French since here the relevant legal term is '*société*' (anonyme) (Ibid., p. 28).

This definition has something to do with the ways the political regime or the French Empire at large organizationally related to its subjects.

Early in the 1950s, Scandinavian scholars, especially Swedish scholars such as G. Heckscher, O. Ruin, and N. Elvander, emphasized in their concept of neo-

corporatism the tendencies of free corporatism in describing the intense cooperation of the state and organized interests that developed during World War II.
That is to say, neo-corporatism implies intense relations between the public and
the private sectors, reflected in organizational participation by government. In
short, as Ruin quoted by Lebmbruch indicated, corporatism is defined in terms
of "a situation where the interest organizations are integrated in the governmental decision-making process of a society (1974, p. 172). This definition implies a
situation of pluralistic interest-negotiating schemes, which constantly take place
among groups to protect and to promote their interests. The above argument can
also be supported by Dahl's concept of American-style political pluralism, in
which he emphasized how power sharing, an essential part of the American democracy as compared to the old European system of solid class consolidation, is
derived from the views of various political elites competing for the public space.

Philippe Schmitter underscores, in his definition of corporatism, the structure of the system of interest intermediation. Corporatism is characterized by
"the dimensions of recognition and the control by the government and the system of interest intermediation (Lehmbruch and Schmitter, 1982, p. 5). In my
view, this system of interest intermediation means that a mutuality of interest
can be identified, discussed, and bargained for. Mutuality of some kinds and
governmental control are among some of the most important characteristics of
corporatism as defined by Schmitter.

Thomas M. Magstadt defines corporatism or the corporatist model as "a
system characterized by an alliance of government, labor, and business forged in
order to shape public policy more effectively (1998, Glossary, G-5)." Hague, et
al., define corporatism in its traditional terms as:

> a system in which the state organizes a series of 'corporations,' each of which
> represents groups of workers and employers, although remaining subordinate to
> the state. As applied to modern states, corporatism refers to the tendency for
> policy to result from negotiations between the government and organized inter-
> ests (1992, p. 460).

For Paul Heywood, the traditional corporatist state implies the establishment of pacts and social concertations (1987). It means the process of producing
and managing pacts between government and social partners in order to produce
predictable outcomes. It should also be stated that in advanced capitalist states
the nature of the social pact varies from country to country.

In general, the foregoing discussion supports the view that corporatism refers to the organization of contemporary corporate or state capitalism exempli-
fied by the United States and Japan. Some political scientists tend to see corporatism or corporate power as conceptually a problematics in political science. It
is perceived as a phenomenon that is related to corruption, abnormality, and
immorality, as it too easily evokes the specter of fascism and authoritarian rule
(Schmitter and Lehmbruch, 1982, p. 263). During the Cold War era, some

scholars connoted the authoritarian politics of Austria, Italy, Portugal, the So-
viet-bloc Eastern European countries, the newly emerging nations in Asia, and
South Africa with corporatism. Few characteristics of corporatism that have led
to intellectual skepticism by some scholars include its monopolistic and hierarchical tendencies. The accumulative processes of the corporate world also tend
to embody and promote efficiency over social justice. Scholars also recognize,
however, that despite the differences among them, the Scandinavian countries,
for instance, are all essentially democratic in their political behaviors and decision-making processes, and they have also developed "social" dimensions of the
corporate world. In general, companies have been participating in collective
actions for the good of the majority of the people in those societies. Thus, it is
possible to have democratic control over special interests.

In the view of this author, one of the most important questions is, How does
one project organized interests in policy in an attempt to correct the dimensions
of corruption, or unethical, authoritarian, and fascist tendencies in the domains
of policy formulation and implementation? How can these tendencies be controlled without completely destroying the meaning or the essence of being a
corporate power? What kind of bargaining takes place between the private sector and the state?

The work of Peter Katzenstein on Austria and Switzerland is a relevant illustration of the concept of democratic corporatism that I have alluded to in the
discussion above, as he wrote:

> The first of the three characteristics of democratic corporatism, an ideology of social
> partnership (rather than class conflict), captures routine politics in societies such as
> Austria and Switzerland. The ideological cohesion that results does not lead to the
> end of political conflict. Rather, conflict is framed within vaguely held but firmly
> shared notions of the public good. Such notions pervade political arrangements, but
> they are to be found in particular in major interest groups, which are both centralized
> and inclusive. The leadership of Switzerland's "peak Switzerland association" of
> business or of Austria's trade union movement enjoys very strong powers over a
> compliant membership….This kind of corporatism, however, retains its democratic
> character through its close links to political parties. Electoral competition is a peri-
> odic shock to and interruption of a potentially dangerous celebration of consensus.
> The third defining characteristic of democratic corporatism is a particular style of
> political bargaining. It is voluntary, informal, and continuous; it coordinates the con-
> flicting objectives of political actors by permitting trade-offs across different sectors
> of policy; and it encourages a predictability in the policy process that is conducive to
> flexibility on the parts of actors (1984, pp. 27-28).

This lengthy quotation supports the view that corporatism is not always
anti-liberal democracy across nation-states. Peter Katzenstein further indicates
that it is "the ideology of social partnership that unites business and unions at the
national level, and a distinctive process coordinates conflicting objectives" (Ibid;
p. 30).

The role of political ideology is a determining factor in social capital making, the trust and the expectation of mutuality in the process of bargaining between the state and the private sectors. This ideology should be functional, with clear rules in civil society. It is the civic consciousness that makes social capital possible. To a certain extent, the win-win theory will not work if there is no notion of benefit mutuality. It would be also necessary to end this section with a brief definition of corporatism from a non-Western perspective.

In developing countries, for instance, in Kenya, corporatism was close to some forms of nationalism. For instance, in postcolonial Kenya the approach Jomo Kenyatta used to rule Kenya can be characterized as corporatist, as T. G. Ramamurty indicated in the foreword to the book *Kenya Under Kenyatta:*

> Evalutions vary as to the character and content of the stability and growth blessed by the Mzee, obviously according to the ideological predilections of the observers. However, there is a general consensus over the approach adopted by Kenyatta. This approach was one of acknowledge and accommodation of group interests, the qualifying groups ranging from traditional ethnic conglomerations through colonial-type 'administrative bureaucratic bourgeoisie to latter-day managerial and entrepreneurial elite. Described differently as 'hegemonial exchange,' 'proportionality principle' or plain political arithmetic, the approach was considered pragmatic and benevolent (1990, p. i).

Julius E. Nyang'oro and Timothy Shaw have also identified some dominant characteristics of corporatism, which are similar to what was already developed earlier as they wrote,

> In "the Third World," the contemporary usage or revival of corporatism sprang up in analyses of Latin America of the 1960s rather than in the Africa of the 1980s. In such a non-European and non-industrialized context, the concept was redefined to allow for the distinctive structures of political economy in the global peripheries or semi-peripheries: essential characteristics of corporatism exclusive and inclusive social relations, organization and accumulation—were applied and adapted to Third World, particularly where industrialization and concentration were occurring (1989, p. 2).

Private corporatism is an essential part of contemporary state formation, its pragmatism, and the dynamics of the global economy. Both state and private corporations have some common interests that sustain their actions. The public and private corporate sectors need one another in order to function effectively. That is to say, the principles of surplus accumulation and of the common good interact in complementary ways in some societies and in contradictory ways in others. How the state and the private sectors articulate the people's or citizens' interests is an object of serious debates, especially in the era of global liberalization.

Capitalism and the Foundation of Private Corporate Power[1]

The ideology of contemporary private corporate power is capitalism. It provides the intellectual and political tools for developing capitalistic society and its values. One cannot have or develop private corporate power in its various forms as a machinery of decision making and control without capitalism. It is argued, however, that the opposite is possible: Capitalism can be incorporated into social systems, such as the liberal or social welfare state or other types of communitarian systems, which can produce social policies. Capitalism can be used for the public interest. The experiences of the social welfare states provide sufficient illustrations to learn from. A brief definition of capitalism should help raise further issues concerning the value of corporate power.

Capitalism in its classical form, as defined by Karl Marx in the nineteenth century, is essentially an economic system. Marx thought that society could be reduced to economic relations. Material well-being and means to gain this well-being are central in the ways society is organized and governed. Further, social relations are considered basically as the relations of economic production. That is to say, the development of society is associated with the quality and the quantity of the forces of production. Those who own the means of production and control them are the ruling classes. The rest of society is compelled to work for the owners of the means of production in order to gain their subsistence. This economic relationship is the foundation of all other institutions in any given society. Government, culture, religion, philosophy, and psychological dispositions (part of superstructures) function as a result of the dynamics of the economic relations between the ruling class and the proletariat. They are shaped by economic power as it is determined by the relationship of the classes. All these organizations are created to reinforce the values and power of the ruling class in a capitalist society; therefore, historical analysis based on them as autonomous phenomena or variables is circumstantial.

Out of these organizations, Marx was essentially concerned with the tensions and contradictions between social relations within two classes and their societal implications: (1) the bourgeois class, the owner of the capital; and (2) the proletarian class, the owner of the labor. This division, which was enhanced by the division of labor, reduces the laborers to a replaceable part of the production process. Further, theories of exploitation and alienation are the explanations of the social division of labor, or division of society. Thus, the theory of labor, and not gender division, explains the origins of the social tensions among human beings in a capitalist world.

Marx believed that labor alone creates value, and the value of a commodity was created by the average socially necessary amount of labor required to produce the commodity under "normal" circumstances. The value of a commodity represents human labor in the abstract, and this abstract labor gives a commodity its exchange value. The fact that all commodities require labor for their production is universal to all systems of production; the differentiating aspect in capitalist production is that labor creates exchange value for a commodity, which is the result of capitalist social relations. The exchange value for a commodity allows one to exchange a commodity for another. Marx also recognized that a commodity possesses the property of use value that it provides a person with utility.

Surplus value is an additional value, or the most important value of a commodity produced by the laborer that is recognized by the capitalists upon the sale of a commodity. It should be noted that his/her "right" to this surplus value stems from the canonized belief in individual property rights and the fact that he/she owns the means of production. The realization that surplus value leads to profit on the part of the capitalist is the motivational force behind the capitalist system. It is the acquisition of surplus value and the authority to allocate it that gives the capitalist his/her power. It should also be emphasized that the capitalist drive to increase surplus value creates the second motivational force behind the capitalist system: accumulation. In short, accumulation of capital makes more surplus value possible and this surplus value makes more capital possible, creating an upward accumulation of capital. The laws of private property endorsed by the capitalist mode of production perpetuate this trend.

As the capitalist system develops, capital is increasingly allocated to a smaller number of people, who then have the power of deciding how best to allocate the surplus of production to their benefit. This process of centralization and concentration results from the nature of the dynamics of the capitalist system. For the purpose of this work, let me briefly conclude with the following concepts associated with Adam Smith's invisible law:

- Resources such as land, labor, machinery, and minerals are always considered scarce. Scarcity is defined as an objective phenomenon by the mainstream definition of capitalist theory. As Franklin states:

  > Whatever their absolute quantity, the resources can in fact be quite inadequate relative to the demand for them. Because people's wants are assumed to generate a demand greater than the means available to satisfy them, choice becomes necessary (1977, p. 24).

- In every so-called "perfect market," there consists a larger number of buyers and sellers, and no one buyer or seller can influence the commodity price by his or her individual action. His or her input is an infinitesimal proportion of the total (1977, pp. 25-26).

- All the social relations are commodified or marketable, that is to say they have prices as goods.

- Free entry and mobility principles stipulate that new firms be free to enter a profitable industry without incurring productive costs or encouraging obstacles from other firms or from the political arena (1977, p. 26).

- All commodities of a given industry or firm or class are said to be homoge-. neous or interchangeable in the eyes of the consumers. This is to say, all commodities are produced for sale.

- The choices made by buyers and sellers are based on a complete knowledge of the market situation and of their alternatives. That is, they know about products, prices, costs, and productivity.

- The assumption of rational self-interest is vital to the functioning of the capitalist system. Basically, producers are thought to seek maximum returns from their productive efforts and consumers seek maximum satisfaction from use of their personal income (1977, p. 27).

As the dominant system, its political expressions and its policy base, as currently articulated in the global liberal economics either through the Maastricht Treaty of the European Union or the classical structural adjustment programs (SAPs) in the developing world, have been against organized labor, against state intervention in subsidizing social services, small enterprises, agricultural firms, and in favor of the free market and free trade.

International Debt as a Policy of the Corporate World in Africa

"Corporate governance is about the way in which we seek to manage the inter-dependencies in which we are all immersed" (Collier, Jane, and Roberts, 2001, p. 70).

One of the direct consequences of the dynamics of corporate globalization in Africa has been the privatization of the state both in its military and economic forms. This privatization means that public affairs have become in most cases the matters of transnational institutions using the state's apparatuses as instruments of actualizing the interests of the private social groups and international companies. The disengagement of the African state from society and its own political base, and further integration of the state in the dependency syndrome on the so-called donors' political will and financial resources, have engendered more poverty and alienation.

Corporate globalization means that transnational and multinational companies have become larger and more important in international relations and world politics than nation-states and their national economies. This importance also implies that the rules of these companies are conceived as the general rules in the arena of politics. For instance, this has become the case with the conditionalities promoted and supported by the World Bank and the IMF as the general rules to be applied to all political actors who are interested in having access to international capital.

As articulated earlier, my analytical perspective is that international debt has to be examined as an essential part of the operations and structures of international capitalism. International capitalism is the most important component of the corporate world. I am interested in this dimension of the corporate world because it is its most vibrant and visible dimension. The various aspects of the national segment of the corporate world and their agencies, especially those in the developing world, have been subjected to the tyranny of international rules. There is a movement concerning the forgiveness of some types of international debt. This section is examined within the framework of this movement.

The African debt crisis is therefore part of a larger world debt crisis. Given the local and regional particularities and historical contingencies associated with the dynamics of the world economy, however, the implications of the African debts should be analyzed through the lens of geopolitical regional paradigms and the role of Africa in world capitalism. International debt issues should inform how capitalism works.

The issue of debt forgiveness, known also as debt relief, has been internationalized since the 1999 G-7 conference in Germany. At the April 2000 conference in Cairo, Egypt, President Jacques Chirac of France announced that France would forgive the totality of bilateral debts to the poorest and most indebted countries and that other countries should follow suit, and that in the next fifteen years, France would make an effort to forgive about $23 billion to heavily indebted poor countries (HIPC). The processes of selecting the first group of countries have been completed. Eleven poor countries have already qualified for debt relief from the IMF, the World Bank, and other creditors. These countries include Benin, $460 million; Bolivia, $2.1 million; Burkina Faso, $700 million; Cameroon, $2 billion; Honduras, $900 million; Mali, $870 million; Mauritania, $1.1 billion; Mozambique, $4.3 billion; Senegal, $850 million; Tanzania, $3 billion; and Uganda, $2 billion (Lumumba-Kasongo, 2003). Since 2001, a debt-relief package has been pending in Congress, which must approve the U.S. share. It should be noted that it is not clear how the IMF and the World Bank arrived at the above figures. However, many speculate that the debt relief scheme is basically part of bilateral debt.

Other countries that are in the pipeline and that were expected to have debt relief before the end 2000 include Chad, $250 million; Gambia, $130 million; Guinea, $1.2 billion; Guinea Bissau, $700 million; Guyana, $1.1 billion; Malawi, $1.1 billion; Nicaragua, $5 billion; Rwanda, $800 million; and Zambia, $4 billion. Countries under consideration are Ethiopia, $1.5 billion; Madagascar, $1.5 billion; Niger, $700 million; São Tomé and Príncipe, $170 million (Ibid.).

Conditionalities set up for debt relief are similar to those of the SAPs as discussed earlier, with an emphasis on electoral democracy, poverty alleviation, and women's issues. But these conditions have been used in an *ad hoc* fashion depending on the unwritten geopolitical factors that shape the major powers' interests and behaviors in the discourse of the global economy and its security paradigms. What do all the above figures represent as a percentage of the total African debt?

In order to have an idea of what debt relief may represent in the African debt saga, and in the absence of the availability of data concerning debt by country in the year 2000, I decided to use the 1998 data to calculate the relief as a percentage of total debt. It should be noted that the selected nations in my sample have likely increased their loans between 1998 and 2004, making the percentage not reflective of reality. Nonetheless, the exercise still gives a general idea of the statistical significance of debt relief (see the annexed tables of the debt in 1998 and the debt relief in 2000). Unless countries selected here doubled or tripled their loans in the past two or three years, it is clear that the debt relief scheme may have a significant reduction of between 20 percent to almost 100 percent in some countries. The effort seems to be on positive side. However, the debt relief impact has been assessed within the framework of the performance and structures of the total African political economy.

Why do nation-states, companies, and people take foreign loans? Who is to pay back these loans in Africa? What is likely to happen if nation-states decide to default, as Mexico attempted to do in the summer 1982? Some simplistic answers are that at any given time, some nations, companies, and people need cash in order to run their businesses and correct their budgetary problems. Or maybe, there is a lot of money around that may need borrowers. In general, it is also obvious that people/taxpayers are paying back their loans with their labor. But in Africa, it should be added that many governments have been paying their financial obligations with people's "blood and lives." Many people are being socially and physically tortured so that governments can repay loans. Many people are dying as a result of policies related to loans and the states' disengagement.

Since the 1970s, along with the oil crises, international debt has become also an issue not only in international relations, trade agreements, and diplomacy, but also in fiscal policy management and resources allocation and distribution. In principle, executive branches of the governments, from the views of both realist and idealist schools of thought, have obligations to secure resources for the well-being and the social progress of their citizens. This complex issue must be examined within a structuralist perspective.

The amount of African international debt, or public debt, has been gradually, annually increasing since the 1970s. Compared to other countries in the developing world, however, especially countries in South America, the total African public debt represents a relatively small percentage of the total public debt of the world. For instance, in 1998, the total public debt of Nigeria represented 3.485 percent ($23.455 billion) of the total public debt of the world. The total public debt of Côte d'Ivoire was 1.608 percent ($10.822 billion); South Africa, 1.579 percent ($10.626 billion); Ghana, 0.828 percent ($5.57 billion); DRC, 1.330 percent ($8. 949 billion); Kenya, 0.836 percent ($5.629 billion); Senegal, 0.487 percent ($3.274 billion); and Ethiopia, 1.429 percent ($9.618 billion). In countries in South America, the percentage of the total public debt was higher than in Africa and Asia. For example, in Brazil it represented 14.707 percent ($98.959 billion); Mexico, 13.076 percent ($87.996 billion); and Argentina, 11.413 percent ($87.799 billion). In Asia, South Korea represented 8.612

percent ($57.956 billion) and Indonesia was 9.948 percent ($66.944 billion). These trends are qualitatively not very different from those of the 1980s. Values in millions of debt in countries as a percentage of gross domestic product (GDP) in 1998 are calculated in the chart annexed at the end of the paper. For instance, in Nigeria, Côte d'Ivoire, South Africa, DRC, Kenya, Senegal, and Ethiopia, these values are 71.1 percent, 116.3 percent, 291.1 percent, 57.9 percent, 44.7 percent, 174.7 percent, and 133.5 percent respectively. A chart showing debt per capita in 1998 is included at the end of the book.

As stated earlier, the issue centers on the availability of resources to pay back this debt and on the origins of the loans. In a simple formula, money that one is paying as debt has to come from some other sources. What are those sources and how do they relate to human conditions?

Why is there a movement toward debt forgiveness or debt relief at this time? The question is complex, as it reflects both cost-benefit analysis and power relation issues. Generally, it is difficult to relate them through nonlinear reasoning. How will Africa benefit from debt relief in the short and long run? What will the "forgivers" gain as a result of their actions? It should be emphasized that in capitalist, pragmatic logic, there is no such thing as a "free lunch." But Africa can take advantage of the principle of mutuality, which should be examined carefully.

I have argued that there is hardly such a thing as "compassionate capitalism." With the constant increase of poverty in the world and emerging opposition to capitalism, to save it from further degradation in terms of labor, market/consumption, and accumulation mechanisms, some decisions must be made at the various orbits of power. The specific scheme of debt relief is not a humanitarian act by the industrial countries. It is a corrective process that should integrate Africa further into the world of international capitalism. Jacques Chirac clearly articulated this situation at the Cairo conference in April 2000, stating that what Africa needs are European investments, further integration into the world economy, and competition with other actors in the world economy. In order to accomplish these interrelated goals, there is a need for political and juridical stability. This is where the role of electoral democracies becomes vital.

Concluding Remarks

The author agrees with Streeck and Schmitter when they conclude,

> The public use of private organized interests requires a strong state rather than a weak state. It is true that an associative social order implies a devolution of state functions to interest intermediaries. But this has to be accompanied by a simultaneous acquisition by the state of a capacity to design, monitor, and keep in check the new self-regulating systems (1985, p. 26).

The question of the capacity of the state or the power of the state to effect decisions and rules, implement policies, and establish legitimacy should be revisited within the context of the origin of the state. The origin of a state, its structures, and its ideological roles in world politics are determining factors in the ways such a state responds to local and international demands. Although this seems obvious, it has been considered a minority view until recently. Thus, there is a need to briefly address it as used in this context.

Scholars associated with the political development paradigm, an important component of the modernization school of thought, have defined the strong state with an emphasis on the importance of its militaristic and coercive behavioral characteristics of a state to make policies and implement them without fearing potential political competition or well-articulated social opposition, as in the 1960s and 1970s. In general, political structures that produced quick decisions were praised and assessed in most cases in a normative manner, that is to say as good versus bad.

Strong states in developing countries, for example, were viewed in terms of their institutional stability but not in terms of the security of the citizenry or in their peaceful development. During the Cold War, military regimes mushroomed in most parts of the developing world, including in newly proclaimed independent nations in Asia and Africa, to crush, alter, or hijack the national agenda and to promote private corporate interests in complex processes of negotiations between industrial nations, multinational corporations, and the local political elites. In Africa and Asia, especially in Southeast Asia, one-party states with their civilian and quasi-civilian regimes also perceived competition and political pluralism as sources of political retardation and wasteful of resources. The concept of the strong state embodied elements of unity, physical and demographic size, and human and material resources. However, this author measures the strength of the state in relationship to how it can advance social distributive justice, gender equality, health and happiness of citizens, and their political participation.

NOTES

1.   With the permission of the Editor, Dr. Habib Zafarullah, most of the ideas and parts of this section were taken from my article, "Capitalism and Liberal Democracy as Forces of Globalization with A Reference to the Paradigms Behind the Structural Adjustment Programs in Africa," published in *Politics and Administration and Change*, No. 34, July-December 2000: pp. 23-52.

Chapter 7

Conclusion:
Summary and New Perspectives

No matter of its strength, its history and its richness, no single institution, idea, individual or social class is capable or is sufficiently equipped to govern, efficiently, effectively, and responsibly alone in any contemporary state.

Who and What Govern in the World of the States? is a study that examines, by using comparative and historical perspectives, the nature of contemporary political institutions and the dominant ideas in the formation of those institutions; the kinds of people who have been producing those ideas and their impact on the construction of the institutions; and the relationship between the processes of building nation-states and the agents of social transformation, citizens. The book is not simply an examination of the institutions and the agents who make decisions and who rule at a given time in a given society (Mosca, 1960 and Michels, 1958).

Hence, this conclusion is more than a summary of the arguments advanced in this book. It is an interpretation of the major arguments with the intention of further clarifying the issues of the origins of the constitutions, citizenry, states, and the implications of liberal democracy as an instrument of global capitalism. One of the main objectives is to project new analytical perspectives onto what should be done in the discipline of political science as we study the ever-changing political institutions, political human beings, and state-society relations within the context of claims for global societal change.

In some cultures, diplomatic traditions, social contexts, and complex human and political discourses, things that have not been communicated to or among people in an analysis, dis/agreements, debates, conventions, social and political formations, and their processes may be considered more important or revealing about a given reality or an issue than what has clearly been explained. All this depends on the nature of the dominant paradigms used for communication. In terms of the results, the relationship between the state and the society reflects many of these aspects of secrecy, mistrust, and the unknown. It is up to people with a high level of consciousness (organic intellectual, organized labor, political parties) involved in a given social context to localize themselves with their discourse and try to understand and appreciate what has been communicated to them or agreed upon and what has not been agreed upon in any public arena.

My analytical perspective is that if one seriously and critically considers the power of the *logos* or what has been or can be communicated, the way in which it was communicated, and the social and linguistic contexts of what was communicated, one is more likely to understand the quality of what has not been told or said. Systematization of knowledge may help one understand not only the nature of the present, but also the past with the possibility of making predictions for the future. This is why we study patterns and trends in social sciences. That is to say, in a given social context, the power of dialectical thinking in world politics can engender critical knowledge. Critical knowledge does not come about only as the result of simple observations. It is a piece of knowledge that is comprehensive, testable, reproducible, and that can be used to understand and solve a social puzzle. In a policy-oriented study as reflected in most chapters of this book, this knowledge has to reconcile and unify the existing conflicts between governance, the governing, and the governed within their past, present, and future in different countries.

In this conclusion, the summary of some major ideas and arguments of selected concrete illustrations that were examined recaptures the significance of the case studies on the question of the origins and sources of constitutions and citizenship, and the nature of the relationship between them and between the state and society. This discussion is also broadened in other parts of the conclusion, which deals with new analytical perspectives.

The illustrations, which have been further examined and clarified by the new perspectives in the rest of the conclusion, come from the concrete cases of the United States, France, the former Union of Soviet Socialist Republics (USSR) and Russia, the People's Republic of China (PRC), Côte d'Ivoire, the Democratic Republic of Congo (DRC), Kenya, and Saudi Arabia. However, these illustrations cover not only the analysis of constitutions and citizenry, but also the role of ideology and corporate power in examining the question of who and what govern. Thus, throughout the text, further illustrations were given from Northern Europe, the United States, Tanzania, and many other countries, as well as from specific political thinkers.

The United States, the French, the Chinese, the Soviet constitutions, and the African socialism of Tanzania significantly influenced various processes of state formation, political thought, and the search for social and political models among many nation-states during the Cold War Era. In this summary, two cases represented liberal democracy, two other cases were taken from the socialist experiences, three cases from the African region with both Francophone and Anglophone illustrations, and one case from the Middle East. Furthermore other historical illustrations, which are not specifically part of the case studies, were also used and discussed in the book.

The United States, a former English colony for 150 years, produced one of the most stable written liberal constitutions in the contemporary world. Its bourgeois revolution was the engine of the implementation of its constitution, but this constitution has various direct and indirect sources, which include the Magna Carta, which was the great charter of English political and civil liberties granted by King John at Runnymede on June 15, 1215; the Petition of Rights of 1628; traditions of constitutional government development in England's representative government, personal liberty, and an independent judiciary; the experience in self-government acquired under the colonial charter and, after 1776, under states' constitutions (Declaration of Independence); the influence and the contributions of the eighteenth-century political philosophers, notably John Locke (1632-1704) and Montesquieu; and lessons learned from the Articles of Confederation (1781) and various experiences related to the struggles of enslaved Blacks against the oppressive social system.

However, with its amendments, clauses, the judicial review, and the role of the Supreme Court, it has been able to deal, at least legally, with the most backward aspect of its political life and history, namely the practices, traditions, and politics related to slavery and its severe ethnic discrimination against Blacks and later against any other ethnic minorities and women. For instance, Blacks as slaves were considered as machines and later valued as three-fourths of a human. What makes the United States' Constitution different and unique is that "all other types of law—rules, regulation practices, statutes, administrative orders, customs—must be in conformity with the Constitution (Barker, 1999, p. 2)." The question of citizenry is clearly defined in terms of blood and naturalization. The principle of the sovereignty of individual rights is capital. A pluralistic elite's interests, individual merit and right, and corporate power rule.

Since 1793, France has produced a total of sixteen constitutions. Based on its dogma of assimilation, which is essentially the French colonial strategy and principle of governance and governing, these constitutions have influenced, in various ways and forms, many other constitution-making experiences in the former French colonies. It was argued that as compared to the American Revolution and its democracy, national struggles in the colonies in Africa and the Caribbean were more influenced and conditioned by the external European powers. The French Revolution of 1789 was essentially centered on democracy as participation but not necessarily as representation, which historically has been described by many scholars as an English invention. Democracy as participation has been an important factor constituting the basis of the French welfare state.

The French Constitution of 1958, which was the focus in this book, was promoted by a unique historical situation (occupation by Germany) and by a high level of patriotism or nationalism. It was a product of the dynamics of a combination of factors: France was engaged in a war against the National Liberation Front of Algeria; the crisis in Algeria was larger and deeper than any crisis of the French colonial experience elsewhere. Furthermore, France's memory of defeat in Indochina was still vivid. Thus, Charles de Gaulle, a nationalist, was recalled by various national political forces to join the government in order to unify France and to make sure that France did not lose her colonies in possible national revolutions that were taking place in most parts of the world, including Africa.

However, in terms of the dominant ideas, the 1958 constitution was consistent with the previous constitution of 1946. Both the nature of the political crisis in French society and the ideal of political and historical continuity shaped the 1958 French constitution. Some scholars go so far as to characterize the French constitutionalism as the embodiment of some elements of "egalitarian socialism." Liberty, equality, and fraternity have become a permanent, powerful moral and political tool in the struggles against the state, the state that is claimed to be national and which creates a rallying arena in French political society.

The Union of Soviet Socialist Republics (USSR) was a vast multinational state organized within a complicated federalist revolutionary framework with autonomous regions. It was indicated that the October Revolution of 1917 in Russia, with the Bolsheviks and the left social-revolutionaries, produced a different model of articulating power relations and building a modern society. The state power was, in principle, defined as belonging to the working class (proletariat). It was highly centralized on the working-class agenda of industrialization. Before the collapse of the Russian empire, all constitutions that were formulated after the one produced by Third Congress of Soviets, which was approved by the Fifth All-Russian Congress of Soviets on July 10, 1918, embodied a proletarian revolutionary agenda and principles. But this constitution was only for the Russian Soviet Federative Socialist Republics (RSFSR). Like any constitution in the world of the states, this one went through amendments to take into account the positions of the leadership and the momentum of the revolution.

The 1977 Brezhnev Constitution became more inclusive and incorporated the principles and covenants of international human rights. What became clear in this case is that the Soviet constitutions were not necessarily conceived as programs of action to be used for advancing a social agenda. They were more of historical documents and legal records for reminding the Soviets of what had been achieved and of the spirit of their journey in the struggles against social injustice and capitalistic oppression. The working class or "the people" was the central unit in the promotion of these constitutions.

The People's Republic of China is a unitary multinational state. After more than two decades of economic reforms, its ideology has become "socialist with a market economy." China was proclaimed the People's Republic of China in 1949, under the leadership of Chairman Mao Tsetung within the framework of the proletarian revolution but projected and conceived as popular revolution. Its first constitution in 1954 was aimed at guiding the revolution and making it "pragmatic." The grand ideas that influenced, in different stages of development of the Chinese society, the Chinese constitutions are Marxism, Leninism, Maoism, and populism. Maoism became the core doctrine of the revolution as it became more popular than Marxism.

The March 1978 Chinese Constitution was examined more deeply because it took effect during the second year after the death of Chairman Mao, which was also the time of the beginning of the economic reforms. In short, despite the momentum of reforms and commitment of the leadership to them, the Chinese Constitutions reflect the Chinese history of political struggle, the role of the Communist Party and the people, and the prominence of Mao in the grand ideas of social revolution in China.

The nature of constitution-making in the Democratic Republic of Congo (DRC) was examined in historical terms as a project for understanding the nature of state formation. The particularity of the state formation in the DRC began with the Congo as personal property of Léopold II after the Berlin Conference of 1884–85. After the Congo became a colonial property of the Belgian State (a colony) in 1910, the process of state formation, including the establishment of the systems of control, formal education, public administration, and the consolidation of the revenues by the Belgian state and private corporations, became philosophically eclectic. The Belgian administration did not prepare the Congo to become an independent state in the 1960s. But through political protests, it won independence albeit with some extreme institutional and administrative weaknesses.

The Congolese crisis since the 1960s has been essentially part of the crisis of the state. It is through the trinity of the state, Catholic Church, and private corporations that the question of who and what govern was addressed. Historically, the political institutions set up after independence planted the seeds of political instability. The Basic Law created by the Belgian government in the early 1960s was itself ambiguous regarding sharing power and power management of the state. The first independent constitution was produced in 1964. The weak political institutions locally, combined with a lack of human resources and the implications of Cold War politics, produced what is known as the "Congo crisis." In this case, the discussion covered the political situation of the 1960s, the rise to power of Mobutu as the head of state through the second military coup d'état (1965), and the capture of power by Laurent-Désiré Kabila in 1997. Mobutu personalized the Congolese politics and all the institutions of decision making and governance. However, even with his camouflaged politics of authenticity, he did not produce any constitutions that were informed by African history and values. The second republic lasted only a very short period, with the assassination of Kabila in January 2001. After a major war with more than 3 million deaths, since August 2003 the DRC has entered into a phase of a fragile political transition, unpredictable, managed within a framework of the struggle for employment and a poorly managed government with lack of political will among its new members.

It is expected that this government will produce a constitution that will be used as a political guide for the country. Some of the elements of the debates will center on whether the Congo should be a federal state or a unitary system and how to define Congolese citizenship. There is no indication so far that the question of African sources or origins of the constitution would be important in the new debates.

Côte d'Ivoire, a former French colony, that was part *Afrique Occidentale Française* (AOF) and which was ruled for more than 40 years by Félix Houphouët-Boigny after independence with his vision of politics and Africa on a one-party-state model, has been through a serious multidimensional crisis of national identity, of power struggles, of political legitimacy, and of economic degradation. It was argued that the root of this crisis can be partially identified in the nature of the Ivorian State.

Félix Houphouët-Boigny ruled the country with the constitution influenced by the French constitutions. However, he never promoted nor did he support a political experiment of the French political culture in the country. Thus, it was argued that both elements of Houphouët-Boigny's nationalism/patriotism or personal frustration for not being fully accepted as part of Paris's project of a clear and true assimilation and integration into the French-dominated francophone African community schemes, did influence the nature of constitution-making in Côte d'Ivoire. The Ivorian Constitution of 2000, made after the passing away of Houphouët-Boigny, and the 1961 Constitution, do not reflect the nature of the Ivorian society, its ethnic composition and its social values and elements, and the history of the Ivorian struggles against the French imperialism. Rather, they were conceived in a universalistic, internationalistic, and French framework as tools of national political exclusion.

In short, the Ivorian state was conceived in the constitution as highly centralized, presidential, and unitary. Given the fact that it did not touch on some important ideas such as the nature of traditional power systems, local/indigenous democracy, and political culture, in my view, it was produced as a working document. And the question of who the Ivorian national (citizen) is has not been totally solved, because this issue was introduced as a legal and strategic instrument of a partisan power struggle and political exclusion rather than a means for a nation building different than Félix Houphouët-Boigny's model.

Kenya, the first British colony in sub-Saharan Africa to gain independence, on December 12, 1963, was also a settler's colony. The presence and the involvement of Europeans, in particular those of British descent and Asians from the Indian subcontinent, made this so-called indirect rule more ambiguous here than in Ghana and Nigeria. Its constitutions retained some aspects of British liberalism (individualism and the free market) as England is considered in Europe as the inventor of contemporary liberal thought.

The role of the Mau-Mau movement was central to the definition of Kenya as a new nation-state. The initial agenda of the Kikuyu struggle to regain their land was transformed into a national struggle for independence through a complex process of recruitment, propaganda, and struggle. Jomo Kenyatta and his political party, the Kenya African Union (KAU), played the key role in state formation in Kenya. Kenyatta's role was defined in a nationalistic way. Nationalism is another element that defined what Kenya is in the beginning of the twenty-first century.

It should be emphasized that the ideas of a welfare state, which were articulated both by KANU and most of its members in self-government, were based on African socialism and inspired by the uprising that broke out in 1952 in Kenya, namely the Mau-Mau movement, as well as by African traditions and cultures. Despite this inspiration, the Kenyan history of constitution-making does not seem to reflect a major breakthrough in the utilization of the African traditions and history as the part of the foundation of the contemporary constitution. Kenya's amended Constitution of 1999 does not start with the ideas of "we the people" but with the definition of the state and its attributes.

Saudi Arabia does not have a written constitution like the United States, France, or Kenya, but in Article 1 of the document promulgated by Royal decree of King Fahd in March 1992, the Kingdom of Saudi Arabia is described as "a Sovereign Arab Islamic State with Islam as its official religion; God's Book and the Sunnah of His Prophet, God's prayers and peace be upon him, are its constitution." And, Arabic is its language. Some of the elements of the answers about who and what govern are derived from Islamic law, called Shari'ah, which is based on five main sources:

(1) The Qur'an (Koran), which is the book God revealed unto Prophet Muhammad;
(2) The Sunnah, the words and deeds of Prophet Muhammad, complementing and explaining the teaching of the Qur'an;
(3) Qiyas, which is an analogy of the Qur'an and Sunnah to new problems not specifically stated in either source;
(4) djma, a consensus by Ulama who are the learned Muslims in religion and juridical matters; and
(5) Idjihad, the use of independent reason and enlightened judgment within the Islamic context on issues and problems.

It was argued in this book that what tends to make Saudi Arabia different from the general and common perspectives is that despite the rhetoric and strong Islamic rules and traditions, Saudi Arabia has not fully produced an absolute theocracy—the God ruled republic—in its classical form.

The historical illustrations summarized above support and enlighten the view that political institutions that govern the world as human-made phenomena have their histories and agendas. In this book, I have carefully examined the intellectual, political, and economic complexities that are part of the question of who and what govern in the world of the contemporary states. I have dealt with this question by using a historical-structural approach within a framework of broad comparative analysis. While this analysis pays attention to particularities and appreciates the uniquenesses which are as important as historical case studies, my perspective cannot be fully understood and appreciated by using only the single logic and paradigms of institutional power. The classical institutional power embodied in the organization of the armed forces (military and police), the parliamentarian systems, the dynamics of the political parties, social classes, religious and cultural forces, the structure of gender relations and the management of the private interests and how these forces organize to capture and/or to influence power and reproduce themselves in a given society.

In every human society—from so-called simple societies to complex societies—someone, some individuals, some social classes, or some institutions are in charge of making laws and policies, managing them, and enforcing their implementation. Some ideas are more powerful or more appealing than others. This book did not deal with individual elites in an atomistic manner. It dealt with the systems of thinking and political institutions that govern the world. What varies among nation-states and societies includes the social contexts and the nature of social and political structures that produce political decisions, the history of these institutions, the quality of social and political values attached to and expected by these institutions, the people's cultural dispositions to participate in their systems, and the capacity of the institutions to solve socioeconomic and political problems.

Who and what govern in the world of the states contains several hidden complex questions about the existence of state–society relations. The work that deals with the above question is not and cannot be a simple intellectualistic exercise. It is a work done to challenge the existing legalistic, narrow, state-centric, and the behaviorist approaches in defining the nature of the relations between citizens, power, and the private sector.

One of the characteristics of world politics and its multiple actors has been, since the European colonial powers started to expand all over the world and began to name the world in their images and exploit its resources for the benefit of the few (economic and political elites), is the inability or uneasiness of citizens and people of a given nation-state to raise the issue of, and pose the questions related to, the origins of the ideas or thoughts that govern them. In many social science traditions, the question of origins has not been systematically addressed. Furthermore, human beings are generally fascinated with the generalized mythologies even when and if there may be agreement that many myths do have some historical foundation. Mythologies tend to make us accept ourselves faster without looking at the issues or contradictions in the views or perspectives that are informed by historical forces. Yet humans in self-reconstructing modes (an existential phase of the human being who is always futuristic and self-made phenomenon) are essentially historical forces *par excellence*. A historical analysis helps to deal with the dialectics of why and how the social phenomena behave as they do.

Until recently, the epistemological issue related to the question of origins of the social phenomena has not been viewed as a centrally important part of the political science paradigms or political studies' typologies. Perhaps this is so partially due to the religious basis of the city-state (as a unit of analysis) as it developed in the Mediterranean region of Europe. This basis made the city-state a very conservative political entity. But gods and the spirits did not govern the agora. Citizens and political elites ruled it under the protection of gods and the spirits.

This book is not about the myths of world politics. It is about the reality of world politics, especially the nature of the relationship between citizens (political human beings), state institutions (agencies of capitalism and manager of the public arena), and the private corporate world (the profit-making agencies operating in the public arena). This disarticulated trinity is real as it shapes human behavior and localizes humans socially. To go beyond the legalistic or behavioral approaches to examine the structures of world politics, this study is primarily an attempt to deal with the question of the origins of social and political thoughts that have been the foundation of the institutions or agencies of politics. Constitutions have their histories, agencies, and agents, which have produced them.

In the contemporary world, all the constitutions we have discussed function both as symbols of the state and citizens' powers and also as the *raison d'être* of these powers. They embody ideas and ideals of the political communities, and in some communities they are used effectively to articulate changes or to deal with real political problems. The state tries to immortalize itself through its constitution(s) and its citizenry. World politics has produced various types of constitutions, which have been dysfunctional in some countries and functional in others. Some have functioned as codes of law (the European model), while others have been used as political frames to guard the state, society, and their values (the United States model). While the European-dominated model is more legalistic and judicial, the American model (despite the fact that American society is a more litigious society) is more philosophical, political, and pragmatic. But in both models, constitutions are not naturally fixed and absolute, even in the case of the United States, whose constitution is used as a divine-like document in a secular, individualistic society. It is interpreted, however, to fit the interests of the dominant political and economic classes and to satisfy general popular opinion and political culture. As it was articulated earlier, revolutionary social contexts and thoughts produced revolutionary types of constitutions such as the American and French bourgeois revolutions, the Chinese popular revolution, and the Soviet proletarian revolution. However, all the constitutions regardless of their origins have some "hidden revolutionary basis" by the fact that they embody elements of futurism, universalism, and human dignity.

Unlike other constitutions that were studied, from France, the United States, the Soviet Union and Russia, and Saudi Arabia, the African constitutions have been influenced more by external factors than internal dynamics. It was also clear that in neocolonial Africa the constitutions have been almost photocopies or juxtapositions of two sets of documents, namely the international conventions, especially those related to human rights issues, and European constitutions, even in the complete absence of European social values or the European level of industrialization and economic development. In general, these constitutions are African in all but their content, traditions, and inspirations. Thus, political instability in many African states is not caused by a deficit of constitutions in numeric terms. It is historically correct to say that African political elites and states have produced too many Americo-European-like constitutions. The problem is that many African leaders have believed that it was possible to progress out of the European interests, traditions, cultures, and structures of the states. Yet, this has not happened in any part of the world, including Japan which has strong traditions of learning from others but integrating what it learns into its own cultural fabric and political objectives.

The study of political thoughts of constitutions, which includes the ideas of the dominant thinkers, the social structures in which these figures have lived, their class economic interests, the vision of their societies, power struggles, and the ideas of national revolutions or political decolonization helped us demystify constitutions. Despite their social validity and the institutional stability they have provided in some countries, and their revered or quasi-divine status in contemporary nation-states, especially after the collapse of institutional socialism (state socialism) in 1992 in many parts of the world, the constitutions by themselves do not solve all social and political problems. For constitutions to work, one has to add the idea of "all things being equal." It was articulated that constitutions—either those which have revolutionary bases like the American, French, Chinese, and Soviet or those with conservative foundations like the Ivorian, Congolese, Kenyan, and Saudi Arabian—are essentially elite phenomena. However, it was also shown that the constitutions that have worked better or more efficiently or socially in some countries are those which have been rooted in, or adapted to, the people's own political culture and history, as compared to those which have been either imposed or adopted without any prior critical mass discussion. The Japanese, for instance, to a large extent, have succeeded to appropriate or own the United States' model of constitution, which was imposed on them.

To understand politics, not only as a process of decision-making, a process of policy formulation and implementation, and governance, but also in its broader sense, one needs to examine and comprehend the nature of the political processes in a given historical and social context. Constitution making is a process that includes political debates, historical understanding of the social context, and a new vision of the political elite related to the nature of the political community to be created. If this process becomes inappropriate or is hijacked by a particular interest group, it can produce an abusive social system. I have discussed how these forces have been constituted and how they relate to other forces and structures to form a whole. The dynamics of history are central to the analysis of why nation-states do what they do. In short, constitutions must be rooted in specific histories and cultures; they also must be informed by the dynamics of the international political economy and its imperatives and by the claims associated with some values of "universal humanism."

The discussion on state, society, and private corporation in this book included theoretical and empirical studies such as those conducted by Philippe Schmitter, examinations of the history of state formation and expansionism and of the World Bank's structural adjustment programs (SAPs).

It was also argued that as we continue to study globalization, capitalism, and the state as interrelated phenomena, we have to revisit our analysis of the nature of state-society relations because historically the European nation-state that has become a global political entity has two inherent dimensions: public and private. Most of the nation-states that expanded outside of Europe started either as private enterprises or as semiprivate enterprises centered on reporting to the monarchs or to the Catholic Church, where later military power played a vital role. There were two forms of private corporations that have dominated state-society relations: first, the private sector as part of the state domain, with the state as a moneymaking agency; and second, the independent private sector that cannot function without the support of the state. The nature of the relationship between the state and private corporations has always been complex. This complexity is due to the fact the state also has an intrinsic private dimension. The nation-state is essentially a public entity but it cannot survive without an external private sector. In the liberal welfare state as developed in Western Europe, the private sector was viewed as an engine of growth; the development of the private economic sector needed to be facilitated so that it could support the necessary activities of the government, including the delivery of some public services. Thus, within this perspective, the private economic sector can play a positive role in the promotion of the common good. The development of this welfarism became possible in part because of the maturity of the European state as reflected in its nationalism and the people's struggles to change the state.

It was indicated that, although its legitimacy is shaky in many aspects, especially in Africa, the Balkans, and the Middle East, liberal democracy has staked a global claim as reflected in the number of presidential and legislative elections that world politics has produced in the past two decades or so. The judicial dimension of this democracy has become more popular than its social implications. Furthermore, transnational economic and financial institutions have been using their power base to redefine the power of the state and the state's frontiers with society. Are these transnationals/multinationals really interested in democracy? The questions are: What kind of democracy and what kind of transnational or multinationals are we talking about? For what specific interests do transnational institutions behave the way they do?

In an attempt to deal with these questions, we avoided speculative generalizations. The effort was to focus on the objectives of global capitalism and see whether this capitalism could produce its own democracy. I argued that although liberal democratic states and societies have some common characteristics, there are various forms of liberal democracy in the world, namely the European models, the United States model, the Japanese model, etc. I also distinguished between liberal democracy, the oldest democracy in the world of the states as a single system, and social democracy. It was also indicated that it is possible for any conscious society to imagine its own democracy between these dominant models.

It was argued that despite complaints about high taxation schemes and a relative lack of individual incentives and some major differences in the ways they define democracy and citizenry, the Scandinavian countries at large have performed better in terms of establishing policy dialogues between the state/people and private corporations and dealing with the gender gap and social inequality. The more direct policy of engaged social dialogue in a complex system of social control has been beneficial to both the state and the society. This has been, for instance, the case of Japan until recently.

Concerning the call for liberal democracy and its effectiveness, it was argued that for liberal democracy to be effective, it has to be substantive, it has to correct and permanently eradicate social injustice, and it has to promote and protect the right-to-life principle. Therefore, the main question is, given its essence and goal and in its current form as practiced in many parts of the world, is liberal democracy with its main components, namely representation and procedures, philosophically and instrumentally capable of fulfilling these criteria? In the absence of compelling philosophical evidence or historical grounds to assert that liberal democracy can positively reach the majority of people (the poor people including women, youth, peasants, and working classes), and structurally transform their living conditions so that they can become socially productive forces who can enjoy dignified living conditions, there is a need to consciously and systematically explore and project social democracy as an alternative to the United States model of "classical" liberal democracy. There will not be any democracy in the countries of the Global South without a built-in development agenda, commitment for human dignity, and collective decolonization.

In its basic legalistic scholarship, the concept of citizenship has been more dynamic within the state-centric and global capitalist approaches than concepts such as gender, labor, and welfare, which are socially more relevant. From the world of the states' point of view, every human being must be defined and must function as a citizen of a country, except in situations defined by international laws, agreements, and conventions or as the result of wars, political displacements, and social and natural calamities in a given social context. Our personal identities, for instance, names, languages, labor practices, and traditions, are defined within the framework of citizenship. The world of the states claims to make people on the planet more "rationally" organized and thus more functionally unified. But in reality, the concept of global apartheid seems to be a more appropriate characterization of the world of the states than the concepts of unity, peace, and social progress as they are associated with the politics of the nation-state.

As noted in this book, in terms of its origins, its interpretations, its meanings, and the different forms it takes, citizenship is one the most complex characteristics of the nation-state. In all the constitutions and family law documents used, people defined as citizens or nationals are proclaimed as sovereign. And they, in principle, ought to rule. Furthermore, in many contexts in its functioning forms, the definition of "citizen" has been used as a source of power struggles. The battle over its control or its redefinition has even led to civil wars and social explosions. In democracies, in principle, people ought to govern. People are defined through their general assemblies as having absolute power to rule. Although the notion of people has been used in most constitutions to define citizens, it is one of the most ambiguous expressions associated with nation-state building. In reality, the instrumentalization of citizenry by the state, social classes, and private corporations depends on the forms of government and historical context into which the citizenry was born and promoted. However, this instrumentalization has also led to political segmentation.

In this book, the discussion on the citizenry focused on the question of the origins of this expression, its meanings, and its contradictions. It was noted that the discourse on citizenry is multidimensional in terms of its socioeconomic, cultural and political meanings. Legal or civil citizenship is a product of the nation-state formation and the consolidation of its power. Despite social and philosophical contradictions in the world of the states, this world defines itself as the world of citizenry. Citizenry is the incarnation *par excellence* of the nation-state. It is used as an instrument of legitimacy for the nation-state. In its ethical and geopolitical senses, the world evaluates the social and technological achievements or the policy outcomes of any government/political elite through the way such a government treats its citizens. In this area, the nation-state claims to proclaim its humanism, which is defined in social and historical terms, its universalism, and its uniformity.

Despite the fact that notions such as "global citizenry" or "citizenship of the world," "global village," or a "world without frontiers" have become popular among bourgeois organizations, intellectuals, and multinational and transnational private corporations, their policy implications and actualization have been at the best minimal or nonexistent in many countries. It was also articulated that the demand for the national citizenship has gradually increased in many countries in the past two decades, even in the European Union. This demand is not only a legal expression of people to belong to nation-state apparatuses; rather, it is about the process of redefinition of the citizenry as a social and economic phenomenon. It is about people acquiring further new identities, identities of protection, participation, and social progress. The demand is reflected in popular social protests.

The civil societies, the states, the working classes, and the ethnic groups, especially in developing countries, have produced different interpretations of citizenship and a citizenry. What is common among all these social formations, however, is that citizenship entails rights and also responsibilities and duties. Citizens have been struggling for protection from social injustices, institutions of discrimination, and the contradictions associated with the development and functioning of global capitalism. The conflict between interpretations of a citizenry and its actual usage have led to serious power struggles in many parts of the world. The rise of the notion of sociological citizenship ("ethnicity" in its political sense) in its practical sense in many countries, especially those in the South, is due partially to the failures associated with legal or civil citizenry and the reductionist interpretations made by segments of the old modernization school of thought, which in the past dismissed ethnicity as an irrational phenomenon belonging to the domain of primordialism.

Judicial activism, which has been promoted by legal and human rights organizations, both professional and grassroots, by civil societies, and by popular movements, has significantly contributed to a redefinition of citizenship and citizenry. Furthermore, the adoption of human rights resolutions and international conventions in constitutions has been generally influenced by the gender and women's movements, the green movements, and the recent bourgeois global movements against global institutions. The new constitutions have taken into account the rise of a new consciousness of citizens' rights. This consciousness, as reflected in the activities of multipartyism and liberal democracy, has also been used as an instrument to challenge the state's sovereignty.

International institutions, especially those associated with the United Nations, have advocated the concept of global citizenship. However, the current trends (since the 1990s) of recapturing the United Nations agencies by the transnational financial institutions, especially the World Bank and the International Monetary Fund, the unilateralism of the American administration in international politics and relations, and the chronic deterioration of human and social conditions the world over, have raised serious doubts concerning the meanings, the practicability, and the acceptability of the concept of global citizenship. However, for this concept and its supported consciousness to be socially and politically effective and functional, some kinds of global and international affirmative action and quota systems should be considered for the creation and distribution of material and social resources. Yet, the neoliberal global political economy and its various forms of liberal and multiparty democracy are essentially anti-welfarism. The state in its current form in many countries is not capable of promoting global welfarism. If any efforts are to be made to redefine citizenship at global level, they must focus on the reconceptualization of the state, global capitalism, and the systems of people's power-sharing dogma as claimed by all constitutions.

Further studies are needed on the nature of the relationship between individual rights as articulated and promoted by liberal democracy with their contradictions, and the collective citizenship that has been articulated by international human rights organizations, the Organization of African Unity, and the charter of the United Nations. To make liberal democracy sustainable, collective rights must be its central policy and political principle. Furthermore, the new conceptualization of citizenship has to be able to solve the permanent conflict and contradictions between the state's search for the actualization of its sovereignty and the citizen's struggle for acquiring his/her sovereign rights.

In theory, many constitutions, through referendums, amendments, and judicial review, have tried to solve the problems of social inequality among citizens and the bad treatment of some citizens, such as women and members of ethnic minority groups, in most societies. But constitutions also have difficulties addressing the foundation of social injustices related to the local/national political culture and international capitalism.

It was argued that the question of who and what govern in the world of the states cannot be fully understood and appreciated through a technical/legalistic analysis of the state's behavior, the structures of the states, and the nature of the political institutions alone. State-society relations and their relations with the structures of the private corporate world determine where the real power is located. The question has a political nature rather than a classical, legalistic one. This book calls for a rethinking—with the object of changing positively—of the state's and people's relations within the framework of recent, post–Cold War popular demands for social welfare state with the mandate to reconcile the conflict between the interests of capitalism and the claims and interests of citizens in the name of humanism, collective social progress, and the safety and stability of the world.

Finally, does ideology matter? It was argued that, since the beginning of the process of the consolidation of the European model of nation-state in 1648 (the Westphalia peace accord) and its imperial expansionism, world politics has always been ideological in its formation and also in the ways actors behave and make decisions to promote their own class interests. Given the contradictions that the state, its economy, and their agencies and agents produce in the distribution and management of resources, as well as in the arena of political control and decision making, the world is moving toward multipolarity. Because of the diversity and multiplicity of its claims, one cannot yet clearly identify the ideological components of this multipolarity. However, some signs of strong regionalism, 'global' nationalism, hybrid nationalism, and primary nationalism similar to the movement of Jean-Marie Le Pen in France, are emerging. In short, one cannot understand the world of the states without relating it to its foundation, which is political ideology. In this sense, political science is most likely to be first of all the discipline that systematically studies the ideology of power in all its complexity.

Tables

Table 1. External Debt of Net-Debtor Africa, 1989-1999

External Debt of Net-Debtor Developing Countries, 1989-1999											
	1989	1990	1991	1992	1993	1994	1995	1996	1997	1998	1999
Africa											
Total External Debt	275.5	288.8	291.1	287.5	290.1	315.6	335.2	330.1	315.4	324.6	---
Long-term Debt	241.5	254.5	257.6	251.6	250.2	275.6	290.3	282.8	269.5	276.5	---
Concessional	77.1	84.9	91.8	95.8	1008	110.6	119.2	125.2	122.8	130.4	---
Bilateral	51.8	56.6	60.1	62.2	64.2	68.8	72.0	76.1	73.0	76.4	---
Multilateral	25.2	28.3	31.7	33.6	36.6	41.9	47.2	49.1	49.8	54.0	---
Official, non-concessional	79.8	81.4	84.1	82.5	81.1	91.5	97.2	90.1	82.7	84.5	---
Bilateral	51.8	50.6	51.7	50.5	47.8	55.3	60.7	55.4	52.0	53.3	---
Multilateral[1]	21.4	24.6	26.6	27.0	28.2	30.4	31.3	29.2	26.1	26.9	---
IMF	6.6	6.1	5.7	5.0	5.0	5.8	5.2	5.4	4.5	4.3	---
Private creditors	84.7	88.3	81.8	73.2	68.4	73.4	73.9	67.6	64.0	61.7	
Of which:											
Bonds[2]	2.	3.	3.	5.	2.	4.	5.	5.	9.	9.	---

	0	6	1	1	9	5	3	9	7	8	
Commercial banks²	31.9	31.1	29.4	22.9	21.3	21.9	22.9	25.1	22.3	21.3	---
Short-Term Debt	34.0	34.2	33.5	35.9	39.9	40.0	44.9	47.3	45.9	48.1	---
Sub-Saharan Africa											
Total External Debt	123.8	140.0	145.9	149.5	153.7	162.5	172.1	170.6	165.8	171.1	175.7
Long-term Debt	108.4	121.3	125.7	127.1	129.2	140.0	147.4	145.1	141.8	147.4	149.9
Concessional	50.0	58.4	63.1	66.3	69.8	77.9	82.2	84.6	84.6	90.5	94.2
Bilateral	29.0	33.0	34.5	35.8	36.7	38.4	39.8	40.3	39.9	42.3	42.7
Multilateral¹	21.0	25.3	28.6	30.5	33.1	39.5	42.4	44.3	44.6	48.3	51.5
Official, non-concessional	33.7	37.4	37.3	36.7	35.3	37.2	39.5	36.6	33.0	33.6	33.0
Bilateral	20.0	22.8	22.9	22.8	21.7	24.7	25.8	24.8	22.6	21.1	22.9
Multilateral	9.3	10.5	10.9	10.8	10.9	11.2	11.1	10.0	8.8	8.7	8.1
IMF	4.4	4.1	3.5	3.0	2.7	1.3	2.5	1.9	1.6	1.8	2.0
Private creditors	24.7	25.6	25.3	24.1	24.1	24.9	25.7	23.8	24.3	23.3	22.8
Of which:											
Bonds²	.4	.3	.3	.2	.2	.2	.3	.2	2.7	2.6	3.2
Commercial banks²	8.1	8.7	8.5	8.2	8.2	8.5	9.3	12.2	10.1	9.9	10.2
Short-Term Debt	15.4	18.7	20.2	22.4	24.5	22.5	24.8	25.5	23.8	23.7	25.8

Data calculated in this chart are from *World Economic and Social Survey, 2000*. Table A.25 (Pg. 276-278), (United Nations).
Source: "United Nations, based on IMF, OECD and World Bank" (p. 278).

---

¹ "Including concessional facilities of IMF" (278);.
² "Government or government-guaranteed debt only" (278).

Table 2. Debt Relief and Debt in 1998 in Africa

Country	Debt Relief (millions)	Debt in 1998 (millions)	Debt minus relief	Relief as % of Debt
Already Completed				
Benin	460	1,044	584	44.1%
Bolivia	2,100	4,933	2,833	42.6%
Burkina Faso	700	826	126	84.7%
Cameroon	2,000	8,198	6,198	24.4%
Honduras	900	3,220	2,320	28.0%
Mali	870	2,183	1,313	39.9%
Mauritania	1,100	1,423	323	77.3%
Mozambique	4,300	2,731	-1,569	157.5%
Senegal	850	2,710	1,860	31.4%
Tanzania	3,000	5,682	2,682	52.8%
Uganda	2,000	2,371	371	84.4%
Expected this Year				
Chad	250	630	380	39.7%
Gambia	130	269	139	48.3%
Guinea	1,200	2,512	1,312	47.8%
Guinea Bissau	700	695	-5	100.7%
Guyana	1,100	1,078	-22	102.0%
Malawi	1,100	1,371	271	80.2%
Nicaragua	5,000	5,238	238	95.5%
Rwanda	800	682	-118	117.3%
Zambia	4,000	5,317	1,317	75.2%
Under Consideration				
Ethiopia	1,500	8,733	7,233	17.2%
Madagascar	1,500	3,273	1,773	45.8%
Niger	700	1,114	414	62.8%
Sao Tome and Principe	170	144	-26	118.1%

Source: World Bank, *Global Development Finance* 2000.

Selected Bibliography

Abramovitz, Mimi. *Regulating the Lives of Women: Social Welfare Policy From Colonial Times to Present*, Boston, MA: South End press, 1989.

Agyeman, Opoku. *Africa's Persistent Vulnerable Link to Global Politics*, San Jose, Lincoln, Shanghai: University Press, 2001.

Al-Rasheed, Madawi. "God, the King and the Nation: Political Rhetoric in Saudi Arabia in the 1990's." *The Middle East Journal*. Volume 50, summer (1996): 359-71.

Ake, Claude. *Democracy and Development in Africa*, Washington, DC: The Brooking Institutions, 1996.

Amin, Samir. *Eurocentrism*, New York: Monthly Review Publishers 1989.

Aristotle, *Ethics,* trans. J. A. K. Thomas, New York: Penguin Putnam Inc., 1976.

Aseka, M. Eric. *Jomo Kenyatta: A Biography*, Nairobi: East African Educational Publishers, 1992.

Agnew, John, Book Review of "Giovanni Arrighi and Beverly J. Silver with Iftikhar Ahmad et al., *Chaos and Governance in the Modern World System*, Minneapolis, University of Minnesota Press, 1999. Pp. 320," *Journal of Historical Geography* Volume 27, 3 (2001): 468-469.

Ball Terence and Richard Dagger. *Ideal and Ideologies: A Reader*, (Fourth Edition,) New York, Boston: Longman, 2002.

Barker, Lucius J., Twiley W. Barker, Jr. Michael W. Combs, Kevin L. Lyles, and H. W. Perry, Jr. *Civil Liberties and the Constitution: Cases and Commentaries*, Upper Saddle River, New Jersey; Prentice Hall, 1999.

Beetham, David, "Key Principles and Indices for a Democratic Audit," In David Beetham (ed.) *Defining and Measuring Democracy*, London, Thousand Oaks, and New Delhi, 1994.

Biddle, Francis and Ugo Carusi. *Commissioner Federal Textbook on Citizenship,* Washington, D.C.: Government Printing Office, 1944.

Bromley, Simon. "Prospects for Democracy in the Middle East," In David Held (ed). *Prospects for Democracy, North, South, East, West,* Stanford, CA: Stanford University Press, 1993.

Brown, R. Lester. *State of the World,* New York and London: W. W. Norton and Company, 1999.

Bulletin de l'Afrique Noire (Paris), No. 67, (30 September 1958).

Chaube, Shabani Kinkar. *Politics and Constitution in China,* Calcutta, K. P. Bagchi and Company, 1986.

Chaudhry, Kiren Aziz. *The Price of Wealth: Economies and Institutions in the Middle East.* Ithaca: Cornell University Press, 1997.

Chantebout, Bernard. *The French Constitution; Its Origins and Development in the Fifth Republic* Trans. By David Gruning,, New Orleans, Loyola University, School of Law, Center of Civil Law Studies, 1998.

Chernow, Barbara A. and George A. Vallasi (eds.) Fifth Edition *The Columbia Encyclopedia.* New York: Columbia University Press 1993.

Chinweizu. *The West and the Rest of US: White Predators, Black Slavers, and the Africa Elite,* New York, Random House, 1975.

Citino, Nathan J. *From Arab nationalism to OPEC: Eisenhower, King Saud, and the Making of U.S.-Saudi Relations,* Bloomington: Indiana University Press, 2002.

Collier, Jane, and John Roberts, "An Ethic for Corporate Governance," *Business Ethics Quarterly,* Volume 11, Issue 1 (2001): 67-71.

Conover, Pamela Johnston, Ivor M. Crewe, and Donald D. Searing, "The nature of Citizenship in the United States and Great Britain: Empirical Comments on Theoretical Themes," *the Journal of Politics,* Volume 53. No. 3 (August 1991): 800-832.

Constitution de la Côte d'Ivoire (AOÛt 2000).

Crowder, Michel. "Independence as a goal in French West African Politics, 1944-1960," in W. H. Lewis (ed.) *French Speaking Africa: The Search for Identity,* New York, 1965.

Dagger, Richard. "Metropolis, Memory and Citizenship," *American Journal of Political Science* (25) (1981): 715-37.

Dekmejian, R. Hrair. "Saudi Arabia's Consultative Council." *The Middle East Journal.* Volume 52, No 2 Spring (1998): 201-18.

De Tracy, Count Destutt, *A Treatise on Political Economy; to Which Is Prefixed a Supplement to Preceding Work on the Understanding, or Elements of Ideology; with the Analytical table, and Introduction on the faculty of Will,* translated by Thomas Jefferson, in John M. Dorsey, *Psychology of Political Science,* Detroit: Centre of Health Education, 1973.

Deetz, S. *Democracy in Age of Corporate Colonization,* Albany: State University of New York Press, 1992.

Diop, Cheikh Anta. *PreColonial Black Africa,* Translated from the French by Harold Salemson, Westport, Connecticut: Lawrence Hill and Company, 1987.

Dorf, Philip. *Graphic Survey of American History.* Editorial Supervisor, Frank J. Dressler, Jr. New York, Oxford Book Co. 1955.

The Economist. "Saudi Arabia Needs a Face-Lift. Prince Abdullah Could be the Man to Clean Up the Family Firm." Volume 338, Jan. 6 (1996) Number 14.

The Economist. "Illusion of Change. New Cabinet Members Only Give Impression of Political Reform." Volume 336 Aug.12 (1995): 37-8.

Earle, M. Edward. (ed.) *Modern France: Problems of the Third and Fourth Republics,* Princeton: Princeton University Press, 1951.

Ebenstein, O. Alan, William Ebenstein, and Edwin Fogelman. *Today's Socialism, Capitalism, Fascism, and Communism* (the Tenth Edition), Englewood Cliffs, New Jersey: Prentice Hall, 1995.

Ehrmann, Henry and Martin Schain. *Politics in France*, Fifth Edition, New York: Harper Collins Publishers, 1992.

Eichengreen, B. "The Tyranny of the Financial Markets," *Current History* 96, (1997).

Elgie, Robert. "Democratic Accountability and Central Bank Independence: Historical and Contemporary National and European Perspectives," *Western European Politics*, Volume 21, Number 3 (July 1998).

Faisal Alhegelan, Sheikh. *Perspective on Saudi Arabia: Excerpts from Public Statements, Arabia to the United States, 1979-1980*, Washington, D.C.: Royal Embassy of Saudi Arabia, 1980.

Femia, Joseph V. *Marxism and Democracy*, Oxford, England: Clarendon Press and New York: Oxford University Press, 1993.

Finer, S. E. Vernon Bogdanor, and Bernard Rudden. *Comparing Constitutions*, Oxford, England: Clarendon Press, 1995.

Franklin, Raymond S. *American Capitalism: Two Visions*, New York: Random House, 1977.

French, Hilary. *Vanishing Borders: Protecting the Planet in the Age of Globalization*, New York: W.W. Norton and Company, 2000.

Foucault, Michel. "Two Lectures," in Colin Gordon (ed.) *Power and Knowledge: Selected Interviews and Other Writings, 1972-1977*, Brighton, Harvester Wheatsheaf, 1980.

Gertzel C. J. Maure Goldschmidt, and Don Rothchild, *Government and Politics in Kenya*, Nairobi: East African Publishing House, 1969.

George, Susan. *A Fate Worse than Debt: The World Financial Crisis*, London: Peguin Books, 1988.

Gittleman, M. Richard and Jacques Vanderlinded, *Constitutions of the Countries of the World: Zaïre*, Dobbs Ferry, N.Y.: Oceana Publications, 1991.

Gong, Ning. *Economic Record*, Volume 74, No. 225 (Jun 1998).

Gutkind, Peter C. W. and Immanuel Wallerstein. (eds.) *The Political Economy of Contemporary Africa*. Beverly Hills: Sage Publications, 1969.

Hague, Rod, Martin Harrop, and Shaun Breslin. *Political Science: a Comparative Introduction*, (2nd edition fully revised and updated), New York, N.Y. Worth Publishers, 1998.

Hague, Rod, Martin Harrop, and Shaun Reslin. *Political Science: Comparative Introduction*. New York: St. Martin's Press, 1992. 1985.

Harmon, Robert B. *Politics and Government in Saudi Arabia: A Selected Bibliography.* Vance Bibls Je, 1981.

Halliday, Fred. *Arabia Without Sultans: A Political Survey of Instability in the Arab World*. New York: Vintage Books, 1975.

Harshé, Rajen. *Pervasive Entetnte: France and Ivory Coast in African Affairs*, New Delhi, India: Mayfair Press, 1984.

Hart, Henry. *Indira Gandhi's India*, Boulder, COLO: West View Press, 1976.

Held, David. (ed.) *Prospects for Democracy: North, South, East, West,* Stanford, CA: Stanford University, 1993.

Heller, Mark. *The New Middle Class and Regime Stability in Saudi Arabia.* Cambridge, Mass. Center for Middle Eastern Studies, Harvard University, 1985.

Helms, Christine Moss. *The Cohesion of Saudi Arabia: Evolution of Political Identity.* London: Croom Helm, 1981.

Hempel, C. "Problems of Concept and Theory Formation in the Social Sciences," in *Science, Language, and Human Rights.* Philadelphia: University of Pennsylvania Press, 1952. Pp. 65-86.

Heywood, Paul. "Power Diffusion or Concentration? In Search of the Spanish Policy Process," *West European Politics,* Volume 21. No. 4 (October, 1998).

Hyette, Summer Scott. *Political Adaption in Saudi Arabia: A Study of the Council of Ministers.* Boulder: Westview Press, 1985.

Hiffe, John. *Tanzania Under German Rule.* London: Cambridge University Press, 1969.

Holston, James. "Urbanization Citizenship and Globalization," Paper delivered to the International Studies in Planning Program, Cornell University, the Department of City and Regional Planning, Ithaca, New York, April 28, 2000.

Howard, Dick. *The Specter of Democracy,* New York: Columbia University Press, 2002.

Huntington, Samuel P. The Clash of Civilizations and the Remaking of World Order, New York: Simon and Schuster, 1996.

Hyden, G. *Political Development in Rural Nairobi.* East African Publishing House, 1969.

Irungu, Kiunjuru. *The Machiavellian Art of Political Manipulation: The Kenyan Experience,* Thika, Kenya: The House of Hedges, 1999.

Islami, A. Reza S. *The Political Economy of Saudi Arabia.* Seattle: University of Washington Press, 1984.

Itoh, Mayumi. "Japanese Constitutional Revision: A New Liberal Proposal for Article 9 in Comparative Perspective," *Asian Survey,* (March 1, 2001).

Jerichow, Anders. *The Saudi File: People, Power, Politics.* Curzon Press Ltd. 1998.

Johnson, Nevil. *In search of the Constitution: Reflections on State and Society in Britain,* Oxford, New York, Toronto, Sydney, Paris, and Frankfurt: Oxford, 1977.

Kamoche, Jidlaph G. *Imperial trusteeship and Political Evolution in Kenya, 1923-1963: A Study of the Official Views and the Road to Decolonization,* Washington, D.C: University Press of America, 1981.

Kaplan, Irving. (ed.) *Tanzania: A Country Study.* Washington, D.C.: The American University Press, 1978.

Kariel, Henry. *The Decline of American Pluralism,* Stanford University Press, 1961.

Katzenstein, Peter. *Corporatism and Change: Austria, Switzerland, and the Politics of Industry,* Ithaca and London: Cornell University Press, 1985.

Kearney, A. T. "Measuring Globalization," *Foreign Policy Magazine,* (January/February, 2001).

Keasey Kevin, Steve Thompson, and Mike Wright. *Corporate Governance,* Oxford University Press, 1997.

Keet, Dot. "Integrating the World Community: Political Challenges and Opportunities for Developing Countries," Paper presented at a workshop on the Future of Partnership Between the ACP States and the EU organized by the Foundation for Globalization

Dialogue and The Friedrich Ebert Foundation, with the Development Bank of South Africa. Pretoria, 1995.

Kegley, Charles W. and Eugene R. Wittkopf. *World Politics: Trends and Transformation* Boston and New York: Bedford/St. Martins, 2000.

Kelleher, Ann and Laura Klein. *Global Perspectives; A Handbook for Understanding Global Issues,* Upper Saddle River, New Jersey: Prentice Hall, 1999.

Killian, Johnny and George A. Costellio. (co-editors), *The Constitution of the United States of America: Analysis and Interpretation: Annotations of cases decided by the Supreme Court of the United States to June 1992,* Washington, D.C. the Congressional Research Service, Library of Congress, 1996.

Kingsbury, Benedict, "Sovereignty and Inequality," *European Journal of International Law* (UK), 9(4): 599-625).

Knight, Franklin W. *The Caribbean: The Genesis of a Fragmented Nationalism,* (second edition), New York, Oxford University Press, 1990.

Kohli, Ritu. *Kautitlya's Political Theory: Yogakshema-the Concept of Welfare State* (Foreword by Professor M.M. Sankhdher, Rajouri Garder, New Delhi: Deep and Deep Publications, 1995.

Kolko, Gabriel. *Confronting the Third World: United States Foreign Policy (1945-1980),* New York, Pantheo Books, 1988.

Korten, D. *When Corporations Rule the World,* Connecticut: Kumarian Press, 1995.

Krasner, Stephen. "Sovereignty," *Foreign Policy Magazine* (January/February, 2001).

Kunkel, Christoph and Jonas Pontusson, "Corporatism versus Social Democracy: Divergent fortunes of the Austrian and Swedish Labour Movements," *Western European Politics,* Volume 21, No. 2 (April 1998).

Lackner, Helen. *A House Built on Sand: A Political Economy of Saudi Arabia.* London: Ithaca Press, 1978.

Lafferty, William M., "The Main Theme/*Thème* Principal of the World Congress," *Participation,* Volume 23. (Autumn/*Automne,* 1999).

Lane, Jan-Erik. *Constitutions and Political Theory,* Manchester, Manchester University Press, 1996.

Lijphart, A. *Democracies: Patterns of Majoritarian and Consensus Government in Twenty-One Democracies.* New Haven: Yale University Press, 1984.

London Times, March 25, 1978.

Loucou, Jean-Noël. *Le Multipartisme en Côte d'Ivoire,* Abidjan, Côte d'Ivoire: Editions Neter, 1992.

Long, Breckinridge, A.B., M.A., LL.M. *Genesis of the Constitution of the United States of America,* New York: The MacMillan Company, 1926.

Lowi, Theodore. "Our Millennium: Political Science Confronts the Global Corporate Economy," *International Political Science Review,* Volume 22, No. 2 (2001).

_____. *End of Liberalism,* New York: W.W. Norton, 1969.

Luger, Stan. *"The Generous Corporation: Political Analysis of Economic Power, The Journal of Politics,* Volume 52. No. 3 (August 1990): 972-974.

Lumumba-Kasongo, Tukumbi. *Political Re-mapping of Africa: Transnational Ideology and the Re-Definition of Africa in World Politics,* Lanham, New York, London: University Press of America, 1994.

_____."Capitalism and Liberal Democracy as Forces of Globalization with A Reference to the Paradigms Behind the Structural Adjustment Programs in Africa," *Politics and Administration and Change,* No. 34, (July-December 2000): 23-52.

_____. "A Reflection on Nationalistic Discourses and Ethnonationalism in Struggles for Democracy in Africa," In L. Adele Jinadu (ed.), *The Political Economy of Peace and Security in Africa: (Ethno-cultural and Economic Perspectives),* Zimbabwe, Harare: African Association of Political Science, 2000.

_____. *Nationalistic Ideologies, Their Policy Implications and the Struggle for Democracy in African Politics,* Lewiston, Queeston, and Lampeter: The Edwin Mellen Press, 1991.

_____. *The Rise of Multipartyism and Democracy in the Context of Global Change: The Case of Africa,* Westport, Conn.: Praeger, 1998.

_____. "Reflections on African Renaissance and Its Paradigmatic Implications for Deconstructing the Past and Reconstructing Africa," *Journal of Black Renaissance* with guest-editors, Mueni wa Muiu and Guy Martin Volume 4. No. 1. (Spring 2002): 110-120.

_____. "Reconceptualizing the State as the Leading Agent of Development in the Context of Globalization in Africa," *African Journal of Political Science* Volume 7 No. 1. (June, 2002).

Lumumba-Kasongo Tukumbi and N'Dri T. Assie-Lumumba. "A General Reflection on the African Conditions in the World System and Their Implications in the Process of the Search for Permanent Peace and For a Functional Democracy in Africa and Côte d'Ivoire," *Journal of Comparative Education and International Relations in Africa (JEDIRAF)* Volume 2, Nos 1-2, (December 1999).

_____. "The State, Economic Crisis, and Educational Reform in Côte d'Ivoire, In Mark B. Ginsburg, *Understanding Educational Reform in Global Context: Economy, Ideology, and the State,* NY: Garland Publishing, 1991: 257-284.

Llyod Duhaimer's Law Museum on the Internet, 2003.

MacEwan, Arthur. *Debt and Disorder: International Economic Instability and US Imperial Decline,* New York: Monthly Review Press, 1990.

Magstadt, Thomas. *Nations and Governments: Comparative Politics in Regional Perspective,* NY: St. Martin's Press, 1998.

Malhotra, Veena. *Kenya Under Kenyatta,* Delhi: Kalinga Publications, 1990.

Mandela, Nelson, *No Easy Walk to Freedom: With a New Foreword* by Ruth First, London, Ibadan, and Nairobi: Heinemann, 1986.

Mannheim, Karl. *Ideology and Utopian,* translated by Louis Wirth and Edward Shils, London: Routledge and Kegan Paul, 1948.

Mansbach, W. Richard. *The Global Puzzle: Issues and Actors in World Politics.* (Third Edition) Boston and New York: Houghton Mifflin Company, 2000.

Masland, John W. "Post-War Government and Politics of Japan," *The Journal of Politics,* Volume 9 (November 1947): 565-585.

Marshall, T. M. *Class, Citizenship, and Social Development,* Chicago: University of Chicago Press, 1964.

Martin, Guy. *Africa in World Politics: A Pan-African Perspective*. Trenton, NJ and Asmara, Eritrea: Africa World Press, Inc., 2002.

Mazrui, Ali. "Capitalism, Democracy and Stability in Africa" (1998, Internet).

McConnell, Grant. *Private Power and American Democracy*, New York: Alfred A. Knopf, 1967.

Michels, Roberts. *Political Parties: A Sociological Study of the Oligarchical Tendencies of Modern Democracy*; Translated by Eden and Cedar Paul Glencoe, Ill.: Free Press, 1958.

Middle East Economic Digest. "Special Report: Saudi Arabia." 38 Mar. 11 (1994): 27-8.

Middle East Reporter Weekly. "Saudi Arabia: Biggest Government Shake-up in 20 Years." 77 Ag 4 (1995): 16-17.

Mitchell, Neil. *The Generous Corporation: Political Analysis of Economic Power*, New Haven, Yale University Press, 1989.

Morgenthau, Hans. *Politics Among Nations*, New York: Alfred A. Knopf, 1948.

Mosca, Gaetano. *The Ruling Class*, Translated by Hannah D. Kahn and Edited with an introduction by Arthur Livingston, New York, McGraw-Hill, 1960.

Mulgan, R. G. *Aristotle's Political Theory*, Oxford: Clarendon Press, 1977.

Mwayila, Tshiyembe. "Would a United States of Africa Work," Nancy, France: The Director of the Institut Panafricain de Géopolitique; Translated from the French to English by Julie Stoker of The Mail and Guardian (Attached Document received from the Congolese Defense Fund); 1999.

_____. "Le Zaïre et la Troisième République: Réflexions sur le Projet Constitutionnel adopté par la Conférence Nationale Souveraine," France, Nancy: Institut Géo-politique de Nancy, 2000.

Namay, Rahshe Aba. "Constitutional Reform: A Systemization of Saudi Politics." *Journal of South Asian and Middle Eastern Studies*. 16 Spring (1993): 43-88.

National Citizenship Education Program, A Joint Program of the Projects Administration and United States Department of Justice in Cooperation with the United States Office of Education, *On the Way to Democracy* (book 3), Washington, DC: Federal Work Agency, January, 1942.

Nelson, Brian R. *Western Political Thought: From Socrates to the Age of Ideology*, (Second Edition) Englewood Cliffs, New Jersey: Prentice Hall, 1996.

Newman, Michael. *Democracy, Sovereignty and the European Union*. New York, St. Martin's Press, 1996.

Newton, Kenneth, "Trust, Social Capital, Civil Society, and Democracy," *International Political Science Review*. Volume 22, No. 2, (April 2001): 201-214.

Nyang'oro, Julius and Timothy Shaw. *Corporatism in Africa: Comparative Analysis and Practice*, CO, Boulder: Westview Press, 1989.

Nyerere, Julius. *Democracy and the Party System*. Dar-es-Salaam, Tanganika, 1963.

_____.*Uhuru Na Ujamaa: Freedom and Socialism*. Oxford University Press, 1968.

_____.*Decentralization. Dar-es-Salaam*, Tanzania: Government Printer, 1972.

Odinga Oginga. *Not Yet Uhuru*. London: Heinmann, 1967.

Ojwang, Jackton B. *Constitutional Development in Kenya: Institutional Adaptation and Social Change*. Nairobi: African Center for Technology Studies (Acts) Press, 1990.

O'Sullivan, Mary. Contests for Corporate Control: Corporate Governance and Economic Performance between the United States and Germany, New York City: Oxford University Press, 2000.

Oxaal, Ivar, Tony Barnett and David Boath (eds.), *Beyond Sociology of Development*. London: Routledge and Kegan Paul, 1975.

Pickles, Dorothy. *Algeria and France*, London, 1964.

Purnendra, Jain and Takashi Inogushi. *Japanese Politics Today: Beyond Karaoke Democracy?* NY: St. Martin's Press, 1997.

Plato. *Republic*, trans. Desmond Lee, New York: Penguin Putnam, Inc., 1987.

Primo, Natasha, and Viviene Taylor. *Beyond the DAWN-Africa Debates: Globalization in Search of Alternatives*. Cape Town, South Africa: SADEP, University of Cape Town, 1999.

Rawls, John. *A Theory of Justice*, Cambridge, MA: Belknap Press of Harvard University, 1971.

Rohr, John A. *Comparative Politics, Founding Republics in France and America: A Study of Constitutional Governance*, Laurence: University of Kansas Press, 1995.

Robertson, A. H. and J. G. Merrills. *Human Rights in the World*. Manchester University Press, 1992.

Sankhdher, M.M. and Maurice Cranston. *The Welfare State*, Rajouri Garden, New Delhi: Deep and Deep Publications, 1985.

Sartori, Giovanni. "Neither Presidentialism nor Parliamentarism" in Jua J. Linz and Arturo Valenzuela (eds.). *The failure of Presidential Democracy, Volume 1: Comparative Perspectives*, 106-18. Baltimore, MD: John Hopkins University Press, 1994a.

Schatant, Jacobo. *World Debt, Who is to Pay?* London, N.J: Zed Books, Ltd., 1987.

Schumaker, E. F. *Small is Beautiful: Economics as If People Mattered,* New York, Hagestown, San Francisco, London: Harper and Row, Publishers, 1973.

Shome, Raka and Radha S. Hegde. "Culture, Communication, and the Challenge of Globalization," *Critical Studies in Media Communications*, Volume 19, No. 2, (June 2002): 172-189.

Simons, B. William. *The Constitutions of the Communist World,* Alphen aan den Rijn, The Netherlands: Sijthff and Noordhoff, 1980.

Smith, Edward Conrad. *The Constitutions of the United States with Case Summaries,* New York, Evanston, San Francisco and London: Barnes and Noble Books, 1972.

Shakir, Abdulmunim Ahmad. *Individual and Social Responsibility in Islamic Thought*, Ann Arbor, Michigan: University Microfilms International, 1982.

Steans, Jill. *Gender and International Relations: An Introduction,* New Brunswick, New Jersey: Rutgers University Press, 1998.

Steger, Mansfield B. *Globalism: The New Market Ideology*, MD: Lanham: Rowman and Littlefield Publishers, 2001.

Stiglitz, Joseph E. *Globalization and Its Discontents* New York; London: W.W. Norton and Co., 2002.

Streeck, Wolfgang, and Philippe Schmitter (eds.). *Private Interest Government: Beyond Market and State*, London, Beverly Hills and New Delhi: Sage Publications, 1985.

Sweet, Alec Stone and Thomas L. Brunnell, "Constructing a Supranational Constitution: The Dispute Resolution and Governance in the European Community," *The American Political Science Review*, Volume 92, No. 1 (March 1998): 63-81.

Trotsky, Leon. *Our Political Tasks,* First published: 1904 as Nashi Politicheskiya Zadachi; Translated by: New Park Publications and Transcribed by Andy Lehrer in 1999 for Trotsky Internet Archive (http://www.marxists.org/archive/trotsky/works/1904-pt/ch01.htm).

The United States Constitution of 1996,

Vyshinsky, Andrei. *The Law of Soviet State,* trans. of 1938 Russian ed., NY, 1948, pp. 87-103.

Wamwere wa Koigi. The *Peoples* Representative and the Tyrants or Kenya: Independence without Freedom, Nairobi: New Concept Typesetters, 1992.

Widner, Jennifer. "Building Judicial Independence in Common Law Africa," in Andreas Schedler, Larry Diamond, and Mark F. Plattner (eds.). *The Self-Restraining State: Power and Accountability in New Democracies*, Boulder, CO: Lynner Rienner Publishers, 1999: 177-193.

_____, *The Rise of a Party-State in Kenya: From "Harambee" to "Nyayo."* CA: Berkley, Los Angeles, Oxford: University of California Press, 1992.

William, Simons B. *The Constitutions of the Communist World,* Alphen aan den Rijn, The Netherlands: Sijthff and Noordhoff, 1980.

Windschuttle, Keith. "Liberalsim and Imperalism," in Hilton Kramer and Roger Kimball, *The Betral of Liberalism: How the Disciplines of Freedom and Equality Helped Foster the Illiberal Politics of Coercion and Control*, Chicago, Ivan R. Dee, 1999.

Wolf Phillips, Leslie. (ed.) *Constitution of Modern States, Selected Texts and Commentary*, NY, Washington, and London: Frederick A. Praeger, 1968.

Yizraeli, Sarah. *The Remaking of Saudi Arabia: the struggle between King Saud and Crown Prince Faysal, 1953-1962*, Tel Aviv, Israel: Moshe Dayan Center for Middle Eastern and African Studies, Tel Aviv University, 1997.

Young Crawford. *Politics in the Congo: Decolonization and Independence*, Princeton, New Jersey: Princeton University Press, 1965.

Zolo, Danilo. "Democratic Citizenship in A Post-Communist Era," in David Held (ed). *Prospects for Democracy, North, South, East, West*, Stanford: Stanford University Press, 1993.

Index

About the Author

Tukumbi Lumumba-Kasongo is a political scientist trained at *Université Libre du Congo* (*Université de Kisangani*), Harvard University, and the University of Chicago. He has taught political science in many universities and colleges including the University of Liberia in Monrovia Liberia where he was also the chair of the department of political science, Roosevelt University, Vassar College, Bard College, Cornell University, and Wellesley College. He is currently Professor of Political Science at Wells College; Visiting Scholar, Department of City and Regional Planning, Cornell University; Visiting Research Fellow, Center for the Study of International Cooperation in Education (CICE), Hiroshima University, Japan; Co-Founder and Director of CEPARRED; and *Chercheur Associé, Institut d'Ethno-Sociologie, Université de Cocody* in Côte d'Ivoire. He has extensively published on democracy and political change in Africa, international relations, social movements, higher education and politics in Africa, and world politics. Some of his books are: *The Dynamics of Economic and Political Relations between Africa and Foreign Powers: A Study in International Relations*, Westport, Connecticut: Praeger, 1999; *Rise of Multipartyism and Democracy in the Global Context: the Case of Africa*, Westport, Connecticut: Praeger, 1998; *Political Re-mapping of Africa: Transnational Ideology and the Re-definition of Africa in World Politics*, Lanhman, Maryland: University Press of America, 1994.

He is the Editor of *African and Asian Studies* (Journal) and Co-Editor of International Studies in Sociology and Social and Anthropology (books) published by Brill, Leiden, the Netherlands and Associate Editor of the *Journal of Comparative Education and International Relations in Africa* in charge of research and bookreviews.

He is listed in *Who's Who Among America's Teachers*, 8th Edition, 2003/2004, Volume 1 and also in 7th Edition, 2002, Volume 1, Austin,Texas:Educational Communications, Inc.; in *Contemporary Who's Who*, Raleigh, North Carolina: American Biographical Institute, Inc., 2002/2003; and in *Who's Who in the World, 2000 Millennium Edition,* (17th Edition), New Providence: Marquis, 1999. He is also the Vice-President of the African Association of Political Science—Representing the Central African Region.